Ph : 320020
THE NEW BOOK DEPOT
18-B. CONNAUGHT PLACE
NEW DELHI-110001
BOOK DEPOT

BENGAL, 1928–1934
The Politics of Protest

BENGAL

1928–1934

The Politics of Protest

TANIKA SARKAR

DELHI
OXFORD UNIVERSITY PRESS
BOMBAY CALCUTTA MADRAS
1987

Oxford University Press, Walton Street, Oxford, OX2 6DP

New York Toronto
Delhi Bombay Calcutta Madras Karachi
Petaling Jaya Singapore Hong Kong Tokyo
Nairobi Dar es Salaam
Melbourne Auckland

and associates in
Beirut Berlin Ibadan Nicosia

SBN 19 562076 3

Printed in India by Rekha Printers Pvt. Ltd.,
A-102/1, Okhla Industrial Area, Phase II, New Delhi 110 020 and
Published by S.K. Mookerjee, Oxford University Press
YMCA Library Building, Jai Singh Road, New Delhi 110 001

For My Parents

Contents

Acknowledgements

About five years have gone into the making of this book, years of many interruptions and spells of complete suspension of work. It is a great pleasure to be able to recall at last how the tedium and uncertainties were shared and encouragement offered by friends to make the book possible.

A scholarship granted by the Indian Council of Historical Research enabled me to start my research on Bengal. I have very pleasant memories of working at the National Library, the West Bengal State Archives and the West Bengal Secretariat Library in Calcutta: the National Archives, the Central Secretariat Library and the Nehru Memorial Museum and Library in Delhi; the British Museum and the India Office Library in London; the Indian Institute at Oxford and the Cambridge South Asian Study Centre at Cambridge. I wish to thank the staff of all these institutions for their ready help and co-operation.

Shri Chinmohan Sehanobis, Shri Gautam Chattopadhyay and Dr Ranjit Das Gupta were extraordinarily generous in giving me access to a great deal of rare material and arranging interviews with revolutionary terrorist, Communist and trade union leaders. Shri Shantimoy Ray often helped me with observations and reminiscences about an active political life.

I was very lucky to get detailed and critical comments from Ranajit Guha on my thesis on Bengal politics, all of which opened up new horizons of thought and work. At the last stages of revision I was fortunate enough to be able to meet him at Canberra and get clarifications on some of his earlier comments. Professor Barun De, who was a teacher at the post-graduate classes at Calcutta University, aroused much of my interest in Bengal history, has looked at my work at various stages and has helped me with suggestions and encouragement. Professor Ravinder Kumar was kind enough to go through the entire thesis and offer valuable criticism. Professor Parthasarathi Gupta supervised my research and I am deeply grateful to him for his kindness and criticism.

I am grateful to Dipesh Chakravarty and Saurabh Dube for their comments on the introductory chapter. Pradip Kumar Datta went through several sections of the work and his criticism and interest stimulated my flagging efforts at revision.

Many friends have encouraged me all this while by wishing to see the book published: Jasodhara and Amiya Bagchi, Sukhomoy and Lalita Chakravarty, Gargi Chakravarty, Gyan Pandey, Veena and Ranen Das, Mohit Sen, Sukumari Bhattacharjee and Ajit Bhattacharjee. Basudev Chatterjee finally got tired of waiting and marched off to the Oxford University Press with the manuscript in the middle of my loud protests.

It is a lasting grief to me that Shri Susobhan Sarkar did not see the completion of the work which I had discussed with him in its early stages. My father did not see even the beginning of my research although he had created my first and strongest notions about the discipline of history and my decision to go in for research.

I do not know whether I should thank Sumit or record my resentment about the way in which he relentlessly bullied me into writing this book. In any case it was fun to have someone who could argue so consistently about everything that I wrote.

I hope Aditya will some day read this book and tell me all that is wrong with it.

The faults of this work are many and they are entirely my responsibility.

List of Abbreviations

GOI	Government of India
GOB	Government of Bengal
RNP (B)	Report on Native Papers (Bengal)
Progs	Proceedings
Poll	Political
RCLI	Royal Commission on Labour (India)
AICC	All India Congress Committee
BPCC	Bengal Provincial Congress Committee
BCCD	Bengal Council of Civil Disobedience
NMML	Nehru Memorial Museum and Library (New Delhi)
IOL	India Office Library (London)
BM	British Museum (London)
CSASC	Cambridge South Asia Study Centre (Cambridge)

Introduction

Few things are as stale as outmoded academic concerns. Since quite some time has gone into the making of this work, many of its arguments have become almost tediously familiar: the inverse relationship between Congress organizational strength and popular militancy would be an obvious example. Fortunately for me, however, most of these questions have not been posed for the period and region covered by this study. They blend well, moreover, with a number of new questions and problems that I have attempted to explore here.

I began my research with a rather simple-minded preoccupation with the Bengal Congress. The burning debate those days was between 'Cambridge school' historians, with their accent on factions, and Indian left nationalists, concerned with the overriding importance of the colonial context and the broad nature of Congress ideology and movements. If I did not consciously equate popular anti-British risings completely with Congress directives, I was at least convinced of the impossibility of documenting the other side of the story: perceptions and actions of men and women who were 'led' by the Congress. I looked for a period of continuous struggle under Congress auspices since such a time span would ensure a relative plenty of records. A focus on movements of mass activity would, moreover, underline the gap left by Cambridge school historians. The year 1928 seemed a convenient starting-point. It marked a revival in nationalist agitations: anti-Simon Commission demonstrations, revival of revolutionary terrorism and new departures in Congress organizational activity. Civil Disobedience then initiated a shift in focus to rural areas and to new forms of struggle. The world depression which, in Bengal, resulted in a massive collapse in rice and jute prices, provided an appropriate overall context. It demonstrated the workings of a colonial control that exposed the country to vicissitudes of global price fluctuations. The relationship between the economic catastrophe and the militant mass upsurge during Civil Disobedience was to add an interesting dimension to the study. 1934 marked the end of both Civil Disobedience and revolutionary terrorism. It provided a logical cut-off point.

I was soon struck by further possibilities within the period. The first two years were highly significant for working class struggles and the growth of Left politics—developments which would, perhaps, be even more meaningful for Bengal than the history of the Congress movement. This dimension had to be incorporated even if it meant an apparent diffusion of a tightly-knit and consistent central thesis. The relationship between the Congress and the Left was to unite the two levels of the discussion.

I certainly did not expect to recover common people as conscious subjects of history who often created movements along lines very different from those laid down by the Bengal Congress or Leftist organizations. The sources made me realize that it was possible to go beyond a historical gaze which can discern the general shape of mass participation but cannot focus on it with any clarity or certainty. Government records—the official discourse of knowledge and control—faithfully tried to preserve every note and inflexion of the common peoples' protest. Gordon, Gallagher and Broomfield must have suffered from a very acute problem of myopia, indeed, to have missed out on this.[1] The path-breaking research of Gyanendra Pandey (I was fortunate to read the manuscript of his book in 1977) and an article of Sumit Sarkar[2] helped me to conceptualize the central paradox of the Congress as both organizer of and brake on mass radicalism. Dipesh Chakravarty's brilliant and provocative study of the cultural constraints on working-class politics gave me a point to hone my own perceptions and generalizations on—the more so, because I did not find some of his conclusions entirely convincing.[3]

[1] L.A. Gordon, *Bengal: The Nationalist Movement 1976–1940* (Delhi, 1974); J.H. Broomfield, *Elite Conflict in a Plural Society* (Berkeley, 1968); J. Gallagher, Johnson and Seal (ed.), *Locality, Province and Nation* (Cambridge, 1973).

[2] Gvamemdra Pandey, *The Ascendancy of the Congress in Uttar Pradesh*, 1926–34 (Delhi, 1978); Sumit Sarkar, 'The Logic of Gandhian Nationalism: Civil Disobedience and the Gandhi-Irwin Pact, 1930–31' (*Indian Historical Review*, July, 1976).

[3] Dipesh Chakravarty, Unpublished thesis on Calcutta Jute Mill Labour, Australian National University (Canberra, 1983).

My interest in the period and theme sharpened when I realized that popular struggles of different kinds, not directly connected with the nationalist or Left organizations, constituted a significant part of contemporary political reality. In different ways they shaped the political future of the province as well. I had to risk a further dispersal of my central thesis and revise the purpose and scheme of my study. I sought to integrate these events within my discussion by exploring the dialectic between the autonomy of these movements on the one hand, and the attempts by various kinds of political leadership to impose controls on them, on the other.

Women are generally rendered invisible in the works of historians on nationalism and subaltern politics. When they are perceived at all, it is not against the broad context of gender relations within a particular movement, but within the somewhat rarefied, exclusive domain of 'womens' studies', within a vacuum as it were. Instead of appending a list of women who 'also ran' in politics, I have tried to tackle the question of womens' political actions in terms of social, political and human relations.

The arrangement of the work has posed major problems. I had to risk a great deal of organizational shapelessness and muddle to convey an idea of the rich variety and complexity of the political trends of this period. Similarly, I hung on to an all-Bengal perspective, ignoring the itch to explore in depth a few individual struggles. A general overview, which necessarily remains incomplete in many essential respects, retains, nonetheless, a certain validity of its own. It indicates the diversity of trends, their interconnections, tensions and mutations.

Another problem related to the strictly chronological framework of the study. It seemed tedious, more appropriate for a text-book and, in any case, unnecessary for such a short time-span. A 'thematic approach' looked a much more tempting alternative. Finally, however, I decided against it. To try and collapse complicated events and developments into a single, unified, cohesive grammar seemed to prune them of their richness, and ultimately, of real meaning. An arrangement of events in a chronological pattern, an understanding of events as process, could best explore their unfolding and maturing even within this brief period.

With its abundant rainfall, innumerable rivers and rich delta soil, undivided Bengal seemed endowed for enviable agrarian prosperity. Famines had been relatively few, even though British rule began with one and ended with another. Bengalis living in other provinces often commented on the relative aridity and wretchedness of rural life outside Bengal.[4]

Yet George Blyn's statistics show a 38 per cent decline in per capita foodgrains output in 'Greater Bengal' between 1901 and 1941.[5] The stopping of coarse rice imports from Burma in 1942 was sufficient to produce a famine of terrible proportions in 1943.

Long-term ecological factors explain a part of the decline. The river system has been shifting steadily from west to east in recent centuries, creating a 'moribund delta' region in the western part of the province as contrasted with the 'active delta' in south-east Bengal. Natural processes were aggravated by human interference under colonial rule. Stagnant rivers and swamps, combined with obstructions to natural drainage by unimaginatively constructed railway embankments, led to devastating bouts of malaria (Burdwan Fever) from the second half of the nineteenth century in large parts of western and central Bengal. A contrast developed between stagnant or declining agriculture in Western districts (particularly in Burdwan Division) and relative agricultural prosperity in East Bengal, intimately associated with the commercial cultivation of jute and double cropping.[6] This relative prosperity had limits and an official investigation found that soil fertility was on the decline.[7]

Ecology apart, agrarian relations, as shaped by the Permanent Settlement and later tenancy legislation, acted as a major constraint. In the course of the nineteenth century, near-absolute private property rights given to zamindars by Cornwallis were balanced by increasing legal protection to an upper category of tenants. The combination of landlordism with some small peasant rights ultimately created a kind of a deadlock: massive surplus

[4] See, for instance, Bibhutibhushan Bandopadhyay's surprised comments on North Bihar in *Aranyaka*, Calcutta n.d. Bandopadhyay was no spoilt urbanite, unfamiliar with Bengali rural reality.

[5] George Blyn, *Agricultural Trends in India 1891–1947, Output, Availability and Productivity* (Pennsylvania, 1966), p. 162. Also Amiya Bagchi, 'Reflections on Patterns of Regional Growth in India during the Period of British Rule', Centre for Studies in Social Sciences, Calcutta, (*Occasional Paper* No. 5, 1976).

[6] GOB, Report of the Land Revenue Commission, Vol. I, Calcutta 1940, Appendix IV, Table I. See also B.B. Chaudhuri, 'Agricultural Production in 19th Century Bengal'; in *Bengal Past and Present*, (Calcutta 1969); Partha Chatterji, *Bengal 1920–1947: The Land Question* (Calcutta, 1984).

[7] GOB, *Report of the Bengal Provincial Banking Enquiry Committee 1929–30*. Calcutta, Vol. II, p. 21.

extraction by zamindars and other tenure-holders blocked possibilities of capitalist farming from below by rich peasants, while landlord-based capitalist agriculture, which would result in total dispossession of land among the peasants, was also precluded.

Zamindars in Bengal had traditionally been tribute-collectors and not organizers of agricultural production. In colonial Bengal they had little incentive to go in for risky investments for the purpose of modernizing agriculture. This was particularly true since revenue, though initially high, was permanently fixed while rent-enhancements remained unhindered till 1859. The growing rent-revenue gap provided the basis for a rapid proliferation of a hierarchy of intermediary tenures.[8] The individual tenure-holder or zamindar was quite often not particularly prosperous and lacked the resources to go in for agricultural improvement; the total burden of rent on actual producers still remained enormous and increased over time.

A similar disjunction between property rights and productive enterprise developed at lower levels of rural society. An upper stratum of peasants acquired stable occupancy rights through Tenancy Acts of 1859 and 1885. There was nothing, however, to prevent them from leasing out their land to subtenants ('Korfa' ryots) or getting it cultivated by sharecroppers ('bhagchashis'). Occupancy rights could also be purchased by urban outsiders. With the development of commercial agriculture this upper stratum of tenants (called by different local names among which the *jotedar* has become the best-known) tended to combine exploitation of subtenants and sharecroppers with moneylending. Even where they employed landless labourers, an increasingly labour surplus situation made technological innovation unnecessary for profit maximization, especially because there were no minimum wages for agricultural labour. Jotedar elements tended to belong to ritually low but locally dominant and often quite prosperous castes—Mahisyas in south-west Bengal, Aguris and Sadgops in Burdwan—unlike the overwhelmingly upper-caste zamindar and tenure-holder; poor peasant categories, sharecroppers and labourers often came from untouchable or tribal groups. A few untouchable groups like the Namasudras had thrust themselves up into enterprising tenant ranks in some areas.

[8] Ranajit Guha, *A Rule of Property for Bengal* (Paris, 1963); Ratnalekha Ray, *Change in Bengal Agrarian Society c 1760–1850* (Delhi, 1979); Partha Chatterji, *Bengal 1920–1947*.

Stratification within the peasantry was most advanced in the economically stagnant moribund delta region of West Bengal. There were exceptions. At Midnapur, the percentage of 'owner-cultivators' was 52.46 according to the 1931 census, indicating a relatively broad middle-peasant development which partly helped to create a broad mass base for nationalism in this district. Another favourable factor for a unified, consolidated mass base was the predominance of a single caste—Mahisyas—among all levels of the peasantry. Differentiation was much less evident in south-east Bengal where jute enabled the small peasant economy to exist in relative prosperity till the depression.[9]

Contradictions and tensions within rural society frequently revealed an anti-imperialist potential. There had been a history of peasant or tribal anti-British struggles, independent of external political mediation, from early colonial times.[10] British rule had created the existing system of property relations and it consistently tried to bolster up the status-quo by giving full legal protection to established property rights. Since colonialism marked a clear break with older patterns of property-holding, in times of stress, peasants could transpose their visions and hopes of a kinder and more responsible patriarchal social order into an imagined pre-British past, and defy contemporary social arrangements in the name of indigenous, traditional and more authentic customs. They had, therefore, their own independent version of the nationalist critique of colonial economy. The police, ill-paid, corrupt and cruel, tended to be universally unpopular as the visible symbol of alien oppression. Confrontations with the police during movements of nationalist upheaval were frequent and easily organized. At the same time, rural tensions carried ample possibilities of divisiveness. The immediate oppressor—zamindar, moneylender, trader or policeman—tended to be a fellow-Indian.

In East Bengal the situation was further complicated by the fact that the bulk of zamindars, tenure-holders and trader-mahajans were Hindus while the peasantry was overwhelmingly Muslim. Social conflict would not necessarily or inevitably coincide with

[9] GOB, *Report of the Land Revenue Commission. Vol. I:* GOB, *Report of the Bengal Provincial Banking Enquiry Committee*; Partha Chatterji, *Bengal 1920–1947.*

[10] Ranajit Guha, *Elementary Aspects of Peasant Insurgency in Colonial India* (Delhi, 1983); Suprakash Ray, *Bharater Krishak Vidraha O Ganatantrik Sangram*, Vol.I (Calcutta, 1966).

anti-British struggles. The State, remote and inaccessible in its final authority, in contrast, could very often seem isolated from local tyrants and injustice. Its distance from local problems therefore vested it with final justiciable and corrective functions. The myth of 'Maharanir rajya'—the rule of the Great Queen—lingered on, and blended with indigenous, traditional faith in the retributive powers of the Great Mother Goddess Durga. The trust in the benevolence of the distant authorities, however, was nowhere as absolute or tenacious as the British fondly imagined them to be. The quick and open defiance by villagers during moments of upheaval was very much a part of the matrix of peasant consciousness.

A clearly worked-out nationalist ideology was initially articulated by English educated urban groups, overwhelmingly 'bhadralok' Hindu in composition, which combined professional jobs with zamindari or intermediate tenure-holding. Numerous schemes were formulated, both in Swadeshi and in Gandhian periods, for village reconstruction. The link with rent-receiving interests, however, generally constrained more effective expressions of concern. Caste and socio-cultural differences created a distance which was a badge of 'bhadralok' honour. Any levelling process would deprive the bhadralok of the insignia of self-respect and constitute a cultural disaster, no less significant than the economic catastrophe. In the 1920s virtually every section of nationalist opinion opposed moves to curb zamindari rights and give some legal protection to bargadars. The Nationalist utopia was, therefore, not necessarily a land of freedom and equality. It was quite often a traditional patriarchal universe—a Ramrajya, envisioned even by modernistic elements in Bengali society.

In its self-image and aspirations, the intelligentsia saw itself as a middle class on the western model, bringing modernity through bourgeois development. Yet, this was a middle class connected, not with industry or even with large-scale trade and commerce, but with the liberal professions and landholding. Its failure to develop into a bourgeoisie proper was caused not so much by faulty values or unsound business instincts, as by the early and massive hold established on the higher reaches of modern commerce and industry by European firms backed by a foreign government.[11] The second rung in the business hierarchy came to be occupied in the twentieth

[11] Amiya Bagchi, *Private Investment in India 1900–1939* (Cambridge, 1972), Chapter VI.

century by Marwari and other non-Bengali businessmen, drawing upon established, all India connections. Efforts to change the situation through patriotic fervour in the Swadeshi period had largely petered out by the 1920s. The decade also saw the decline of Bengali entrepreneurship in the coal industry[12] in the face of European and Marwari competition and the discriminatory treatment by British-controlled railways and banks. Civil Disobedience would not be associated in Bengal with anything like Swadeshi enterprises. The autobiography of the patriotic scientist-cum-Swadeshi entrepreneur P.C. Ray—published in 1932—complained bitterly that Bengalis were cornered and pushed out of business by Marwaris.[13] At a totally different level, a folk-song in 1930 complained:

Here (in Calcutta), Bengalis count for nothing
They lag behind all.
From Dalhousie to Chowringhee
is controlled by the 'feringee',
The Marwaris boss over Burrabazar
How many Bengalis are even rickshaw-pullers,
carters or porters?
Even cooks come from outside.[14]

The last lines of the song refer to another problem. Casual labourers as well as the greater part of the industrial working-class came from outside Bengal. Distress at growing economic insignificance had its counterpart in political frustrations: by the 1930s Bengal had clearly lost her earlier leadership in the national movement.

On this rickety structure fell the massive blow of world depression. It aggravated the already growing problem of educated unemployment. The professional urban middle class, with its fixed incomes, would still be over-compensated for this by falling prices. Men and women of that generation recall the 1930s not as years of crisis or depression but as a time of plenty and prosperity, as a kind of a golden memory. The real disaster was for the direct producers who derived the bulk of their income from land. Bengal's small-

12 C.P. Simmons, 'Indigenous Enterprise in the Indian Coalmining Industry, c 1835–1939' *Indian Economic and Social History Review,* (Vol. XIII, ii, April-June 1976).

13 Prafulla Chandra Ray, *Life and Experiences of a Bengali Chemist* (Calcutta, 1932).

14 *Bangabani*, 10 April 1930. Song composed by the 'Sang' (Folk entertainer) of Jelepara.

peasant economy received a shattering blow in many areas. The development of a broad middle peasant stratum, connected with jute, also suffered a decisive setback.[15]

Depression constituted such an overwhelmingly important phenomenon that almost all rural protest in this period may seem to be linked to its effects. This impression is heightened by the fact that due to the compulsions of a province-wide study I could not go into the specifics of the movements that I have referred to. Cultural determinants have, therefore, been missed out frequently, constituting a huge gap in my study. Let me make amends by stating that I did not intend any form of economic determinism. To give two obvious examples of how an upswing in rural protest is not a mechanical product of an economic crisis, one can refer to the events in 1921–2 and 1943. In 1921–2, a rise in rural protest occurred at a time of relative improvement in the situation for direct producers. 1943 was the year of the worst famine in colonial Bengal: the countryside saw a virtual Dance of Death. Starving, uprooted, ruined peasants went through it all without any obvious struggle or serious protest.

Official records, with all their limitations, have constituted a decisive part of the source material for this study. Their slants and prejudices are naively transparent and can easily be seen through. Administrative necessity, however, made it imperative to record events as precisely and vividly as possible. A similar authenticity and immediacy of experience is conveyed through British-owned newspapers and the private papers or memoirs left by contemporary English officials and non-officials. The India Office Library and the Cambridge South Asian Study Centres have good collections of such papers. The accuracy of their information can be cross-checked by contemporary private papers, oral records, newspapers and writings of Indian nationalists which I have used in equal proportions. A large number of local histories of districts, police stations, even villages were prepared at that time as well as later. I found in them extremely useful and interesting material. Bengali literature of the 1920s and 1930s provided crucially important evidence; not only did it carry social and political perceptions and attitudes, it also created them. A whole series of proscribed literature—books, pamphlets and leaflets in English and Bengali—preserved in particular at the India Office Library and the British Museum, shed

15 B.B. Chaudhuri, 'The Process of De-peasantisation in Bengal and Bihar. 1885–1947', *Indian Historical Review* Vol. II, July 1975.

valuable light on programmes and activities of Congressmen, terrorists, Communists and of Hindu and Muslim communal politicians. Pamphlets and booklets written in different dialects on local issues by barely literate people constituted a source for perceptions at the grass-roots level. I read through a large number of such fascinating documents at the India Office Library and at the National Library in Calcutta. Interviews with several men and women who either served in an official capacity or played a role in Congress, terrorist or Communist activities in the 1920s and 1930s often provided new insights.

The years that I have written about were years that were lived and experienced by my grand-parents and my parents. I have been steeped in the ambience of these years, been constantly washed by a flow of living memory. I have, along with my generation, been created by them. This has defined the real, most intense engagement with my theme as also the problems, the difficulties of the painful and often unsuccessful process of necessary distancing.

CHAPTER 1

1928–29

Radical Swarajists

The Non-Cooperation struggle of 1921–2 saw a unique conjuncture of political forces in Bengal. Workers and peasants, tribals and the bhadralok, Gandhians and terrorists, Muslims as well as Hindus, knitted together their varied hopes and aspirations into a broadly common aim of immediate Swaraj. Swaraj, however, did not come in a year, the many millenarian hopes that had informed the upsurge faded away, and Gandhi's unilateral withdrawal of the movement ultimately led to widespread demoralization and stagnation.

Two political alternatives replaced the phase of active struggle. A section of the Congress, the 'No Changers', retired to village bases and followed Gandhi's programme of constructive rural and social work. Another section, the Swarajist Party, accepted Chittaranjan Das' programme of Council entry and of wrecking dyarchy from within. Along with Das' Hindu-Muslim Pact of 1923, which gave substantial electoral and job concessions to Muslims, these provided a positive line of action for the time being. An optimism and a sense of promise were reflected even in the poetry of Jibanananda Das, where a mournful nostalgia usually constituted the dominant mood. Instead of evoking the gently-decaying beauties of a moribund Bengal, he wrote with uncharacteristic jubilation in 1925: 'The crisis in Bengal's life is now over'.[1]

The mood did not last very long. Even in Das' lifetime Council obstructionism had gone stale. He died in 1925, and prospects of united action, even on a limited scale, ended when the Hindu-Muslim Pact was rescinded in 1926. The vicious riots of 1926 wiped

[1] Jibanananda Das, *Rupashi Bangla* (Calcutta, 1932), p. 31.

out the memory of the common fight. A large number of nationalist Muslims were alienated because of the growing links that had developed between the Congress and the Hindu communal organizations. An acute problem of succession almost split the Swarajist Party right down the middle after Das' death. It eventually led to the ouster of B.N. Sasmal, a valued lieutenant of Das and the leader of a powerful peasant agitation in Midnapur. Subhas Chandra Bose and Jatindra Mohan Sengupta, however, continued a squabble which ended only in 1933 with Sengupta's death. The situation was not more hopeful outside Swarajist circles. Gandhian rural ashrams, formed in the first flush of Non-Co-operation enthusiasm, seemed to have reached their most creative peak and were now on a course of decay and decline.[2] The massive spate of arrest after Das' assassination in 1924 had thrown the revolutionary terrorists into complete disaray. They did not recover until the late 1920s.

The Congress decision to boycott the all-white Simon Commission in 1927 provided a way out of the general rut. The Congress organization began to pick up, the release of terrorist prisoners from 1927 led to fresh reorganization, a formidable youth and volunteer movement developed in Calcutta and mofussil towns, recovering their militancy through anti-Simon Commission demonstrations and hartals. A powerful strike wave swept over the railway workers, the jute millhands, the Corporation scavengers and the oil depot workers at Budge Budge. Most of these movements were organized by the Workers' and Peasants' party, an open front of the Communists. A few Congress leaders like Bose began to take an interest in this and there was some possibility that the two movements might draw closer. By 1929, however, such prospects had been defeated by Congress intransigence, by official repression which smashed the labour organizations and by the sixth Comintern line which instructed the Communists to revise the broad-front strategy. Even so, the 1928–9 period did end the political lull and provide a fitting prelude to Civil Disobedience.

Das's death created the need for a new provincial leader, for a cult figure. The choice lay between Subhas Bose and Jatindra Mohan Sengupta. Bose was unconditionally released from Mandalay prison in May 1927. He had been kept there in atrocious conditions since 925.[3] Critically ill in prison, he had already be-

[2] N.P. Bannerji, *At the Crossroads* (Calcutta, 1950), p. 202.

[3] N. P. Mitra (ed.), *The Indian Quarterly Register, The Chronicle of Events*, 16 May 1927 (Calcutta, 1928).

come an embodiment of suffering and of self-sacrifice—attributes indispensable for nationalist heroes of the Gandhian era who, because of their non-violence, were unable to appear as conquering heroes. Apart from the aura of near-martyrdom, his assets included the support of several important political forces. He had close links with some terrorist groups like the Jugantar and the backing of the powerful big Five of Bengal politics—Bidhan Chandra Ray, Nalini Ranjan Sarkar, Sarat Chandra Bose, Nirmal Chandra Chunder and Tulsi Charan Goswami. Highly successful professional men with large-scale business and zamindari interests, the big Five exercised considerable influence over the Swarajists mainly through financial support. Sarat Bose was Subhas's brother and this probably helped him to secure their confidence.

The charismatic appeal that Bengali political traditions assign to Bose derives largely from the fact that he is seen as Bengal's own alternative, even challenge, to the Gandhian leadership. The activities of the 1928–9 period went a long way in putting together this image. It was in these years that he defined the contours of the movement that he was to lead: its social base, the main issues and a particular idiom of nationalist discouse that was common to a wide range of middle class militants. Along with Jawaharlal Nehru, he constituted a radical pressure group within the Congress. Nehru had put forward the Independence resolution at the Madras Congress session to oppose the Dominion Status goal. Bose was unwilling to make his disagreement with the old guard public but his sympathy for Nehru's resolution was well known. The resolution was finally watered down to a vague announcement of ultimate goals. A recognition of the strength behind the demand is still indicated by the appointment of Bose and Nehru as General Secretaries of the Congress in 1928.[5] They also planned to set up an Independence for India League after a Delhi meeting in November 1928.[6] The formation of the League indicated the emergence of an 'avant-garde' that held the possibility of eventually broadening and radicalizing the Congress. In Bengal Bose had arrived as a rebel, as the hero of the urban youth. His open adherence to the Independence goal, moreover, endeared him to new groups of revolutionary terrorists.

[4] For a study of factional politics in the Bengal Congress see Bhola Chatterji, *Aspects of Bengal Politics in the Nineteen-Thirties* (Calcutta, 1969).

[5] S. Gopal, *Jawaharlal Nehru: A Biography, Vol. I 1889–1947* (Bombay, 1976), p. 11.

[6] Subhas Chandra Bose, *The Indian Struggle, 1920–42* (Calcutta, 1964), p. 153.

Organizationally this was perhaps the most creative phase in Bose's life before the formation of the Azad Hind Fauj. A stridently militant idiom and keen interest in agitational politics recruited large numbers of urban youth and students as his volunteers. Bose welcomed this as 'the most encouraging sign of the year'.[7] And, indeed, this was to be his most significant contribution, his most powerful weapon, his real base. He fulfilled the longing of a forcibly disarmed people for martial romance when at the Calcutta Congress session he gave a para-military look to his volunteer corps and paraded in Khaki on horseback as General-Officer-Commanding. His volunteers went on 'route marches' in the South Calcutta suburbs in glittering Khaki uniforms and Bose duly inspected them and took their salute, giving quite a display of military pageantry.[8] The All-Bengal Young Mens' Association had been founded in 1922 and in 1928 its name was changed, under Bose's direction, to All-Bengal Youth Association so that women would also be eligible as members. With Bose as the President of the Bengal Provincial Congress Committee, the hold of the more militant youths on the organization increased noticeably and the distinction between radical young volunteers and actual revolutionary terrorists was often blurred. Confirmed terrorists would have no objection to working as Bose's volunteers in his youth organizations, infiltrating into the District Congress Committees and occasionally capturing them on his behalf. An All-Bengal Khadi Exhibition was held in Calcutta in October 1929 with patriotic magic lantern shows, anti-Government posters and portraits of nationalist martyrs. Demonstrations of dagger play were an added attraction for the youth.[9]

An extremely militant agitation grew up around the boycott of foreign cloth. Bose's style of campaign, however, did not meet with Gandhi's approval. Gandhi possibly resented his enterprise at a time when he himself did not feel ready to launch a movement. In a letter written to the Bengali Gandhian leader Satish Dasgupta he mocked the 'sensational reports about boycott' and described them as 'perfectly useless'.[10] Bose, however, was able to involve a variety of groups in this movement. Hindu and Muslim labourers organized a meeting at Tala on 24 February. There were a number of

[7] Bose, *The Indian Struggle*, p. 125.

[8] *Fortnightly Reports on Bengal*, first half of June 1929, GOI, Home Poll/17/1929.

[9] GOB, *Report on the Administration of Bengal, 1924–28* (Calcutta, 1929).

[10] Letter to Dasgupta 10.3.28, *Collected Works of Mahatma Gandhi*, Vol. XXXVI, February-June 1928 (GOI, 1973), p. 166.

meetings by upper and middle class Calcutta women, at one of which two thousand women took the boycott pledge.[11] Women were largely instrumental in deciding the main items of consumption within the household and a special effort was necessary to convince them about the issue. Bose was more interested in using the issue to draw them out into more public and activist roles like picketing of foreign cloth shops. A section of Marwari and other non-Bengali traders from the Burra Bazar area (the business heart of Calcutta) supported his efforts enthusiastically. Their co-operation was vital for the success of boycott since the movement depended very largely on export-import traders. The Hindu Sabha, which already had a strong base within this section, canvassed for Congress support and the two organizations worked in close and perfect harmony.[12]

Excitement over the boycott issue received a very powerful impetus and spread rapidly to the districts after Gandhi was arrested in Calcutta on 4 March 1929 when he was presiding over a public bonfire of foreign cloth at Shraddhananda Park.[13] The dramatic spectacle of cloth burning immediately captured popular imagination. The spectacle of fire and violent destruction was perhaps a necessary cathartic release for a very militant and emotional kind of struggle which had to function within a framework of non-violence.

Cloth burning and boycott pledges, however, remained more of a symbolic gesture since the actual decline in foreign cloth consumption was minimal. An official confidently stated at the end of 1929 that Khadi and boycott got only 'spasmodic support' and that 'there was no mass movement in support of the Congress programme'.[14] Boycott pledges remained largely verbal and were no longer reinforced by a resurgence in Swadeshi enterprises. There was some fall in the Calcutta import trade in cotton goods and liquor in 1929 but at the same time there was a rise in the import of tobacco, sugar, and machine goods. The fall in cotton goods was ascribed by officials to a dullness in demand due to an accumulation of stocks since 1927–8 rather than to the boycott movement.[15]

The hartal called on 3 February 1928 to protest against the arrival of the Simon Commission in Calcutta created a tradition of confron-

[11] *Forward*, 2, 22 February, 3, 13 March 1928.

[12] *The Amrita Bazar Patrika*, 8 January 1928

[13] *Fortnight Reports on Bengal, first half March 1929*, GOI, Home Poll 17–1929.

[14] GOB, *Report on the Administration of Bengal, 1928–29* (Calcutta, 1930).

[15] Ibid.

tation whose pattern would be repeated throughout the next two years. A feverish spate of meetings, largely under Bose's auspices, had prepared Calcutta for 3 February. 'I am afraid', wrote Bengal's Governor Jackson to Viceroy Irwin, 'that Bose is the real cause of the trouble.'[16] Extremely elaborate police precautions on the day of the hartal had turned 'Calcutta into a state of siege.' From dawn to dusk police and military patrols kept on their rounds and four aeroplanes hovered above the city. A few tramcars were dragged out on the streets under police escort but buses more or less stopped functioning throughout the day. The streets wore a deserted look with most of the shops shuttered and none of the mills in North Calcutta operated. In extensive parts of central and north Calcutta—Russa Road, Bhowanipur, Dharamtalla, the Hogg Market and the College Street areas—crowds of pedestrians and volunteers clashed with the police and Gurkha troops. Houses of Sikh transport workers were attacked by the police at Bhowanipur.[17] Students of Presidency College 'stoned the police for several hours.'[18] Even though the most sensational triumphs were achieved in Calcutta, a number of district towns in eastern and south-western Bengal responded quite gallantly—Mymensingh, Dacca, Chittagong, Faridpur, Rajshahi, Pabna, Bogra, Howrah, Burdwan and Bankura being some of them.[19]

Hartals, however, are a predominantly urban form of struggle. They can really make an impact on densely populated localities and in the areas of public transport, large bazars, offices and educational centres. Even within these limits, however, it was not an unqualified success. A number of district towns stayed out and the failure seems to be connected with the nationalist leaders' inability to mobilize Muslims. Muslims of Noakhali brought out counter-demonstrations and provided a feast to the street beggars to celebrate the arrival of the Commission. Even though Barisal had long been a hot-bed of nationalist agitation, it hardly participated in the hartal. It seems clear that the Congress failure here was a direct legacy of the Hindu-Muslim riots of 1926 and the prolonged Patuakhali Satyagraha (to be discussed later) within the district. The Satyagraha was undertaken over a basically communal issue which had made local Muslims deeply suspicious about Congress

[16] Jackson to Irwin, 13.2.28. *Halifax Collection*.

[17] *Forward*, 4 February 1928.

[18] Jackson to Irwin, 12.2.28. *Halifax Collection*.

[19] *Forward*, 13 February 1929.

bonafides. Even in Calcutta many Muslim groups—Chitpur Road shopkeepers and Circular Road 'biriwallahs' for instance—flouted the hartal call and did brisk business.[20]

Electoral campaigns for Corporation and Legislative Council seats were fought vigorously, with a fair measure of success, as a platform for anti-Government propaganda. The slogan for the Congress candidates for the Howrah municipal elections was, 'Will Howrah fail to join freedom's battle?'[21] Capture of Corporation seats provided a much needed source of financial patronage and a real power base to the Congress. Appointments in Corporation schools and offices were used to subsidize nationalist and terrorist families in distress. The celebration of important patriotic occasions by the municipal authorities seemed to provide at least the shadow of a parallel authority.[22] Bose was defeated in 1928 by an alliance of Muslim and non-Swarajist Councillors. The situation was reversed in 1929 when Sengupta was elected for Mayorship with the support of the Muslim Councillors. The Swarajists won another major triumph when their no-confidence motion was carried in the Council which was dissolved in April and fresh elections were called for. They won in all non-Muslim constituencies.[23] The electoral campaign, however, made it clear that elections were no longer a particularly lively political issue.[24] The Swarajists had already made their point about the hollowness of Dyarchy and repeated evidence of the same kind ceased to engage public interest to any serious extent.

Sections of mill and transport workers had been extremely active in hartals and demonstrations. Bose reciprocated their interest by addressing labour meetings to protest against the victimization of Tramways workers at the Bamangachhi loco shed at Howrah.[25] He became an office bearer in several new labour organizations—the All Bengal Automobile Society and the Oil & Petrol Workers' Union at Budge Budge. He formed a labour organization committee within the Bengal Provincial Congress Committee, which, however, seemed to have existed only on paper.[26] He also led a strike

[20] *The Amrita Bazar Patrika*, 4 February 1928.

[21] *Forward*, 27 March 1928.

[22] For an account of Congress use of Corporation funds, see GOB, *Terrorism, Civil Disobedience and the Calcutta Corporation* (GOB, Calcutta, 1934).

[23] GOB, *Report on the Administration of Bengal, 1928–29*.

[24] Ibid.

[25] *Forward*, 28 February, and 1 April 1928.

[26] Note by Petrie. GOI, Home Poll 257/I & KW, 1930.

at the Tata Iron & Steel Works at Jamshedpur in 1928 in which he had become somewhat accidentally involved.[27]

Such interest, however, was not very sustained. Jawaharlal had to reprimand Bose and urge him to collect funds for the Bauria jute mill strikers struggling in his home province. Government officials found his statements after the arrest of labour and communist leaders in the Meerut conspiracy case 'quite mild'.[29] At the Calcutta Congress session of 1928 a large demonstration of workers marched up to the Congress venue to demand that the Congress should represent their case more adequately. Bose, the GOC of the volunteer corps, harshly refused them entry.[30] It was widely rumoured that he had suggested asking for police help.[31] The procession to the Congress session was largely composed of workers struggling against railway and jute mill authorities. If that was any indication of the limits of his solidarity for workers pitted against the State or European capitalists, it was inevitable that he would be far more sensitive about the interests and fears of Indian capitalist groups, many of whom supported the nationalists. The point was shrewdly made by G.D. Birla who wrote to Thakurdas: 'Mr Bose could be relied upon to help the Tata Iron & Steel Works whenever necessary, provided properly handled . . . Mr Bose appreciates the necessity of co-operation with reasonable and advanced types of capitalists . . . His main object in labour matters . . . is no doubt service to the labour but not necessarily inimical to the capitalist.'[32]

Reduction of jute cultivation was the sole concrete issue that Bose used for rural mobilization. In a permanently settled Bengal, a discussion of most agrarian problems was likely to carry overtones of class conflict. Jute was a rare issue which could bind all rural strata together against the extraction of profits by foreign agencies.

[27] For an account of the strike see Vinay Behl, *Tata Iron & Steel Company ke Sramik Andolan, 1920–28* (Translated by Prabir Bhattacharya) in *Anya Artha* (October 1978).

[29] *Fortnightly Reports on Bengal*, 2nd half of March, GOI, Home Poll 17/1929.

[30] N.P. Bannerji, *At the Crossroad*, p. 212.

[31] This is mentioned in a contemporary satire on Bose, Narayan Chandra Bandopadhyaya, *Shree Bhaonta* (the Honourable Hoax) (Calcutta, 1930) PP Ben B 59 (IOL). The book also claimed that Bose's group crushed a press strike at the *Forward* (a pro-Bose newspaper) at a time when he was loudly proclaiming support to the working class in general.

[32] Birla to Thakurdas, 16.7.1929. Thakurdas–Birla Correspondence, FN 42, Purushottamdas Thakurdas Papers (NMML).

In March 1928 Bose issued an appeal to zamindars to reduce the acreage devoted to jute and to release more land for paddy.[33] An Anti-Jute Propaganda Committee was formed in April. It opened about thirty branches in the different jute-growing districts each equipped with one paid lecturer and two or three volunteers. They visited village 'hats' (markets) and went to 'baithaks' (village gatherings) where they talked about the jute issue, advised on health and sanitation, and occasionally, brought in the theme of Swaraj.[34] Jute growers were asked to exploit Bengal's world monopoly position in jute production and, by reducing the acreage devoted to the crop, to hike up prices to reduce the profit margin of European jute manufacturers. It was a return to a technique of rural mobilization that had been used in the Noakhali and Barisal districts at the beginnings of the Non-Co-operation movement.[35]

The continued use of jute reduction schemes by generations of Bengali nationalists linked up a nationalist device with certain deeply-rooted peasant attitudes towards different kinds of crops. These attitudes have been reflected in a host of 'panchalis'—verse-narratives composed and circulated in jute-growing districts. Generally ill-spelt and clumsily-written, these constitute a peasant discourse on the place of food crops and cash crops in rural life. Many of them go on to make wider generalizations about the purpose of peasant cultivation and the meaning of peasant existence. All reflect an acute fear that jute might actually uproot and displace paddy—the source of nourishment, a life-giving crop which is identified with nurture, with Lakshmi, with the most tangible expression of domestic prosperity. The fake lure of a crop that simply brought in hard cash, in contrast, would break down peasant self-sufficiency and contentment. Its quick and dubious profits would collapse one day, leading to hunger and scarcity. Profits would corrupt the pure and simple tenor of an ideal village community, increase stratification and create aspirations and ambitions among simple peasants whose practical wisdom teaches them otherwise not to outstrip the collective pace.[36] Self-sufficiency and guaranteed plenty that were associated with paddy and other food crops would give way to new, uncertain links with a totally unpredictable,

33 *Forward*, 23 March 1928.

34 *Forward*, 24 April 1928 and 12 March 1929.

35 *History of Non-Cooperation Movement in Bengal*, GOB, Poll Confidential 395 S. NI-I of 1924.

36 Abdul Chhamed Mian, *Desh Boka*, Part I (Mymensingh, 1930).

temperamental world market.[37]

Congress appeals, therefore, could find some resonance in the villages. A jotedar, from Chandura Hat at Brahmanbaria in Tippera, remarked approvingly: 'So the Congress has begun rather late what I was crying for all these years.'[38] At the same time such rural literature seemed to be largely normative and prescriptive, while actual peasants found it difficult to overlook the fact that jute prices were rising steadily for the last six years,[39] and that increased acreage would immediately bring in more profits. The appeals angered the more politicized Muslim rural groups. Mohammed Moizuddin Hamidi from Khulna referred sarcastically to 'those Congressmen who dress up as liberators of the homeland and constantly try to appear as friends and sympathizers of the ryot with their propaganda for reducing jute cultivation. These are the men who in the last Council were responsible for the Ryot Destroying Bill, alias the Zamindari Rights Bill, alias the Tenancy Amendment Bill.'[40]

The statement refers to the unanimous Swarajist stand on the Tenancy Amendment Bill debates in the Legislative Council.[41] The Bill had been before the Council continuously since 1926 and divisions on various proviso had generated intense controversy within the house. It was re-introduced in a revised form by Sir P.C. Mitter in August 1928. The main points of discussion and debate centred around the transferability of occupancy holdings, the rights of under-raiyats and the adjustment of certain landlord and tenant rights on matters like the cutting of trees. Another significant point was the determination of the status of the sharecropper: whether he was an agricultural labourer or an inferior under-tenant, and the fixation of his rights accordingly. At every step the Swarajists unequivocally advocated the protection and even the extension of existing landlord privileges vis-a-vis tenants. Jitendra Lal Bannerji was the lone

[37] See, for instance, Munshi Kumar Ali, *Jatiya Gan*, (Comilla 1926) BEN B 4314 (IOL) which reflects the nationalist use of thie peasant discourse. For more authentic verisons of the rual discourse itself, see Abedali Mian, *Desh Shanti*, (Rangpur, 1926) BEN/B 4381 (IOL), and Abdul Chhamed Mian, *Desh Boka*, Part I (Mymensingh, 1930).

[38] Notes on Jute Propaganda P-28/11 of 1928, *AICC Papers* (NMML).

[39] Ajit Das Gupta, 'Jute Textile Industry' in V.P. Singh (ed.) *Economic History of India* (Bombay, 1965), p. 265.

[40] Muhammed Moizuddin Hamidi, *Krishaker Unnati* (Khulna, 1929), p. 40.

[41] On the configuration of political interests behind the debates see Partha Chatterji, *Bengal 1920–1947*.

nationalist who differed with the Swarajist stand on the landlord's fee on transfer of holding or the right of pre-emption in such cases. He, too, toed the line when it came to the rights of under-tenants and bargadars. All suggestions about upgrading their status were scotched by a firmly united Swarajist group and the only opposition came from a few Muslim Councillors.[42] On this one occasion the Swarajists even reversed their consistent strategy of council obstructionism. In all the debates and voting they bent over backwards to support Government motions and arguments. 'Government was generally successful', wrote an official, 'with the support of the Swarajist Party in defeating the amendments in favour of tenants' interests.'[43] Large parts of Bengal were affected at this time by powerful movements of tenants and Muslim or untouchable sharecroppers. The Swarajist line had its consequence, therefore, in loss of support or bases in these sectors. The growth of active Proja Samitis and their capture by anti-Congress Muslim politicians received an impetus from the clear-cut class affiliations of Swarajists.

The Jute Reduction campaign was the entire sum and substance of Bose's specific message for the peasantry. The Bengal Provincial Conference at Rangpur in 1929 laid down a fairly comprehensive plan for mobilizing factory labour, youths, students and women. Jute propaganda remained, even here, the lone item meant to recruit the peasant.[44] Such omission contrasts strangely with Bose's Lahore Congress speech which called upon the Congress 'to undertake at once the task of organizing the peasants and other oppressed sections of the Indian People, on their own grievances.'[45]

Organizationally, the BPCC was not on a sound footing under Bose. The AICC auditor complained in 1929 that cash books did not balance, the Secretary had never signed the books, vouchers were often unsigned and contained no details about travel expenses. No salary registers had been kept and none of the District Congress Committees had submitted any accounts.[46] Bengal failed to fulfil the Congress quota of membership recruitment: by September 1929 she had recruited only 52, 283 out of a projected

[42] Bengal Legislative Council Proceedings, 30th Session, July-August 1928. Calcutta, 1929).

[43] *Fortnightly Reports on Bengal,* GOI, Home Poll 1/28, 1928.

[44] *Forward*, 31 March 1928.

[45] Speech at the Lahore Congress, Report of the Indian National Congress, 44th session, Lahore (December, 1929), p. 93.

[46] *AICC Papers*, P 28/11, 1929.

total of 124, 403 members.[47]

By the end of 1929 the contours of the movement inspired directly by Bose emerged quite clearly. Urban bhadralok youth constituted his most important field of concern. Herein lay his greatest strength as well as his weakness. Unlike his rivals Sasmal and Sengupta, who had attained provincial leadership by organizing major peasant and labour movements, Bose lacked experience in sustained constructive organizational work from a well-defined local or regional base. The lack of a concrete social base gave a peculiarly amorphous character to his urban radicalism.

Jatindra Mohan Sengupta did not represent a course of action or ideology that was markedly different from that of Bose. The personal differences between the two leaders, however, were of crucial importance within the factional politics of the Bengal Congress. Sengupta worked among the very same sections that consituated Bose's main base—students, youth, terrorist groups, and to a much lesser extent, the workers. His closer ties with the rural Gandhians, however, gave him a potential foothold in rural areas.

Sengupta rose to political prominence at Chittagong when in April 1921 he organized a strike by the Burma Oil company employees. He went on to organize relief for the tea garden coolies stranded at Chandpur after their exodus from Sylhet.[48] With these local achievements behind him, he became a close associate of Das after whose death he inherited his 'Triple Crown'—leadership of the Swarajist Party, Presidentship of the BPCC and Mayorship of the Calcutta Corporation. After Bose was released from gaol, Sengupta relinquished the BPCC Presidentship to him.

After Bose's release both the leaders vied for Das' status and gathered different political groups around themselves. Antagonism burst out into the open over the issue of Congress exhibition accounts after the Calcutta Congress Session. Sordid accusations and counter accusations were flung at each other through the two nationalist dailies—the *Forward* (under Bose's control) and the *Advance* (founded by Sengupta in 1929 to reply to Bose's charges). The big Five remained firm on Bose's side while Sengupta was more certain of AICC support. Preoccupations with these intrigues, however, cost him his Chittagong base which was captured by terrorist volunteers who admired Bose's militancy and voted against

[47] GOB, *Report on the Administration of Bengal, 1928–29* (Calcutta, 1930).

[48] Surendrachandra Dhar, *Deshapriya Jatindra Mohan* (Calcutta, 1933) BEN 1153 (IOL) p. 99.

Sengupta in the 1929 BPCC elections. Bose was elected BPCC President and Sengupta's faction brought charges of election irregularities against him. Until the AICC arbiter Aney published his award in 1930 and imposed a resolution of the dispute, letters carrying endless charges and counter charges flew to the AICC from both sides.[49] Sitaramayya, sent earlier by the AICC to investigate the matter, wrote in horror: 'It gave me an insight into the character of the leading men in the province.'[50]

Sengupta played a very important role in Corporation and Council level politics. These spheres of political action, however, were becoming increasingly marginal to the unfolding of agitational politics. Students and youths, therefore, remained an important source of support to him. The All-Bengal Students' Association was loyal to him. In October 1929 its Secretary opposed Bose's call for a general strike in schools and colleges. Bose promptly formed his own group—The Bengal Provincial Students Association.[51] He also outdid his rival in forming a militant volunteer corps and in a somewhat wider range of activities among the workers. Sengupta's stand over the Tenancy Amendment Bill within the Council was indistinguishable from Bose's: both stuck to the Swarajist line with equal fervour. The alternative leadership, embodied by Sengupta, had therefore much the same content as Bose's albeit in a less dynamic form.

Radical Congressmen and terrorists shared a range of idioms and expressions, which made up an internally consistent patriotic discourse for urban middle class Hindu nationalists. The pivotal point was youth power—youth being necessarily urban, Hindu and middle class. Bose referred to youth awakening in contemporary China, Turkey and Germany as the most positive signs of progress. Surendramohan Ghosh, a terrorist leader from Jugantar, described youth as inevitably reckless, self-sacrificing and freedom loving. Purna Chandra Das, another important Jugantar leader, saw the future of the country in youth action alone. The *Gita* was frequently cited to evoke a death-defying mood among the youth. The language of such addresses was steeped in a kind of torrential, fast-flowing emotionalism, an effusive, hyperbolic rhetoric. 'He alone is young', wrote Bose, 'who can lose himself in the eternal sport (Lila) of creation and destruction.' A more concrete message

[49] *AICC Papers*, G 120/1929, G 2/1929, G 39/1929.

[50] Ibid. G 120/1929.

[51] *Deshapriya Jatindra Mohan*, p. 332.

was to ignore all imported ideas and thought. Bose claimed that both republicanism and socialism were essentially Indian concepts and that the Indian youth need not search for direction anywhere outside India. Trilokyanath Chakravarti, a terrorist leader, reminded them of another important duty: freedom struggle was the sole need of the hour, youth should not be distracted by social reform or rural reconstruction schemes.[52] Such appeals had two covert targets. Glorification of indigenous concepts above foreign 'isms' seems to be an attack against communistic ideas which were beginning to interest a section of the urban intelligentsia. Stress on shelving social reform projects was a concealed denigration of Gandhian strategies.

The novelist Saratchandra Chattopadhyay, perhaps, more than any other contemporary figure, articulated and justified the self-image of middle class Bengali Hindu nationalism. His presidential address at the Rangpur All-Bengal Youth Conference in 1929 filled out Bose's ideological statements and gave them a somewhat more extreme form. He postulated a clear-cut polarization: Bengali youth = revolt vs All India Congress = caution and compromise. Unambiguously critical of Gandhian leadership, he claimed that Bengal had sacrificed more than others during Non-Co-operation: 'The Bengali youth loves his country more than any one else' with the possible exception of the youth of Punjab. He expressed a deep pessimism about the prospects of the coming struggle. The significance of the Bardoli Satyagraha was lightly dismissed. 'The only ray of hope is the awakening of youth power in Bengal.'[53]

Pather Dabi, politically his most significant novel, reflected as well as influenced several very important dimensions of this brand of nationalist thinking. The novel began to appear serially in *Bangabashi* from 1922—that is, just after the Non-Co-operation movement. It came out in the form of a book in 1926 and was immediately banned. It inspired generations of radical nationalists and revolutionary terrorists. The hero, Sabyasachi, is a revolutionary who moves in a mysterious manner all over South Asia but his plans and real activities are never definitely spelt out. The mystery somehow enhances his personality. Capable, literally of everything, he is the first superman in serious Bengali fiction, always a million times larger than life. The function of such superhuman attributes

[52]All these references are taken from a collection of patriotic addresses in *Jaubaner Dak* (Calcutta, 1929), BEN/B 68 (IOL).

[53] *Taruner Vidroha*, in *Sarat Sahitya Sangraha*, Vol. XIII (Calcutta, 1960).

seems to be to exalt him as a viable alternative to Gandhi, the real-life charismatic leader of the national movement. Using this fictional superman as a yardstick, all other alternative forms and agents of nationalism are cut down to size and ridiculed. Sabyasachi denies the peasant—whom Gandhi had brought into the Congress movement—any role in the freedom struggle. The working class—largely neglected by Gandhi—on the other hand does have an important function though as cannon-fodder for the liberation struggle and not as its conscious agent. 'My sole concern is about the educated middle class bhadralok', he proclaims, 'for they alone can die for an idea'. The process of 'substitutism' in political action has to move up another rung, for it is the charismatic leader who alone strikes the final blow. 'Let me carry the whole burden of the freedom struggle on my shoulders', cries Sabyasachi. Such proclamations seem to vie with Gandhi's unilateral decisions and supreme leadership.[54]

Pather Dabi came out in 1926. After the communal riots of 1926 Saratchandra added another dimension to his political thinking. He read out *The Hindu-Muslim Problem of Today* at a Hindu Sabha meeting in 1926. 'Hindustan is the land of the Hindus', he said, and Muslims must be excluded from the national movement. Gandhi's attempt to involve both the communities in a common fight had ruined the Non-Co-operation movement. New leaders must not even dream of unity since 'unity can only exist among equals',[55] and Muslims are doomed to remain inferior to Hindus.

If radical Congress leaders did not openly come up with such sentiments neither did they display any very strong convictions about unity or equality. They saw the defence of Hindu religious interests as a political and moral duty which the Congress was bound to accord very high priority. A communal fracas had developed in 1927 at Patuakhali in Barisal over a school Puja and cow-slaughter. Local Hindus went on a prolonged satyagraha in protest against Government and police attitudes. Satindranath Sen had earlier built up an extremely sound base among local Muslims through constructive activities. An anti-union board agitation had been launched here in 1926 with full Muslim participation.[56] He chose to give up these fronts and devote himself fulltime to the satyagraha. Congress leaders did not seem to perceive any danger

[54] *Pather Dabi*, in *Sarat Sahitya Sangraha, Vol III*, pp. 234, 298–9, 253–5, 264.

[55] *Bartaman Hindu-Mussalman Samasya*, in *Sarat Sahitya Sanghaha* Vol. XIII (Calcutta, 1972), pp. 68–75.

[32] Hiralal Dasgupta *Swadhinta Sangrame Barisal* (Calcutta, 1972), pp. 68–75.

or incongruity about the use of a basically communal issue for anti-Government mobilization and propaganda. The *Forward* issued a strident appeal: 'All the Hindus of India should come forward to help the Satyagraha movement with men and money'.[57] There was, therefore, something more than a lapse in such insensitivity: there was a real, if unconscious, identification between nationalism and Hinduism.

Rural Gandhians

The Swarajist—terrorist syndrome gave a certain orientation to the resurgent Congress movement. Another segment of the Congress—Rural Gandhians or erstwhile No-Changers—worked in villages, giving a very different dimension to the Congress movement and adding to its possibilities. After the formation of the Swarajist Party, they had detached themselves from the heady excitement of electoral politics to retire to village bases or 'ashrams' formed during or just after the Non-Co-operation movement. There they immersed themselves in local Khadi centres which acted as pivotal points for broader rural reconstruction schemes—arbitration courts, relief work and anti-untouchability campaigns. The quiet, sustained, constructive work and a deeper and more genuine involvement with village life stood in sharp contrast to the hectic electoral and agitational turbulence that characterized the rest of BPCC activities. They provided a thread of continuity between Non-Co-operation and Civil Disobedience.

Gandhians did not constitute a completely homogeneous, unified alternative to the Swarajists. There was, as we shall see, considerable and significant internal variation among different rural bases.[57] They still shared certain assumptions about present-day political options and the shape of the future Ramrajya. The core of this shared body of thought was non-violent, constructive rural work, concretized through Khadi, national education and social service. Rural handicrafts were the central motif in their scheme of rejuvenation and growth. The exposition of an alternative model of growth progressed through a critique of modern urban industries as well as through arguments for small scale, rural handicrafts produc-

[57] *Forward*, 15 March 1928.

[57a] This is a point that has not been sufficiently emphasized by the otherwise very valuable detailed studies of several Gandhians bases in south-western Bengal by Hiteshranjan Sanyal. See Sanyal, 'Dakshin-Pashchim Banglai Jatiyatabadi Andolan' *Chaturanga*, Vaisakh-Ashar, 1384/1977.

tion. The arguments, however, did not pursue their inner logic entirely: the range of exclusions within the discourse is illuminating. Criticism of modern industries was not premised on a systematic analysis of the capitalist system of production and labour relations. On the contrary, several important Gandhians visualized the co-existence of the two systems.[58] Concern about problems of Indian workers was confined to a few vague sentimentalities about the wretchedness of the 'Kuli-majur' (worker and labourer) without exploring its origin or meaning.

Nor was any concern expressed about the growing problem of educated middle class unemployment. The entire class, in fact, came in for a great deal of impassioned censure. Rural Gandhian literature developed a consistent image of Calcutta: a snare of glittering corruption, with no organic links with real Bengal, a centre of hedonistic consumption draining the countryside of its wealth and sons, a fake world of alienating western education and values. The city was represented as a sort of a Scarlet Woman in contrast to the virtuous and pure rural Bengal.[59]

The positive alternative to such decadence was the image of simple rural peace, the repository of all true virtues. The central figure in this picture was the self-sufficient, honourable peasant who dominates a rural scene which seems strangely untouched by any serious internal contradictions or conflict. The binary opposition between the city and the country, the bhadralok and the 'chashi', actually reinforced the status-quo in villages. Satish Dasgupta's *Bharate Samyavad* (Communism in India) encapsulated an entire spectrum of attitudes. Written in 1930 by a man who was known as Bengal's Gandhi, this is, on the surface, an attack against the faction-mongering demagogues of Calcutta. They are criticized for their lack of communication with the masses, for their vicarious sympathy for the cult of violence which often leads to communal conflict. A deeper purpose, however, was an ideological reply to the challenge of the Soviet model of development. In a manner strikingly Slavophile, it argues that the caste system, in its pristine purity, captured the essence of socialism since 'all effort and intention favour the community although individual distinctions are not

[58] See for instance Dr I.B. Ghosal's speech at the 3rd session of the 24 Parganas District Political Conference, Budge-Budge. Proscribed Pamphlet, June 1931, PP BEN/B2B (IOL).

[59] See for instance Satish Chandra Dasgupta, *Bharate Samyavad* (Calcutta, 1930), p. 59; or the plays of Mukunda Das like *Karmakshetra* (Kasipur, 1930). Proscribed book, PP BEN/B3I (IOL).

to be ignored...'. Such a system overcomes notions of private accumulation and possessive individualism more successfully than anything achieved in the Soviet Union.

Dasgupta insisted that a perfect caste system rules out contempt for untouchables and lowly castes—a distortion introduced into Hindu doctrine only after Muslim invasions. The vocation of all these orders may look humble but they remain honourable and useful. The Ramrajya that he envisaged is one in which the peasant's prosperity will be assured. It is also an order where he will be firmly kept in his proper station. A perfect system of education is designed specially for the peasant. 'They will have to be taught in such a way that they will contentedly stay on villages and live blameless lives....Their syllabus must not be too heavy. They will learn the alphabet, some elementary arithmetic and, at the most, how to read the *Ramayana*... that is enough for the common run of peasants.'[60] The ideal peasant then aspires towards contentment rather than knowledge and awareness. Mukunda Das, the Gandhian village bard from Barisal, summed up significant peasant virtues: 'Those who sacrifice their lives to save their masters and hope for nothing but a place in heaven.'[61]

Dasgupta attempted to redefine the motives, functions and role of the zamindar in the present rural world. Any fundamental incompatibility between landlord and tenant interest is denied. If the zamindar does not fulfil his traditional obligations any longer (such a possibility is admitted, albeit somewhat hesitantly), that is because he is now reduced to the status of a 'tax daroga'—a mere middle-man who collects taxes, keeps his own commission and hands over the rest to the State. The substantial and varied burden of abwabs and cesses surprisingly do not find mention. The absentee landlord too is exempted from blame since under changed conditions his role is a limited one and old expectations no longer apply.[62] Oppression and exploitation, then, are not related to the system of expropriation of surplus under feudal zamindars: the decline of the system and the erosion of the traditional zamindar are the roots of the problem. The disappearance of this ideal type did in fact haunt a wide section of Bengali nationalists interested in agrarian problems. A mythical rural past was woven around the central figure of a benevolent paternal despot; he administers justice, lays down norms, disseminates culture and binds the whole village to and around him to

[60] Dasgupta, *Bharate Samyavad*, pp. 8, 61, 65.
[61] Das, *Karmakshetra*, pp. 86–7.
[62] Dasgupta, *Bharate Samyavad*, p. 64.

constitute patriarchal family networks. Extraction of rent, interest, unpaid labour or eviction of tenants became marginal and negligible facets of the total picture. Once colonial revenue and local government arrangements have destroyed this set-up, rural Gandhians are at a loss to suggest an alternative except for a simple return to the past.[63]

Fire is reserved for the rising stratum of rich jotedars or intermediate tenants. This could be a concealed attack against a major political rival—the men of the Proja movement with their base among richer tenants. The criticism is linked up, however, with the urban bhadralok which allegedly grows out of this group. That zamindari and tenurial interests characterized the urban elite even more than jotedari ones is a fact which again is not mentioned.[64]

The communal riots of 1926 deeply disturbed the Gandhians. Many had occurred in Eastern Bengal villages where Gandhians had built up important bases among the Muslim poor. During Non-Co-operation, the Congress had distributed large numbers of charkhas among Muslims in Comilla, Chittagong, Nadia (then Kushtia) and Noakhali villages. This had been done on such a large scale that the tradition of charkha spinning survives even today in these places. Maulvi Fazlul Huq had set up a 'Khilafatist Weaving Centre' at Noakhali which had a considerable Muslim youth membership. An enthusiastic Muslim Khadi promoter, who carried its sales to Chittagong, was nicknamed Khaddar Mian.[65] After the violence of 1926 co-operation and joint endeavours practically disappeared. Dasgupta sought to turn the tide through sincere reiterations of respect for the Islamic faith—a note that was becoming extremely unusual in Bengali Hindu, even Congress, circles from the mid-1920s. Gandhians also insisted that all manner of concessions would have to be made to Muslims to assuage their fears and suspicions. Dasgupta very perceptively indicated how revolutionary terrorism might unintentionally widen the communal gulf; violence may equally well be used against each other and terrorist

[63] See portrayals of the zamindar in short stories and novels of Tarasankar Bandopadhyay, *Jalsaghar*, *Chandimandap*. Bibhutibhushan Bandopadhyay, who wrote extensively on rural experiences but who had no overt nationalist associations, on the other hand, portrays a very different kind of zamindar: a petty, rather insignificant figure with small, scattered holdings, dependent on his agent for extorting from tenants the necessary props of a rather crude and unadorned philistine existence: neither the cultural standard-bearer of *Jalsaghar*, nor the powerful and benevolent father-figure remembered by Debu in *Chandimandap*.

[64] Dasgupta, *Bharate Samyavad*, p. 66.

[65] Mohammad Waliullah, *Yugavichitra* (Dacca, 1967), pp. 141–3.

centres could have a vicious role to play during peak points in communal violence.[66]

The theme of brotherhood occupied a major place in the plays that Mukunda Das wrote at this time. The point got somewhat fudged, though, by the consistent depiction of Muslim social subordination and their willing acceptance of it. A Muslim rich peasant, for instance, generously sacrifices his property to retrieve the fortunes of the Hindu zamindar whom he treats as his lord and master.[67] Mutual esteem and toleration were not, however, an entirely adequate antidote to the communal divide. The problems and grievances of a broadly Muslim peasantry, pitted against a largely Hindu zamindar-moneylender combine, could not be tackled by most Gandhians, committed as they were to the rural hierarchical scheme. The force of their very sincere appeals for brotherhood and unity was mitigated by the persistent use of Hindu scripture and imagery that was structured into the Gandhian discourse on Ramrajya.

There was no single uniform model of rural Gandhian activities. Much variation characterized the pattern of bases, local linkages, patronage and forms of work undertaken by different ashrams. The Swaraj Sevak Sangha at Barisal was financed by the rich mahajan Gopeswar Saha and the Ramchandpur zamindar, Kaliprasanna Guha-Chowdhary. It focused entirely on charkha, tree planting and national education.[68] At Outshahi village in Vikrampur, Dacca, the Palli Kalyan Ashram that was set up after Non-Co-operation was patronized by the local zamindar Indubhushan Gupta. Gandhians were successful professional men from the dominant Vaidya caste. Village welfare work was their primary concern.[69] The Malikanda Ashram at Nawabganj in Dacca had been founded by Dr Profulla Chandra Ghosh who had built up a powerful tradition of welfare work since the Non-Co-operation days. The ashram was generously patronized by two rich trading families—the Poddars and the Sahas—of Kalakopa village. Most local mahajans helped with funds from time to time. Dr R. Ahmed, a successful Calcutta-based dentist from Bardhanpara village, was another prominent patron.[70] Khadi, arbitration and national education efforts were

[66] Dasgupta, *Bharate Samyavad*, p. 119.

[67] Das, *Karmakshetra*, p. 84.

[68] Hiralal Dasgupta, *Swadhinata Sangrame Barisal* (Calcutta, 1972), p. 34.

[69] Outshahi Sammilani O Balya Samiti, *Outshahi Gramer Itibritta Ebang Svadhinata Sangrame Gramer Abodan* (Calcutta, 1965), pp. 39–49.

[70] Sureshchandra Dey, *Swadhinata Sangrame Nawabganj* (Calcutta, 1971), pp. 12–14

particularly successful at Bankura. The Gangajalghata Jatiya Vidyalay (a national school) was set up by the son of the local zamindar. Gandhians at Jaipur village were dependent for funds on a big jotedar. A retired engineer set up Khadi and agricultural centres at Brindabanpur village. At Sonamukhi and Patrasayar, Gandhian efforts were initiated by the local zamindar, at Simlipal by a wing of the local Raja family.[71]

A very different pattern of work marked Gandhian activities elsewhere. At Sutahata in Midnapur, the Gandhian leader Kumar Chandra Jana was not very successful at first in his national education and social service work. Local interest mounted only after he associated himself with agitational politics. Gandhians took a prominent part in the Simon Commission boycott movement and made imaginative use of Swadeshi 'jatras' or roving theatres based on the plays of Mukunda Das.[72]

Interesting departures were seen in other parts of Bankura. Congress arbitration courts flourished at Khatra, particularly among tribal and untouchable groups. These people were brutally exploited by a local combination of mahajans, jotedars and pattanidars (intermediate tenure-holders). The Congress appealed to moneylenders and jotedars and tried to intervene on behalf of the peasants. Arbitration court decisions, however, were frequently flouted by village bosses. In 1927 the exasperated peasants killed two mahajans. Although Congress work was hardly directly responsible for this development, the District Committee felt uneasy and eventually recalled its volunteers from the locality.[73] A broad support base among the exploited and militant tribal peasantry gave this Congress ashram an unusual dynamism which was broken by the higher levels within the provincial leadership. At Arambagh subdivision in Hooghly, Gandhian leaders like Prafulla Chandra Sen formed powerful bases through Khadi and welfare work which could have considerable value for an exceptionally depressed poor peasant economy.[74] The influence that Gandhians came to reap here survived virtually untouched until the 1967 West Bengal Assembly elections. Sen's base remained intact till the late 1970s. A

[71] Sanyal, *Dakshin-Pashchim Banglai Jatiyatabadi Andolan, Chaturanga*: pp. 77–82

[72] Bankim Brahmachari, *Swadhinata Sangrame Sutahata* (Midnapur, 1977), pp. 27–8.

[73] Sanyal 'Dakshin Pashchim Banglai Jatiyatabadi Andolan', *Chaturanga*.

[74] Sanyal, 'Arambagh Jatiyatabadi Andolan', *Anya Artha*, September-October 1974.

report from the Hooghly Congress claimed in 1930: 'Zamindars and village notables do not co-operate with the Congress and in fact often oppose it. Most educated and professional men of the locality have nothing to do with it'.[75] The links here revealed quite a different approach to agrarian relations and problems and made anti-zamindari work possible in the locality in the mid-1930s.[76]

The Khadi Pratisthan at Sodepur in the 24 Parganas constituted a very different model. A well-organized institution founded by Satish Dasgupta, this was run in a highly business-like manner on a commercial footing and continued the tradition of nationalist enterprise and industry of Swadeshi days. Dasgupta had served an earlier apprenticeship in the pioneer Swadeshi enterprise, the Bengal Chemicals under P.C. Ray.[77] Gandhi mediated between him and large-scale Indian business concerns to obtain their patronage for the Khadi Pratisthan. 'I hope you will succeed with Mr Birla', he wrote to Dasgupta, '. . .he should have all the assistance that you can give. . . .'[78] And again: 'Of course the mill-owners would gladly give whatever may be wanted if only we would undertake to advertise their wares, but it is not possible for us to do so unless they accept our terms. . . . you will please treat the whole thing as strictly confidential'.[79] Gandhi himself had the closest contact with this group of Gandhians. He in fact deputed Dasgupta to challenge the BPCC authorities, albeit in an oblique manner: 'I did indeed know that Congress Committees were practically sleeping. It would be a great thing if you can put life into them without giving rise to any suspicion.'[80]

Such variation and departures notwithstanding, Gandhian activities remained carefully confined within particular issues and programmes that intended to improve the quality of rural life without challenging basic power relations. In Gujarat, where this stream of rural nationalism ran deepest, Gandhian constructive work has been described as not particularly successful in the field of socio-economic reforms. Politically it still was of great importance in building up Congress support and establishing its hegemony over

[75] Report of the Hooghly Congress Committee, *Bangabani,* 15 October 1930.

[76] Sanyal, 'Arambagh', *Anya Artha,* October-November 1974.

[77] Aparna Basu's interview with Dasgupta, 5.1.1969, NMML.

[78] *Collected Works of Mahatma Gandhi,* Vol. XXXVI (Govt. of India, 1970). Item 425, 30 May 1928.

[79] Ibid. Item 198, 1 April 1928.

[80] Ibid. Item 53, 25 February, 1928.

low caste and untouchable peasants.[81] Its strength and success in Bengal were definitely far less. The aspirations, nonetheless, remained the same.

Revolutionary Terrorists

Revolutionary terrorism reappeared as a serious political force after four years of nearly complete inactivity. The new Governor Jackson found things so quiet on his arrival in Bengal that he insisted on a gradual release of detenus and prisoners from March 1927.[82] Virtually all detenus had been released by 1928 and reorganization became possible. Enforced inactivity in gaol had, as always, stimulated creative self-questioning. Release led to a situation of flux: regrouping, rethinking and planning along new lines. This then was a period of adjustment and preparation, rather than the beginning of a new phase of action

Officialdom had always worried about the possible links—ideological, emotional and organizational—between revolutionary terrorists and the Bengal Congress. Nationalist control of the Corporation enabled many terrorist families to make a living as teachers or clerks in Corporation schools and offices.[83] Congress leaders made no secret of their admiration and sympathy for terrorists. They openly mourned terrorist martyrs like Gopi Nath Saha in 1925 and Jatin Das in 1929. More serious was the brisk enrolment of terrorist activists as BPCC members. This had begun in the Non-Co-operation days when the terrorists suspended their own activities to participate in the Congress movement. Their leaders had been responsible for much of the Non-Co-operation work in districts like Mymensingh, Barisal, Dacca, Faridpur, Chittagong, Tippera, Jessore, Nadia and the 24 Parganas. The association continued to persist even when terrorists revived their separate line of struggle.[84] Bhupati Mazumdar, a Jugantar member, has described the ease with which he could join the Bengal Congress in 1928 even though he never professed any faith in non-violence.[85] A Gandhian Swaraj Ashram at Khalispur village at Khulna was put under the complete charge of a known Anushilan member who used it entirely

[81] David Hardiman, *Peasant Nationalists of Gujarat, Kheda District 1917–34* (Delhi, 1981), Chapters 6, 8.

[82] Jackson to Irwin, 12.1.1928, *Birkenhead Collection*, EUR D 703/22, IOL.

[83] GOB, *Civil Disobedience, Calcutta Corporation and Terrorism.*

[84] Bhupendra Kumar Dutta, *Biplaber Pada Chinha* (Calcutta, 1953), pp. 215–17.

[85] Aparna Basu's interview with Majumdar, 21.1.1969, NMML.

for Anushilan work. [86] Pannalal Dasgupta, a terrorist from Barisal, later described Bose as 'a link more or less between that open thing (Congress organization and volunteer activities) and the underground thing.'[87]

The two parent terrorist organizations—the Anushilan and the Jugantar— began to lose their grip on the new generation of activists. The deadweight of the inherited inter-party quarrel appeared totally irrelevant to the rank and file. A three-day joint session discussed the possibility of merger in 1927 but no concrete solution emerged at the end of the deliberations. [88] Convinced of the futility of old rivalries, which continued to absorb the older generation, younger activists now began to strike out their own path and formed small, semi-autonomous groups, only loosely associated with either of the parent bodies. There were fundamental tactical differences as well to reinforce the generation gap. Both Anushilan and Jugantar leaders strongly discouraged immediate and isolated acts of violence and insisted on a long period of preparation. This, to impatient younger men, seemed to postpone action indefinitely. [89] An Anushilan member from Rajshahi later recalled the many sessions of criticism and discussion which led to 'a crystallization of rebellious feelings among young members against the "dadas" ' [90] The full flavour of the debate has been captured in *Jiyanta*, a novel on those times. It vividly describes the secret, late night meetings among young terrorists in a district town and the endless heated arguments exchanged in urgent, hushed whispers. [91] Demands for Purna Swaraj by the Congress organization itself, the escalation of agitational politics since 1928 and the frequent clashes and confrontations in Calcutta and smaller cities and towns during hartals seemed to vindicate their optimism.

Small activist cells began to plan for action in the very near future. Surya Sen's group worked out a plan for military operations in Chittagong in October 1929. [92] The Shri Sangha at Dacca sent

[86] The author's interview with Pramatha Bhowmick, 7.7.1978.

[87] H.D. Sharma's interview with Dasgupta, 26.6.69, NMML.

[88] D.M. Laushey, *Bengal Terrorism and the Marxist Left* (Calcutta, 1975), pp. 49–51.

[89] ***Terrorism in India 1917–36,*** **GOI, Home Intelligence Bureau (reprinted, Delhi,** 1974), p. 21. See also Jackson's letter to Irwin, 10 May 1929, *Halifax Papers*, MSS **EUR C** 152 **IOL.**

[90] Satyendranarayan Majumdar, *Amar Biplab Jignasha* (Calcutta, 1973), p. 79.

[91] Manik Bandopadhyay, *Jiyanta, Manik Granthabali*, Vol. VII (Calcutta, 1971).

[92] Ananta Singh, *Agnigarbha Chattogram* (Calcutta, 1968), p. 283.

Dinesh Gupta to Midnapur to organize a branch on its behalf.[93] Many of the 'revolt groups' (Niranjan Sen's Barisal group or the Chittagong group for instance) remained formally affiliated to the Jugantar, although the headquarters knew practically nothing of their secret plans. Similarly Anushilan branches in Dacca, Mymensingh, Barisal and other places eluded central control.[94] Social service leagues, youth and student organizations, physical culture associations or 'akhras' and newly-formed women's organizations provided them with an open forum for recruitment. District and local-level Congress organizations sometimes gave them cover.

Debates were not entirely restricted to questions of tactics. Ideological self-questioning and a measure of painful self-criticism were also beginning in some circles. At times the very method of individual terror was questioned; more often, the basic creed was sought to be braided with other issues and methods. In the early 1920s, the Indian Communists M.N. Roy and Virendra Chattopadhyay (both of them ex-terrorists) had sent their emissaries from Moscow and Berlin to put Indian revolutionaries in touch with international Communism. The contact bore valuable fruit in the recruitment of a few important terrorists like Dharani Goswami and Gopen Chakrawarty.[95] More immediately, the recent achievements of the Communists at home created a problem of choice. Bhupal Panda, then a Bengal volunteer member from Contai College, remembers the powerful visual impact that the Lillooah workers' demonstration had made on him in 1928.[96] Ranen Sen, who was then a follower of the revolutionary leader Bepin Ganguly, describes how the speeches of the visiting British M.P. Saklatvallah, the poems of Nazrul and a few pro-Marxist books (Hardayal's *Karl Marx: A Modern Rishi* and two books by Ryazanov) left him dissatisfied with the conventional confines of terrorism. On the other hand, he found Indian Communist literature insufficiently nationalistic. Quite a few Anushilan members like Gopal Basak, Moni Singh, Jyotirmoy Sharma and Dharani Goswami crossed over to the Communist youth front and joined the Young Comrades' League.[97] Dr Bhupendra Dutt, one of the earliest founders of

[93] Narendra Nath Das, *History of Midnapur*, Part II (Calcutta, 1962), pp. 108, 116.

[94] Suprakash Ray, *Bharter Baiplobik Sangramer Itihas* (Calcutta, nd), p. 158.

[95] *India and Communism*, Confidential report of H. Williamson, *Hallet Collection*.

[96] The author's interview with Bhupal Panda, May 1978.

[97] The author's interview with Ranen Sen, May 1979.

Bengal terrorism, and now a firm believer in Marxist ideology, conducted study circles among students. His addresses on Marxism and on the limitations of individual terrorist methods made a profound impression on young terrorists like Pramatha Bhowmick and Satyendranarayan Majumdar.[98] Very sharp attacks on conventional terrorist ideas, particularly their religious, even obscurantist moorings, were made by another first-generation terrorist leader, Hemchandra Kanungo, whose autobiography, *Banglay Biplab Prachesta*, came out in 1928. It exposed the limitations of a number of extremely important leaders like Aurobindo Ghosh. It also declared the author's new convictions about atheism and Marxism.[99] The same convictions were reaffirmed by the great terrorist leader Bhagat Singh in his immensely moving *Why I am an Atheist*, which was written in gaol where he was awaiting execution in 1929. His group, the Hindustan Socialist Republican Army, which was formed in 1928 in Delhi, brought out a manifesto to present radically new alternatives within the overall terrorist tradition. It criticized the religiosity of all terrorist groups and hoped to mobilize peasants and workers for armed revolt.[100] Several Anushilan members were in touch with the HSRA and the manifesto made them rethink about their own ideas.[101] It seems that Anushilan activists were relatively more open to new ideas and influences than Jugantar members who were entirely committed to immediate terrorist action.

A slight wind of change seemed to blow over terrorists in general. Initiation vows occasionally did away with the Hindu ritual which used to constitute the most important part of the ceremony.[102] Larger numbers of women became involved in the movement at least as sources of logistic support if not yet as full comrades.[103] A few Muslim youths contacted terrorist groups for enrolment and received some encouragement although they were eventually rejected.[104] An official report, however, records the enlistment of a handful of Muslims and Sikhs, probably for the first time.[105]

98 The author's interview with Bhowmick. Also Satyendranarayan Majumdar, *Amar*, p. 98.

99 Hemchandra Kanungo, *Banglay Biplab Pracheshta* (Calcutta, 1928).

100 Bhagat Singh, *Why I am an Atheist* (ed.) Bipan Chandra (Delhi, 1979).

101 Satyendranarayan Majumdar, *Amar*, p. 119.

102 The author's interview with Santimoy Ray, 7 June 1976.

103 Basu's interview with Kamala Dasgupta, NMML. Also Laushey, *Bengal Terrorism*, p. 43.

104 Mohammed Waliullah, *Yuga Vichitra* (Dacca, 1967), p. 257.

105 *Terrorism in India*, p. 4.

The changes as yet lightly touched the surface without making any real dent into the old traditions. The religious idiom was retained almost everywhere in some form. Muslims, on the whole, were systematically excluded from the akhras.[106] Social composition hardly changed. School and college students from Calcutta and district towns with upper caste and upper and lower middle class origins remained the standard cadres. Contact with Marxist ideas yielded, as yet, only a few individual recruits. The contrast with HSRA aspirations becomes clear when we compare the HSRA's *Philosophy of the Bomb* with *Youths of Bengal*—a pamphlet issued by Barisal revolutionaries. The former identified independence with not just the overthrow of foreign rule but with 'a new Social Order' that will 'ring the death-knell of capitalism and class distinctions and privileges.... Above all it will establish the Dictatorship of the Proletariat'. There is also a very severe condemnation of all sorts of 'religious superstitions'. In the latter, revolutionary awareness consists of convictions about martyrdom and a pledge to overthrow the 'bloodthirsty English'.[107] On the eve of the new, final and most intense phase of the terrorist saga in Bengal, the conventional theory and practice of individual terror proved, on the whole, fully resilient and able to hold back pressures for change.

Peasant Agitations

The close interaction that had developed between the peasantry and the Bengal Congress during Non-Co-operation did not survive the movement.[108] Since the late 1920s was a very active period in peasant struggles, this disjunction would seriously limit the scope of Congress activities. The existence of a parallel stream of protest opened up new possibilities and options. Their eventual exclusion defined the scope of the Congress movement in new ways.

Sources of rural tension and conflict were manifold. The introduction of the Tenancy Act Amendment Bill in 1923 aroused great hopes as well as major apprehensions. Tenants saw a possibility of

[106] Interview of Muzaffar Ahmad by P.C. Joshi, n.d. courtesy, Gautam Chattopadhyay.

[107] *The Philosophy of the Bomb* signed by Kartar Singh, January 1930; *Youths of Bengal*, Mechaubazar leaflet, December 1929, Both have been cited in *Terrorism in India*, pp. 200, 214.

[108] On this see Sumit Sarkar, 'The Conditions and Nature of Subaltern Militancy: Bengal from Swadeshi to Non-Co-operation, 1905–22, in Ranajit Guha (ed.) *Subaltern Studies III: Writings on South Asian History and Society* (Delhi, 1984).

improvement in their general status and security. The bill held out a promise for sharecroppers too who expected to be reclassified as tenants. Landlords, on the other hand, greatly feared all this. There was a spate of eviction of sharecroppers since it was feared that continuous occupation of the same plot of land might lead them towards the status of occupancy tenants.[109] Rising agricultural prices created another problem. They encouraged landlords to push up the rent burden: rent enhancement suits went up from 19,232 to 45,415 between 1928 and 1930.[110] Illegal cesses and abwabs were yet another source of constant annoyance if not of actual conflict. The publication of some of the terms of the new Tenancy Bill spread an awareness about the illegality of these cesses. The riots of 1926 added a fresh dimension to the tension. Since cesses were often extracted in the name of religious and ceremonial expenses, they could serve as a basis for conflict between zamindars and tenants belonging to different religious communities. Within the same community, however, tenants had a far higher tolerance threshold for such demands. In some areas in Dacca, for instance, Muslim zamindars extracted a 'Khilafati Salami' from Muslim tenants to defray personal expenses. They passed themselves off as representatives of the Khalifa of Turkey. The custom continued for years after the Caliphate itself had been abolished.[111] In contrast to the post-slump pattern of agrarian unrest, the right land and the share of crops were the most vital issues in pre-depression years. These issues lost much of their importance after the slump when the collapse of agricultural prices would considerably reduce the value of both land and crop.

A highly significant strand within peasant resistance at this time was constituted by the struggles between Hindu landlords and Muslim or Namasudra (an untouchable caste) bargadars at Dacca, Khulna, Faridpur and Jessore. Muslim bargadars could and, often did, perceive these conflicts in religious terms while Namasudra sharecroppers almost invariably linked them up with broader social movements for caste upliftment. In all these districts Namasudras made up the largest Hindu caste and were overwhelmingly employed as bargadars or agricultural labourers—that is to say, they were at the bottom of both economic and social hierarchies. At the

[109] B.B. Chaudhury, 'Agrarian Movements in Bengal and Bihar 1919–39', in B.R. Nanda (ed.) *Socialism in India* (New Delhi, 1970), p. 198.

[110] *Census of India 1931*, Vol. V Pt. I, Ch. I, p. 17.

[111] *Report on the Land Revenue Administration of the Presidency of Bengal, 1929–30* (Calcutta, 1931), pp. 6–23.

same time, they were generally endowed with industry, thrift, good health, expanding numbers and a rigorous work-ethic—in other words, with all the features of an ambitious peasant caste.[112] The incompatibility between aspirations and imposed status led, not so much to Sanskritization, as to an active struggle against deprivation. If there was emulation of the ways of social superiors, it was more of the new opportunities like western education and not really of the traditional social and ritual practices of the upper castes. Khulna Namasudras had long been interested in modern education and social improvement along such lines.[113] At Faridpur 'of late years they have shown many signs of rebelling against their degraded position in Hindu society.'[114] Jessore Namasudras had been noted for 'their independence and self-reliance and their efforts to rise in the social scale.' A huge Namasudra Conference had been held here in 1908 to evolve elaborate plans for educational and social reform measures within the caste. Groups of Jessore and Khulna Namasudras did occasionally try to improve their status through the usual means; they claimed an original superior ritual ranking which, for various reasons, had got distorted and degraded in later traditions. In this case Brahmin origins were claimed and they called themselves descendants of Kashyapa.[115] It is interesting that for an untouchable caste they aspired straightaway to the highest possible rank and did not aim at attaining the relatively more plausible position of an intermediate middle-ranking caste. On the whole, however, the stress was not on fresh appeals to the orthodox tradition. There seemed to be a challenge flung at the tradition itself and a search for alternative strategies for social improvement outside its confines. Unlike other depressed castes which sought to improve their rank within the given hierarchy, 'the Namasudras (have) adopted a sturdier attitude and leaders have laid less stress on the social rank of their own caste than on the claim of all classes to a general equality of rights. They have advocated adult suffrage, though for men only, as one means of securing equalities'.[116] A gender hierarchy thus persisted even if the caste hierarchy had to

[112] See *Bengal District Gazetteer:* L.S. O'Malley, *Jessore* 1912; O'Malley, *Khulna,* 1908; B.C. Allen, *Dacca,* 1912; also J.C. Jack, *Final Report of the Survey and Settlemernt Operations in Faridpur, 1904–14, 1916.*

[113] *Bengal District Gazetter: Khulna*, p. 66.

[114] *Bengal District Gazetter: Faridpur* p. 7.

[115] *Bengal District Gazetter: Jessore*, pp. 50–1.

[116] *Report on the Administration of Bengal, 1928–29* (Calcutta, 1930), p. 17.

go. Even the dispossessed would not tolerate the notion of complete human equality.

Agrarian unrest in Jessore in 1928–9 inherited and largely continued a pattern of struggle that had been laid down much earlier. Namasudra and Muslim bargadars of the Narail subdivision in 1909 had gone in for 'practical protest' against caste Hindus. For months they had organized a combination to refuse working as menial servants or to eat food cooked by high caste Hindus—the last aspect being a nice ironical inversion of established norms about pollution. At places within the Magura subdivision they had also refused to cultivate lands of higher castes. At the Sadar subdivision the same year there was a 'general strike' in a village by Muslim cultivators who would not cultivate lands of Hindu landlords unless they were paid a 2/3 share of the crop in the place of the customary half share—an interesting anticipation of the Tebhaga demand of bargadars in 1946–7.[117] A Muslim-Namasudra bargadar combination against the Hindu zamindar was organized again at the Narail subdivision in 1923—a development that the Bengal Congress chose to interpret as a purely communal conflict.[118]

Muslim and Namasudra bargadars of Jessore went on strike against high caste Hindu landlords in February 1928. Muslim bargadars of Manikganj subdivision of Dacca refused to cultivate the lands of Saha landlords.[119] The Saha trader caste was particularly numerous at Manikganj. It included highly prosperous moneylenders and traders who had recently started to invest in landed property.[120] It is interesting that Sahas in the pre-depression situation were attacked as zamindars; during the depression, with its acute shortage of credit and cash, the same group would be attacked in its capacity as traders and moneylenders. By April the Jessore situation looked threatening; men on 'strike' successfully intimidated bargadars who were willing to work. Negotiations began at Narail on a settlement on the basis of a 9 annas-7 annas share of the crop, the former going to landlords and the latter to bargadars.[121] The movement spread to the Sadar subdivision; by May it had reached out to the Daulatpur Thana in Khulna and the Gopalganj

[117] *Bengal District Gazetter: Jessore*, pp. 53, 81.

[118] The author's interview with Pramatha Bhowmick, 26 June 1976.

[119] *Fortnightly Report on Bengal*, st half of February 1928, GOI, Home Poll 28 1928.

[120] *Bengal District Gazetteer: Dacca*, p. 82.

[121] *Fortnightly Reports on Bengal*, 1st and 2nd halves of April 1928, GOI, Home Poll 17/1929.

subdivision in Faridpur.[122] Bargadars held out till the end of the year and resisted all overtures for a settlement. A temporary decline set in from late December at Jessore with the harvesting of an extremely good crop,[123] but in May 1929 it flared up again. This time a clear-cut demand was put forward for a 1/3 crop share for the landlord instead of the customary 1/2 share. The demand was to be reinforced with a total strike or a complete withdrawal of all services from high caste Hindus of the locality. The Commissioner reported that the bulk of the land cultivated under the barga system lay untouched.[124] Sharecroppers of the Boersing Khas Mahal at Khulna supported these demands and tactics. The Commissioner of the Presidency Division reported: 'The tenants of the Boersing Khas Mahal are in a turbulent mood and there is the *Tebhaga movement*.'[125] (italics mine). Muslim tenants of Pabna also withdrew labour services from Hindu jotedars.[126] A general strike by peasants combined economic issues with a wider social protest by Ajlaf (inferior ranks) Muslim and Namasudra bargadars. It provided a very different kind of alternative to the caste upliftment moves by Gandhians and Hindu organizations which ignored the problems of class relations that structured the existence of the untouchables. Congress volunteers for instance went on a temple satyagraha in August 1929 for the right of the Namasudras to enter the Munshiganj Kali Temple.[127] It remained a lone and distant issue somewhat remote from the concerns of even the local untouchables. It never became the radical social upheaval that temple entry movements broadened out into in other parts of the country.[128]

Conflicts between zamindars and more protected categories of peasants very easily led to severe clashes and violence. There was a large-scale confrontation between the zamindar and tenants in Ap-

[122] Ibid, 1st and 2nd halves of May.

[123] Ibid, 2nd half of December.

[124] *Fortnightly Reports on Bengal*, st half of May 1929, GOI, Home Poll 17/1929.

[125] Commissioner to Chief Secretary, GOL, 28 9 29, GOB, Home Confidential, Poll Poll, 403 (Sl. Nos. 1–10) of 1929.

[126] *Fortnightly Reports on Bengal*, 2nd half of June 1929, GOB GOI, Home Poll 17 1929.

[127] Buddhadeva Bhattacharyya, *Satyagrahas in Bengal, 1921–39*, (Calcutta, 1977), pp. 159-64.

[128] On this see Robin Jeffrey. 'Travancore: Status, Class and the Growth of Radical Politics 1860–1940' in Jeffrey (ed.), *People, Princes and Paramount Power*, (New Delhi, 1978).

ril 1928 over the disputed possession of a piece of 'char' land at Sagar Kandi in Pabna. 'Chars' are fertile tracts of islands on rivers which get submerged under water for considerable periods of time each year. Since the land disappears periodically, rights of possession are difficult to establish. An armed band of 300 ryots attacked the zamindar's 'Kutchery' or administrative headquarters which they thoroughly looted. Police had to be called out and the crowd was fired upon to stop the raid.[129] Another band of armed ryots attacked the zamindar's men at a Khulna village in December 1928. They were led by 'a half-witted individual claiming rights to portions of the zamindari property'.[130] That a body of tenants would identify itself so strongly with the personal claims of a single individual is striking in itself; it probably encompassed the defence of certain community notions about property rights and limits to the zamindar's expansion.

A simple case of transfer of zamindari property had curious repercussions at Raipur thana of Narayanganj subdivision in Dacca. In February 1928 the Paharmahal Zamindari was sold off by the local Muslim zamindar to a rich Hindu merchant. Serious problems of rent-realization immediately beset the new incumbent. Most of his refractory tenants were Muslims and devotees of a Mymensingh Pir who advised them to withhold rent from the 'interloper' and to donate it instead for the welfare of the poor in Allah's name. A writ of attachment for rent arrears was served on the tenant leader Sahebali. He not only refused to accept it but beat up the Civil Court peon who had come to serve the notice. Police constables were sent off to arrest him but he assaulted them and threw them out of the village. A large and heavily armed force of policemen then moved in to get him. Along with other villagers and 'armed with lethal weapons' Sahebali fought a pitched battle with them. He was able to elude the police for quite some time but eventually he surrendered.[131] A whole body of villagers was temporarily transformed into outlaws over this issue. The starting point of the conflict—the no-rent issue—knitted together several diverse compulsions and convictions. Resentment over the removal of the traditional zamindar probably provided a basic factor in the situation: the newcomer being both an outsider and a non-zamindar (a trader) could not claim comparable authority. The fact that the

[129] *Forward*, 27 April 1928.

[130] *Fortnightly Reports on Bengal*, 1st half of December, GOI. Home Poll 1-28 1928.

[131] *Forward*, 29 April 1928.

old zamindar was a Muslim and the 'interloper' a Hindu probably hardened the will to resist. The Pir, however, advised non-payment on grounds of poor relief and resisting an interloper; no explicit mention or use was made of the obvious communal divide even though that was the general context of the struggle. The great authority wielded by the Pir from Mymensingh, his voice in the internal developments within a Dacca village, reflected the role that Pirs frequently assumed as decisive political factors in rural East Bengal. The personal jurisdiction of each Pir cut across villages and districts and constituted parallel communities of believers or brotherhoods intermeshing with local and broader religious or class units.

Communal divides still did shape many other peasant struggles. The Bengal Congress took up a consistently pro-landlord stance and much of the organized tenants' movements came under rival political leaders who were generally Muslim and quite often anti-Congress. There was nothing necessarily or intrinsically sectional in their programmes. The broad configuration of rural interests in Bengal, however, was such that on a general level exploiters could easily be identified as Hindus. Large-scale landholding and tenurial interests were overwhelmingly under Hindu control. Rich traders and moneylenders, too, tended to be Hindus. 'With the exception of a few Pathans, Muslims kept out of moneylending activities, partly because of a religious taboo on usury'.[132] The authority of the rural rich was defended by lawyers, most of whom again happened to be Hindus and closely dependent on zamindar patronage. About 89.13 per cent of lawyers in Bengal were Hindus. Almost all Bar Association members defended the zamindari system before the Floud Commission.[133] Social relations in the countryside were largely shaped by such clear coincidence between class and communal divides. Abul Mansur Ahmad has described the sublime confidence with which upper caste Hindus assumed their superiority and the sneer that coloured their everyday contacts even with the better-off Muslims in his Mymensingh village.[134] The social envy and anger this provoked would be shared by all Muslims to a greater or lesser degree. It would still be most acutely resented by the

[132] *Report of the Bengal Banking Enquiry Committee 1929–30* (Calcutta, 1931) vol. I, p. 194). See also Partha Chatterji, *Bengal 1920–1947* (Calcutta, 1984).

[133] Cited in Jatin De, *The History of the Krishak Proja Party of Bengal, 1929–47* (Unpublished thesis, Delhi University, 1978).

[134] Abul Mansur Ahmad, *Amar Dekha Rajnitir Panchash Bachhar* (2nd edn., Dacca, 1970).

relatively affluent tenants. 'The Muhammadan peasant considers himself a gentleman' at Mymensingh and employed labour from outside to replace family labour on the fields to prove it. They also demanded a greater share in education and government posts to compete with Hindus.[135]

Such resentment informed a discourse of protest that assumed a coherent shape around the mid-1920s. It postulated the ideal type of a perfect Muslim peasant who fulfilled his vocation diligently but who was cruelly thwarted by the Hindu landlord/trader/moneylender syndrome. A village bard 'Palli Kavi' from Barisal lamented in 1926:

'All loan contracts fatten on Muslims. They have lost their land, savings and home'.[136]

A book of poems from Chittagong, written in the narrative verse metre 'Payar' in highly Islamicized Bengali, made the same point. It advised the Muslim peasant to stick to his simple way of life and to cut down on conspicuous consumption, the standards for which had been set by corrupt Hindu baboos. He would then escape the traps set by the wily Hindu moneylender.[137] Another Muslim village poet from Malda was lyrical about the virtues of the simple cultivator who was the main prop of the rural economy and mourned his bondage to the moneylender and zamindar.[138] A highly communal collection of folk ballads which lashed out at the falseness of Hinduism, strengthened its arguments by referring to Hindu exploitation and domination over trade, services and moneylending.[139] The image of the self-sufficient and virtuous peasant, ensnared and ruined by urban corruption and hedonistic consumption is reflected, (as we have seen), in the rural literature on jute propaganda and in Gandhian teachings. The same basic dichotomy between the city and the country is replicated here; the term peasant is interchangeable with creative and productive labour, virtue and innocence, while urban elements represent corruption, falsehood, parasitism. The archetypal peasant is hardworking, self-sufficient and independent; he is seen as neither the owner of the labour of others, nor as serving others with his labour. This widely accepted image or self-image of the peasant, however, is not en-

[135] F. Sachse (ed.), *Bengal District Gazetteer, Mymensingh* (Calcutta, 1917), pp. 43, 68.

[136] Palli Kavi Munshi Kumar Ali, *Jatiya Gan*, Vol. I (Comilla, 1926).

[137] Mohammad Faizul Kabir, *Jatiya Kabita* (Chittagong, 1926).

[138] Maulvi Sheikh Idries Ahmad, *Krishaker Marmavani* (Malda, 1921).

[139] Makbul Ahmad, *Hindu Moshalmaner Hangamar Kabita* (Chittagong, 1933).

tirely uniform in all cases. In the case of the Muslim peasant, contradictions and exploitation are brought in within rural life and are identified with religious distinctions. The other is not just the urban baboo; he is also the rural landlord/usurer, he is the Hindu rich who very often seems to speak through the disguise of the Congressman—on the Legislative Assembly floor for instance, to crush the aspiring Muslim peasant. Muhammad Moizuddin Hamidi warned against Swarajist pretensions in his *Krishakar Unnati* (Betterment of the Tenants); he argued that given the Swarajist line on tenants within the Council, the Government remained the best ally of the peasant.[140]

Compared to the Western and Northern districts, the percentage of occupancy ryots was much higher in Eastern Bengal and the process of differentiation much less advanced. There was a considerable and growing body of substantial tenants many of whom were Muslims. They were located primarily in the jute-intensive districts of Dacca, Faridpur, Rangpur, Tippera, Mymensingh and Pabna. The Proja movement was inspired by the interests of this section. Fazlul Huq inaugurated the first Proja Conference at Kamariarchar at Jamalpur in Mymensingh in 1914. The charter reflected the concerns of the upper categories of ryots; there was complete silence about bargadars, for instance. In 1926 a 14 point demand charter was formulated which continued the silence.[141]

After the Council elections of 1929 Huq announced the formation of the Proja Party with the support of eighteen Muslim members in Council.[142] The new Party was carried upwards on the crest of an active peasant movement at Dacca, Mymensingh, Barisal and Faridpur.[143] In its early stages it needed to consolidate itself by broadening its base and linking itself up with movements from below with larger possibilities. It achieved this by capturing the leadership of several ongoing agitations carried on by local leaders. One such movement was the tenants' struggle against the Hindu zamindar Rajeswar Ray Chowdhury of Kalaskathi village in Barisal. Mohammad Yasin Howladar had written a book to describe the variety of torture and illegal cesses that were inflicted on local tenants. It also referred to various forms of unpaid labour or 'begar' extracted from them. Widely distributed and free of cost, the book tried to advise tenants on legal redress and to educate them about

140 Hamidi, *Krishakar Unnati* (Khulna, 1929).

141 Jatin De, *Krishak Proja Party*.

142 *Report on the Administration of Bengal, 1928–29*

143 B.P. Habibullah, *Sher-e-Bangla* (Barisal, 1962), pp. 32–33.

their legal rights. It stirred up a powerful agitation in 1924–5. Howladar did criticize the use of 'begar' (unpaid labour) by Muslim zamindars as well but the edge of the attack was definitely turned against the exaction of unpaid service from Muslim tenants to assist in Hindu religious ceremonies. 'Look at the unfairness of it all. The zamindar does the Puja, he acquires merit, why do we pay him a cess? Such payment is "harami" (sinful) for a Muslim'.[144] The movement was directed against zamindari oppression in general; but since tenants were mostly Muslims and the zamindar was a Hindu, the specific form of struggle was cow-slaughter and refusal to help out with the immersion ceremony[145]—a struggle that would mobilize Muslim tenants alone.

Lines were similarly drawn up between indebted Muslim tenants and Hindu Saha moneylenders at the Manikganj subdivision in Dacca in 1926. A large number of tenants had been evicted for non-payment of debts and Proja leaders advised them to stop the cultivation of Saha lands. The 'strike' proved so successful that peasants were reinstated in their holdings.[146]

These agitations strengthened the Proja movement and led to its rapid spread. Huq, however, did nothing concrete about bargadar agitations or about the protection of lower categories of tenants. Eventually the annexation of the local bases and movements strengthened the bargaining position of substantial tenants and Calcutta-based Muslim politicians.[147] The Proja movement, therefore, contained within itself several interlocking layers of interests and aspirations like the Congress movement which, too, spanned a wide spectrum. It is equally necessary to distinguish between the different levels here, between the aims and functions of the top leaders and the grassroots movements from below.

Some tenant struggles were linked up with a very different kind of religious and social movement. Santal sharecroppers and poor tenants of the Barind tract in eastern Malda had to face an unusually oppressive burden of cesses and abwabs. Zamindars manipulated subtle legal devices to cheat them out of their holdings. Though the original tribal settlers had cleared up jungles and begun cultivation on extremely low rents, once cultivation was properly established

[144] Munshi Mohammad Yasin Howladar, *Jamindarer Daya Prajar Sashan* (Barisal, 1926), p. 5.

[145] Habibullah, *Sher-e-Bangla*, p. 31.

[146] Ibid, pp. 59–60.

[147] The surrender of control by more grassroots leaders has been explored in *Yugavichitra*, p. 288.

zamindars began to deprive them of their earlier rights.[148] In 1924 an anti-landlord movement began at the Barind which involved large numbers of Santal peasants. A Swarajist pleader, Kashishwar Chakravarti, visited Malda from time to time with Hindu proselytizing aims. Jitu Santal from Kochaikandar village in Habibpur thana became his disciple and organized a 'Sanyasi dol'.

By 1926 Jitu had become the supreme and independent leader of a widespread movement committed to the 'making of Santals into Hindus.' By giving up the use of pigs and fowl they would be raised to the status of intermediate 'Jal Chal' castes whose water was acceptable to the high castes. They were to acknowledge Jitu as their sovereign authority, accept his 'bichar' (justice) and instead of paying rent to the zamindar they would pay him one 'kula' (about 5 seers) of paddy. Under Jitu's new order, 'those who cultivate in adhi from another will get the lands.' Sharecroppers (or 'adhiars') were advised to delay the payment of the 'adhi' share; the new Settlement was coming when the lands that they now tilled would be bestowed on them as their own 'jotes' or holdings. Rumours circulated all over Barind that Jitu's Raj will start from Phalgun. Jitu said he would go to the 'gar' at Pandua and that from there 'larai' would begin which was to drive out Mohammedans and others who do not join them.[149]

In September 1928 Jitu instructed Santal adhiars to loot the 'bhadoi' (autumn) crop from tracts of land in the Gajole/Bamangola Habibpur thana areas which had recently been expropriated from them but which would be restored through this action. They were promised that they would be put down on the coming Settlement records as tenants and not as 'aḍhiars'. Several incidents of paddy looting followed and in one case about a hundred and fifty Santals took away the crop from a six-'bigha' plot. The District Magistrate and the Superintendent of Police rushed there with armed policemen and after several clashes Jitu was arrested with sixty of his men.[150]

Jitu's Hinduization movement did not inevitably or necessarily involve feelings of Hindu fraternity or customary respect to caste

[148] Report of Malda SP, 26 12/1926, GOB, Pol Conf. FN (1–2)/1926, Enclosure I.

[149] Evidence of Faisa Mondal, Puran Ghatwal, Surendra Talukdar and Salu Santal, Ibid.

[150] GOI, Home Poll 1–2/1928, *Fortnightly Reports on Bengal*, 2nd half of December 1928. For a connected account of this struggle as well as Jitu's other movements see Tanika Sarkar, 'A Study in Tribal Protest: Jitu Santal's Movement in Malda, 1924–32', in Ranajit Guha (ed.), *Subaltern Studies, Vol. IV* (Delhi, 1985).

superiors. To Jitu, the Hinduized Santal, his own Sanyasi Dol probably remained a category apart and the only meaningful unit of loyalty. 'The English and the Musalmans would go and... Shikarpur will be rescued for the Sanyasis. There will be no more zamindars.' Not only was the 'dol's' message directed at Santals exclusively, it was meant really for Santals of a special category—the sharecropper or the landless Santal. 'All the land will be ours' was a slogan repeated again and again, evoking visions of a lost Champa, the mythical homeland of freedom and joy of the Santals, and striking a strong millenarian messianic note in a movement that might otherwise be termed as vitalist.[151]

The immediate context to the rumours about major changes in land relations was provided by the Survey and Settlement operations in the mid-1920s. Apart from forming a part of a pattern of rumours that evoked great, generalized hopes of a radical transformation, every time a minor administrative reform was contemplated, the message also tied up with a traditional Santal concept of legitimacy. 'Land belongs to those by whom the original clearings in the forest were made and passes through the male line to their descendants, remaining always within the same clan.'[152]

The limited no-rent plans of 1926 grew into the much more militant action of crop-looting in 1928 as a proof of continuity in land ownership. It is interesting that the Santal is not trying to work out a larger or fairer share of the crop for himself; he is claiming stable occupancy rights over the land itself, no less, a determination very strongly rooted in his moral economy. Seemingly, there is a confusion in aims: in 1928 the main motive was to get themselves recorded as tenants, to carve out a more secure niche within the given structure. Simultaneously, however, there had been, even earlier, a vision of a new order which would entirely do away with old proprietorial rights; the colonial administration, judiciary, property relations—all would disappear. But implicit in Jitu's message was a distinction between the short term goal of a limited struggle and the final overturning of the old order and the creation of a new millenium for which a last battle (to be waged at Pandua) would be necessary.

The variety, frequency and intensity of the agrarian struggles of these years received a setback for a while in 1930 when price trends

[151] See the classification used by Stephen Fuchs, *Rebellious Prophets* (Bombay, 1965), pp. 145–6.

[152] Culshaw and Archer, *The Santal Rebellion (Man in India*, Vol. XXV, December 1945), p. 218

changed, bringing about a connected shift in the nature of agrarian problems. The autonomy which had been a marked feature of these peasant struggles would partly be subsumed for a short while, within more organized movements decided by external political forces both nationalist and sectional.

Working Class Movements

The late 1920s constituted a major landmark in the growth of working class movements and organizations in Bengal, adding considerably to the general militancy of these years. The post–war economic boom was over and the mid-1920s saw the onset of an industrial depression. Difficulties of industrialists were compounded by the deflationary policies of the Government of India whose efforts to preserve the 1s–6d ratio led to a further fall in demand.[153] A general capitalist offensive was soon on its way in the shape of rationalization and retrenchment. In the railways sector, for instance, the Inchcape Committee had advised reduction of expenditure as early as 1920 [154] and the Vincent Raven Committee recommendations of 1926 threatened retrenchment of 75,000 workers in railway workshops. In jute the situation was further complicated by a substantial spurt of demand in 1925–9 which had encouraged the Indian Jute Millowners' Association (IJMA) to switch over to a policy of increased production. The 54 hour week was consequently abandoned from 1 July 1929 for a 60 hour week. But the decision coincided with a fall in jute prices and a decline in the industry's profit rate.[156] To cope with the drastic collapse of expectations, 10 per cent of the looms were sealed, working hours were reduced and a wage cut of up to 15 per cent was imposed.[157] The process of retrenchment came to a head at a time when the depression in agricultural prices had not yet begun to make its presence felt—that is to say, when the threat of wage cuts and dismissal had not yet been even partially offset by falling prices.

Like the preceding wave of labour unrest in the early 1920s this period too coincided with a revival of the nationalist agitation.

[153] A.K. Bagchi, *Private Investment*, p. 65.

[154] V. Dubey, 'Railways' in V.B. Singh (ed.) *Economic History of India 1857–1956* (Bombay, 1965), p. 34.

[155] Sukomol Sen, *Working Class of India, History of Emergence and Movement* (Calcutta, 1977), p. 243.

[156] Ajit Das Gupta. 'Jute Textile Industry' in V.B. Singh, *Economic History*, p. 226.

[157] Sukomol Sen, *Working Class*, p. 243.

Calcutta remained the major arena where the two movements coincided and overlapped, with very often the same target—the colonial state, visibly represented in its police force.

The upsurge of 1928–9, however, surpassed the earlier wave in the more sustained and cohesive nature of the strikes which were fewer in number but which lasted longer and had a greater impact.[158] There was much less of sporadic violence and new departures were made in the formation of strike committees and alliance with broader political organizations. Interesting new forms of collective action were experimented with—long marches and demonstrations, sustained satyagrahas, and so on.

There were four major groups of strikes during 1928–9. In 1928 there were two rounds of strikes among scavengers of the Calcutta Corporation which spread among the scavengers amd sweepers of Howrah and some other district municipalities. There were frequent and highly-organized strikes in railway and engineering workshops in Howrah and the Ondal-Asansol area in Burdwan in 1928. Some jute mill strikes began in 1928 which were followed by a prolonged general strike in 1929. Finally there was a strike at the Budge Budge oil depot in 1929. Apart from such serious and fairly large-scale action there were also strikes in Dacca and Calcutta cotton mills as well as among dock and transport workers in Calcutta. Notably silent were miners and tea plantation workers who had been very militant in 1921. The area of unrest was an exceptionally close-knit one: Calcutta and its industrial suburbs in the surrounding districts of Howrah, Hooghly and the 24 Parganas, with some incidents in Burdwan.

Labour organization was the work of a fairly wide spectrum of leaders. Nominated Council members like Latafat Hossain and K.C. Roy Choudhury of the Kankinarah Labour Union were closest to the authorities. 'We have been encouraging him (Mr K.C. Roy Choudhury) in his work in connection with labour as he appeared to be reasonable and sensible', wrote Governor Jackson in June 1929.[159] Roy Choudhury responded to this trust by criticizing the general jute mill strike and by trying to keep his own union insulated from the strike wave. He later admitted that his own Union members did not turn up for work while the strike was on.

[158] *Royal Commission on Labour in India*, Vol. V, Part I (London, 1931) Henceforth RCLI.

[159] Jackson's letter to Irwin, 3 June 1929. *Halifax Collection*, MSS EUR C 15: IOL.

Even though his union was properly registered and safe, it had only about a thousand members at its height while it covered the Bhatpara area with approximately 50,000 workers.[160]

Subhas Bose had built up a few labour organizations although none of them really seemed to function. He was in charge of the Budge Budge oil depot strike which began when the tinplate workers from Golmuri in Bihar, (who were also on strike then under Bose's leadership) sent a deputation to the Budge Budge oil depot workers asking them to go on strike. This was meant to pressurize the tinplate authorities since the Burmah Shell Oil Company had a controlling interest at both Golmuri and Budge Budge. The Union at Budge Budge was financed and helped by a local trader and rice mill-owner. The strike lasted for 3 months and then the workers began to return to work even though the Golmuri strike had not been settled.[161]

Bose's ambivalence about labour organization flowed perhaps from his acute sensitivity to the larger fears of the Indian capitalist groups, many of whom were committed, with qualifications, to nationalism. Some non-Bengali Burrabazar business groups were closely attached to Bose's faction within the Bengal Congress. In this connection the perspective of the Bengal National Chamber of Commerce—on the whole a nationalist body of Bengali businessmen—is worth commenting on. With little investment in large-scale industries, it was not really directly affected by the strike wave . Yet its attitude towards labour problems and protest was rigidly hostile. It demanded a ban on the entry of political agitators into the labour field and blamed the workers's own improvidence for their problems. 'The bhadralok is indebted for want', it pontificated, 'whereas the worker is indebted for want of economy'. On these grounds it categorically ruled out any provisions for workers' health, education, insurance and general welfare.[162] During the first round of the Calcutta Corporation scavengers' strike in March–April 1928, when the Swarajists were in charge of the Corporation, the Congress insisted that the demand for a minimum monthly wage of Rs 10 was entirely unreasonable.[163] The Corporation opened negotiations only when it was clear that deliberate intimidation was having no effects on the scavengers' morale and that civic life was fast becoming

160 Evidence of K.C. Roy Choudhury, RCLI, Vol. V, Parts I and II.

161 RCLI, Vol. V, Part II.

162 Ibid.

163 *The Amrita Bazar Patrika*, 9 March 1928.

impossible. Negotiations were extremely half-hearted and the Corporation authorities dragged their feet over the observance of the terms of the agreement.[164]

Much more significant was the role of a few Congressmen and Non-Co-operation veterans like Bankim Mukherji and Radharaman Mitra who worked in perfect harmony with the Workers' and Peasants' Party and who later joined the Communist Party. Individual leaders of no definite political affiliation often played a crucial role, especially in the initial phase of mobilization. This was generally done through constructive welfare work, or more simply, through prolonged and close association with workers—a combination of Gandhian techniques and a radical perspective. Prabhabati Das Gupta, a student who had returned from the U.S.A. in 1926 with a keen interest in labour issues, built up a base among Calcutta scavengers almost single-handed. She visited them regularly at their slums and ate at their 'dhabas'—taking food that was absolutely taboo for upper caste Hindus. Regarded at first with amusement, she soon earned their confidence and the epithet 'Dhangar Ma' (mother of scavengers).[165] A Scavengers' Union of Bengal was set up in November 1927 with Das Gupta as Secretary and Muzaffar Ahmad as President.[166]

Shibnath Bannerji was arrested in the Meerut Conspiracy Case for his role in the jute general strike. Although there is a curious reference to him in an official document as 'the Judas Iscariot of the Meerut Case',[167] the importance of his contribution to the initial mobilization process in the jute belt cannot be overestimated. He made a thorough study of the rarely-implemented Workmen's Compensation Act and offered to fight compensation claims at Union expenses if the workers enrolled in the Union. Managers at first refused to pay up the compensation but Bannerji deeply impressed the Commissioners with his superior grasp of legal points and a Claims Bureau was set up. Later, Managers too began to prefer to pay up so as to avoid inspection. His success with the claims suits gave him a formidable foothold among the general body of workers and helped the later process of union-building under WPP auspices.[168]

[164] Muzaffar Ahmad, *Amar Jiban O Bharater Communist Party*, Vol. II (Calcutta, n.d.), p. 22.

[165] Interview with Das Gupta, NMML. For the last detail I am indebted to Shri Chinmohan Sehanobis.

[166] Ahmad, *Amar Jiban*, p. 22.

[167] Williamson's report, *Hallet Collection*, MSS EUR E. 251–3 IOL.

[168] Interview with Shibnath Bannerji, NMML, 10 February 1976.

Kiran Mitra (he was known among the workers as Jatadhari Baba) was a major leader of the 1927 East India Railways strike at Kharagpur. At his insistence, the WPP and other Leftist leaders were invited to take part in discussions among all-India trade union leaders on the future of the strike. Mitra agreed with the Leftist leaders' decision to spread the strike wave along the railway workshops in Bengal. He worked out and implemented a remarkably efficient strike strategy particularly at Lillooah.[169] Nagendra Chatterji, a Barrackpore pleader, began to contact jute workers and taught them the 'Cacanny' or go-slow methods of expressing protest. Later, he began to work with the WPP dominated Bengal Jute Workers' Union.[170]

Whenever the question of large-scale organization came up, irrespective of their political views and affiliations all leaders approached the WPP. The WPP, too, readily accepted their help since this was a time of non-sectarian, broad, anti-imperialist front in the Comintern strategy. A very small group as yet, it was still the only organized party that could provide a body of fulltime cadres for the labour field and co-ordinate the work of other leaders outside the Party who lacked assistants of their own. The success in the Calcutta belt was attributed largely to Muzaffar Ahmad whom officials regarded as an 'extraordinary organizer'.[171] The British Communist Philip Spratt was commonly regarded as having as important an influence as Ahmad but Spratt himself later denied this: 'My part was to appear on the strikers' platform to keep up their morale. The prosecution in the Meerut Case exaggerated my part. Muzaffar was the strong man in Bengal'.[172] Another WPP leader, Radharaman Mitra, was largely responsible for the remarkable extension of the solidarity strikes along Ondal and Asansol workshops in 1928.[173] In Dacca, Gopal Basak, a WPP activist, owned a bookshop which imported and circulated Communist literature. He developed certain lines of activities which were somewhat unusual in WPP circles in those days: work among sections of Mymensingh peasants, study circles for Dacca labourers and lectures on world history where he criticized conventional history-writing for ignoring the everyday

[169] Ahmad, *Amar Jiban*, pp. 15–16.

[170] RCLI, Vol. V. Part II.

[171] Williamson's report, *Hallet Collection*.

[172] Spratt's letter to Gautam Chattopadhyay, Madras, 23 5 70. Courtesy Gautam Chattopadhyay.

[173] Gautam Chattopadhyay, *Communism and Bengal's Freedom Movement* (Calcutta, 1970), p. 40.

experience of the common people.[174] An official noted with relief that he had to work practically single handed in Dacca; but for this Dacca might have become, under his influence, as troublesome as Calcutta or Bombay.[175]

In official perception as well as in their self-image, vanguard leaders from outside were the real organizers of the strike wave—the sparks, the hidden fire, while workers merely provided dead timber to be set alight. Some episodes during the strikes may indeed be construed as confirmation of passivity and blind obedience. During the March 1928 strike of Calcutta Corporation scavengers, the WPP not only sent a notice and a list of demands to the Corporation but circulated them among workers as well. Workers were instructed to answer any Corporation officer who came to interrogate them with these words: 'These are our demands. You may address our Anjuman (union). We know nothing'.[176] The Lillooah workshop strike too seemed to be an imposition from above, the result of a decision made by all-India trade union leaders to strengthen the East India Railways strike by involving the workshop labourers as well. A union was set up by the leaders for the express purpose of directing the strike, which began when the authorities dismissed four union members.[177]

Our own period, however, encompasses a point of time when external political ascendancy and organization were just beginning. There seems to be ample material to confirm, again and again, that at least in this formative period, workers did behave with a fair degree of autonomy and that very often they laid down the terms of their relationship with external political agencies. In almost all the cases the decision to launch a strike actually came from the workers and nearly always the strike caught the leaders unawares. In March 1928, even after a regular union had been formed, the scavengers went on strike first and then informed the WPP office. 'And suddenly there was a strike', reported the founder of the union with great surprise.[178] This is not just an indication of political immaturity or an insufficient understanding of the concept of union. Workers at this stage held on to the idea that a strike decision could only

[174] Meerut Conspiracy Case Progs. l.c. 250–7.

[175] *Communists and Labour*, Isemonger's Report, 29/8/1928–GOI, Home Poll 18 XVI/28 of 1928.

[176] Report on a Deshbandhu Park meeting, 4/3/1928–Meerut, Sl. No. 201, 1925.

[177] Gautam Chattopadhyay, *Communism*, pp. 137–8.

[178] Interview with Das Gupta, op. cit. Ahmad also confirms the element of surprise. Ahmad, *Amar Jiban*, p. 22.

arise out of a consensus from within their own community. The strikes at Chengail and Bauria jute mills in July 1928 similarly began with an autonomous decision by workers, a group of whom then went to the WPP office and invited the leaders to come and organize the strike on their behalf.[179] When the 1929 general strike began in the jute mills almost all WPP leaders were behind the bars, thanks to the Meerut Conspiracy Case and the remaining leaders were deeply divided. In September 1929 there was a split in the union, Prabhabati Das Gupta was dismissed for her alleged high-handedness in union affairs and she set up a parallel union with Bakar Ali Mirza and Nripendra Chaudhuri.[180] The union, then, was not in any position to dictate or even very carefully plan out the details of the strike.

Just as workers often began strikes on their own, so they also ended these themselves, in defiance of Union discipline. Their own independent assessment convinced them of the limits, of reaching a point beyond which the struggle could not be continued. At such a stage they would go over to a completely new set of leaders—usually much more moderate and eager for compromise—and ask them to help settle the strike.

C.F. Andrews was completely ignored when in 1927 he opposed the Leftist leaders' decision to spread the EIR strike to the railway workshop. In August 1928, however, after the Lillooah workshop strike had exhausted its momentum, the workers approached Andrews and dissociated themselves from confirmed and far more respected Leftist leaders who intended to continue the strike. Andrews acted as the chief negotiator in mediating between the workers and the workshop Agent and a very moderate settlement was finalized with his help.[181] Similarly the jute general strike of 1929 was concluded by Prabhabati Das Gupta who negotiated a compromise without consulting the more established WPP leaders.[182] It seems that at this stage the general notion about unions was to see them as a group of professionals to execute and manage the technicalities of decisions which would be taken by workers themselves who reserved the power to initiate and terminate movements; unions were yet to be seen as a reified expression of the collective will of the workers with rigid claims on their absolute obedience.

[179] Interview with Das Gupta.

[180] GOI, Home Poll 1-28/1928, 2nd half of June. Also see Abdul Momin, *Chatkal Sramiker Pratham Sadharan Dharmaghat* in *Dainik Kalantar*, 10–12 August 1970.

[181] Gautam Chattopadhyay, *Communism*, p. 317.

[182] RCLI, Vol. V, Part II. See also NMML interview with Das Gupta.

A very vivid example of how vital their own assessment and understanding were to the final decision-making process is the response of the Ondal workshop labourers when Radharaman Mitra appealed to them to extend the Lillooah workshop strike. On 23 May 1928 he addressed the first meeting there with the words: 'We have come with a message from the brethren of Lillooah.... If all the brethren of Jamalpur and Ondal strike work at this last moment for a few days only the Agent will be upset and compromise will be effected'. The police reporter noted that his audience kept totally silent. When he issued a more insistent appeal—'if 30,000 men can live for 2-1/2 months (at Lillooah) you can surely live for 15 days',—a voice from the crowd interjected: 'A strike can be made if you provide us with 3 months' food. First, let the bigger workshops go on strike'.[183] There was, then, initially a strong reluctance against action, induced by the normal and understandable caution of men who lived perilously close to the subsistence level. The meeting broke up without reaching any decision and the workers dispersed to argue and thrash out the issues among themselves. In the privacy of mutual discussion and consultation they finally reached a decision that was entirely their own. The next morning, Mitra, unaware of any new developments, started the meeting with a cry of despair: 'For God's sake, for the sake of yourselves and your children it is necessary that you should go on strike'. The whole crowd then startled him by shouting in one voice: 'We will surely strike.'[184]

Union discipline and techniques of sophisticated collective action were usually very successfully superimposed on pre-union, sporadic protest and were quickly internalized by workers who, for instance, mastered the art of satyagraha thoroughly. During the Lillooah strike satyagrahas could mobilize thousands and could continue for days on end, astonishing the authorities. 'It is a game', wrote Jackson, 'which this particular class of Indian workers delights in'.[185] But discipline would sometimes break down, throwing up more elemental and indigenous forms of self-expression. All through the strikes there were stray cases of violent physical assault on blacklegs and the European management staff. At the Asansol workshop strike in June 1928 blacklegs were beaten up and the Police Superintendent Holman was injured during a scuffle.[186] In

[183] Mitra's speech, Ondal, 23/5/28-*Meerut Conspiracy Case Progs.* P 1930 (IB) (T).

[184] Mitra's speech, Ondal 24/5/28.

[185] Letter to Irwin, No. 456, 20 May, 1928, *Halifax Collection*.

[186] Home Poll 1–28/1928–*Fortnightly Reports on Bengal*, 2nd half of June 1928.

July 1928 the workers at the Fort Gloster jute mill at Bauria beat up European assistants and had a severe clash with the police who fired, wounding 23 workers.[187] Women workers, always less closely associated with Union functioning and hence far less amenable to union discipline, usually turned violent very quickly. During the Ludlow jute mill strike at Chengail in June 1928, they clashed with the police, looted the local bazar and stoned an European mill assistant. An entirely novel form of protest stunned the police when in April 1928 during the Howrah municipality scavengers' strike a major clash developed between the Anglo-Indian police sergeants and the women scavengers who threw pots of excreta at them. The sergeants fled, tearing off their uniforms and vowing never to return until they got the permission to fire.[188] The act showed how the very symbols of ritual and occupational degradation could be turned into weapons of strength.

Lal Paltan (Red Army)), a journal brought out by the Lillooah workshop union and a very rare example of union journalism, gives us a possible indication of the range of interests and concerns of workers. A copy of the 11 December 1928 issue, for instance, consists of four, thin, pink sheets with the hammer and sickle emblem and 'workers of the world unite' inserted in English on the front page. There is an obituary of Lala Lajpat Rai and a general report on the state of the nationalist movement in Bengal. This is followed by a detailed report on the Bauria jute mill strike and criticism of Congress indifference to it. On the second and third pages are bits of local news and gossip—scandal about officers and local grievances—but there is also news about the Titagarh paper mill-workers and Howrah coolies. The range of topics covered certainly transcends the bounds of narrow economism. Written in chaste Bengali and edited by Bimal Ganguly (who must have written almost all of it himself), it could not have precisely reflected the state of the workers' general knowledge and interests. But since it obviously circulated among the workers and could have been read out to large numbers it must have at least reached a fair approximation of it.[189]

Sometimes a gesture or a name extracts from the depersonalized struggle of the mass of workers a sharper individual focus and serves briefly to illumine the entire range of meaning and experience

[187] GOB, *Annual Report on the Administration of Bengal 1927–28, p. 23.*
[188] Ahmad, *Amar Jiban*, p. 21.
[189] *Meerut Conspiracy Case Progs.* S 17.

connected with their struggle. At an extremely tense moment during the jute general strike, when the mill bustees were ringed round by a very hostile police force, some leaders like Moni Singh tried to put heart into the workers by breaking into a song:

> 'We have built happily with our hands
> Now let us smash things up joyously with our feet
> Take up your hammer, take up your spade'.

There was a moment of silence, then the workers' feet started tapping and their bodies swaying to the rhythm of the music. Their voices picked up the tune and soon the tense, nervous crowd was dancing joyfully.[190]

A march was organized by Lillooah workers in April 1928 which went up to Chinsurah in Hooghly, accompanied all the way by trucks of military police: 'We have become governors', chanted the workers, 'for only they are given such military escorts.' In May 1928 Lillooah workers went on another march from Howrah and reached Dalhousie Square late at night, where they were immediately surrounded by mounted police. On getting news of this large gathering, Police Commissioner Tegart rushed out in his nightshirt. Highly entertained by this spectacle, the workers quipped: 'Tegart Sahib's pants are coming down in fear'. The ridicule was flung at a man who was dreaded all over Bengal for his brutality and who, at that very moment, had all his forces spread out around the demonstrators. The sharp earthy humour that flowered at the height of a crucial and risky struggle, gathered into it the good cheer and warmth of solidarity. It had an obverse side as well. During the marches, workers of different castes and communities who had struggled and even died together, refused to eat together for fear of pollution: 'We can give up our lives but not our religion.'[191]

Santiram Mondol, a sardar at the Lillooah workshop, had a long career as a Union activist and at the time of the strike had reached the position of the Union Secretary. Through repeated overtures to the police picket he had managed to establish some sort of a rapport with them and during a satyagraha on 30 July 1928 he could even manage to persuade the police to leave the spot.[192] After the strikes, sections of Howrah policemen, who had developed quite a sympathetic attitude towards the workers, came up to the strike

[190] Momin, *Chatkal Sramiker*.
[191] Gautam Chattopadhyay, *Communism*, pp. 139–41.
[192] Fortnightly Reports on Bengal, 1st half of June 1928, Home Pol 1-28 1928.

leaders and asked them to help organize a union for the local police.[193]

Apart from certain basic economic demands the issues that brought workers out into large-scale action almost always included a defence of the right to form unions. Union recognition was a major demand in the charter of the Corporation scavengers.[194] Victimization of union members was the immediate factor that brought about the very powerful strike at the Lillooah workshop in 1928. The demand charter, pressing for a minimum monthly wage of Rs 30, accommodation and leave facilities and old age pension, was drawn up well after the strike was off the ground.[195] The Chengail jute mill strike of 1928 began when Mahadeo, a sardar of the spinning department, carried a letter from the union to the Manager to protest against the repression of union members. The Manager dismissed Mahadeo on the spot and trampled upon the letter without reading it. The strike that followed was as much over the victimization of union members as it was over the insult flung at the 'big union'.[196]

Defence of union rights meant, very broadly, a strong and real sense of solidarity that often extended beyond the individual factory or even the particular industry, and could encompass, however vaguely, the entire class of factory workers. An Urdu word Anjuman, (which literally meant an association) came up very early to fit the new concept of unions. A sense of community therefore had preceded the workers' exposure to proper unions. Leaders who organized unions found an immediate resonance to their message from within the workers' experience. Since unions seemed to correspond to, or embody, the notion of community rights and obligations, their defence was vigorous from the beginning.

The remarkable strength of the solidarity strikes is also explained by a fairly uniform level of low skill-formation among workers. The high degree of homogeneity that this produced within the workplace cut across different factories quite easily. Most groups of workers filled up the lowest and the most menial jobs in factories; a very low technological level was expected from them as technical and managerial jobs were almost entirely reserved for Euro-

193 Radharaman Mitra's speech, 23/3/1928-*Meerut Conspiracy Case Progs.* P 1932 (I).

194 *Meerut Conspiracy Case Progs.* P 1938 T.

195 Ibid. p. 2103 (T).

196 RCLI. Vol. I, Part II.

peans.[197] The case of the Corporation scavengers is self-evident. In jute, the structure of production ruled out the need for industrial skill. The stagnation in the general technological level within the industry as a whole was reinforced by the lack of competition and by a guaranteed profit margin that jute industrialists enjoyed due to their monopolistic status.[198] Occupational differences, therefore, had little impact on internal differentiation within the labour force. This does not, of course, steamroller all variations in work patterns and political experience out of existence. The jute general strike was led everywhere by weavers who constituted the highest-paid category in the mills.[199] The new production schedule, involving a changeover to the single-shift system from July 1929, affected them the worst and, being relatively highly paid, they also had more staying power.[200] On the whole, however, such internal differences were smoothed over by the much greater range of shared experience. Workers came from certain distinct rural pockets of Bihar, Eastern UP, Orissa and parts of Madras.[201] The trauma of being forced into the milieu of a strange factory and mill bustee existence, radically different from the rural agricultural work habits, were again vital experiences shared by all.

A chronic labour surplus situation and the ready availability of a large 'badli' or reserve labour force ruled out the need to ensure a stable and skilled labour supply. This explained the management's indifference to, and even ignorance about, the living and working conditions of their employees. On the rare occasions when they had to ponder over these problems, employers could easily reach the comforting conclusion that if workers lived badly, it was entirely due to their intemperate habits (for instance drinking), exorbitant and irrational ceremonial expenditure, and a skewed budget with very low spending on food as they wanted to remit most of their money home. The deep and persistent connections with home villages also meant frequent leaves and absences to help out during harvest time. While this was perceived as a problem that inter-

[197] For instance, in the case of Tramways in Calcutta this is stated very frankly by Daines, RCLI, Vol. V, Part I.

[198] Dipesh Chakravarty, *Bengal Jute Mill Labour*, section V.

[199] RCLI, Vol. V, Part II.

[200] Momin, *Chatkal Sramiker*.

[201] Most immigrants came from some well-defined areas; Gaya, Patna, Shahabad, Muzaffarpur, Monghyr, Darbhanga, Saran and Hazaribagh in Bihar; Cuttack and Balasore in Orissa; Benaras, Ghazipur, Balia, Azamgarh, Jaunpur, Mirzapur & Fyzabad in UP; Bilaspur, Nagpur and Raipur in Central Provinces; Ganjam, Vizag and Madras city from Madras. Gilchrist's report; RCLI, *passim*.

rupted a perfect adjustment to the urban, industrial tempo, it was still favoured by the state and the employers on the grounds that village links provided them with occasional rest, some medical care, a home after retirement and protection against emergencies; simultaneously they exempted the State and the capitalists from all responsibility in providing for such contingencies.[202]

The entire body of evidence, if read from a different angle, suggests very different explanations for the problems of the workers and the rationality of their devices for dealing with them. Scavengers had an average monthly income of Rs 15 without any prospects of additional sources of income. They lived in complete absence of any social security arrangements or credit facilities. As a result about 90 per cent of them were indebted to the Kabuli money-lender who extracted an exorbitant rate of interest.[203] In the railway workshops, a large proportion of workers and union activists were Muslims from UP who were similarly thrown upon an alien city without any expectations of insurance, sickness benefits, pension or leave facilities.[204] In bustees catering to jute mills, workers lived in back to back, ill-ventilated, one-room shacks with no open windows or chimneys. Electric light was unheard of and 'in none of them sunlight could penetrate through'. Each room (about 8 ft × 8 ft to 10 ft × 10 ft in size) would be occupied by three or four people. Slums, set at a greater distance from mill-sites fared even worse as regards drainage, water supply and sanitation. Workers spent about 16 rupees a month at the most on food which caused grave deficiency of necessary vitamins, fat and protein in their diet. Karu, a landless labourer from Mungeli in Bihar and a spinner at a jute mill, had a non-earning wife and children to support. He earned Rs 5.2 as, per week when his weekly house rent was Rs 1. 4 as. He had no savings and a total debt of 23 rupees.[204] Since there were no supplementary sources of income, some 75 per cent to 90 per cent of them were in debt, with interest rates varying between 72 per cent to 150 per cent. Their general health had deteriorated markedly in the ten years preceding the general strike even though these were years of rising wages. During the 1929 general strike the manager of the Anglo-India Mill asked the workers at a meeting: 'You used to get very little wages before but you didn't make any

[202] RCLI, Vol. V, Pt. II.

[203] RCLI, Vol. V, Pt. II.

[204] Gautam Chattopadhyay, *Communism*, p. 38.

[205] RCLI, Vol. V, Part II.

trouble then. But why are you agitating now since you are getting much more?' Workers replied that prices had gone up substantially in the meantime, cancelling out all the advantages of the wage increase.[206]

Coming to the Calcutta factories very often implied for the workers a drastic and violent disruption of family life and personal relations. Caste prejudice, lack of privacy in living quarters and costs of transportation combined to force most migrant workers to leave their wives and families behind. An acute sex-imbalance was created, leading to a great deal of blatant prostitution. This was a vicious circle since the prevalence of prostitution stiffened the resolve to leave women in home villages and imparted a ruthless and brutalizing promiscuity and a good deal of violence in slum existence. Living unprotected among an overwhelming male population, the single woman worker was forced to seek the protection of a single man at a time and her state became difficult to disentangle from that of a prostitute. 'There are women who come with men from outside Bengal, who are not their wives and who live very often with these men and work under their protection at the mill.'[207]

The position of the few married women workers who came and worked with their husbands at the mill was in no way better. Referring to work hours under the double-shift system in jute mills, Babuniyah, a woman worker, wanted paid maternity leave and creche facilities: 'I leave my house at 5 in the morning to come to work at the mill and go home at 9.30. I come again to work at 11. I do not get sufficient time for proper cooking. If I am a little late in coming to work the baboos reprimand me. I feed my children after 9.30'. Muthialu, another worker from the same factory, had taken her pregnant daughter (also a jute mill worker) to a doctor attached to the mill: 'The lady doctor wrote something and told us to go to the Sahib at the mill. He read this paper and tore it. We did not know what to do'. The daughter eventually went back to work and lost her child.[208] Managers, however, stuck to a comforting piece of traditionalism, insisting against all evidence that even if creches were provided, working mothers would never make use of them.[209]

All this partly helps to explain the ready participation by women

[206] Ibid.

[207] Evidence of the Bengal Presidency Council of Women, ibid.

[208] Evidence of Babuniyah and Muthialu.

[209] Evidence of IJMA representative. Ibid.

in strikes and their violence. What is remarkable, however, is that there was no corresponding extension of such militancy in union-building or strike-organizing activities which remained the preserves of men and middle class union leaders from outside. The problem cannot be explained away by the fact that leaders and male workers knew and represented women's grievances adequately. Their specific demands were routinely placed towards the bottom of all charters but strikes never developed over these issues. In speeches of leaders we do not find appeals or messages directed at women in particular, no moves to debate and discuss their grievances for consciousness-raising purposes.[210] Subsuming the special problems of the woman worker within a general list set the pattern for a similar use of these issues in labour and other political movements in general; there would always be an even-ing out of complexities, a certain failure of perception which marginalized the specific implications of her existence.

Since employers accepted no responsibility for the minimum security or welfare measures for men and women workers, the importance of village ties remained undiminished—a fact accepted, even welcomed by the state and the capitalists. What they chose to overlook, however, was the fact that migrant workers were overwhelmingly landless labourers who had come to the Calcutta mills only because their village homes could not support them any longer. The extremes of poverty which would send off a man to the dreaded jute mills have been vividly described in the celebrated short story, *Mahesh*, by Saratchandra: when landlord oppression had snatched the last bit of land and the last beast of burden from the peasant Gaffar, only then did he think of the jute mills. It was an act of absolute despair, almost of suicide.[211] Once in the alien city and living out a life of inhuman, unrelieved toil with nothing but stark insecurity at every corner and at the end of it, the workers indulged in heavy bouts of drinking which would not only temporarily assuage their fears and uncertainties, but which might also underline, among the community of fellow-drinkers and sufferers, the fellow-feeling that remained their only hope and comfort. Drinking together would then be an act of solidarity, a pledge of mutual dependence and reassurance. Similarly, the investment in ceremonial expenditure that seemed to clinch the argument about

[210] This is borne out by an examination of speeches and writings of union leaders in *Meerut Conspiracy Case Progs*.

[211] *Mahesh*, *Sarat Granthabali*.

the worker's basic irrationality and irresponsibility for the employer, was linked to ritual observances that were essential for varying the daily monotony. Deference to ritual might also reflect a desperate bid to clutch at the norms of the life of the respectable, settled householder. Rituals would preserve the much–needed illusion that their lives were anchored in known customs and habits, regulated by inflexible laws. Such illusions alone, could mitigate the fear of drifting.

Through its aloofness from the workers' existence the European management lacked a concrete reality and hegemony in the workers' cognitive scheme. A large part of the masters' functions then came to be assumed by the jobbers or sardars at the factories; who, for better or for worse, emerged as the most decisive and important men in their lives. The role that the sardar assumed was an extremely ambivalent one. An enumeration of the many functions that he was supposed to undertake will give us an idea about the range and strength of his influence. As late as 1937 virtually all recruitment at jute mills was done by the sardars, and, on occasions, by the higher rank of Bengali 'baboos' or clerks. Recruitment, whether at the catchment area or at the factory gate, was on the basis of community, caste and kinship ties that the sardar and the worker would share.[212] So, even before he entered the factory floor, the worker had entered into a direct, personal relationship with the sardar, based on deference to and dependence on what seemed to constitute the natural, visible authority.[213] Often the sardar advanced him the initial travel expenses to get him to the mill area from home, arranged his accommodation, trained and supervised his work within the factory and punished breaches in discipline. He would have the sole charge of allotment of work, grant of leave, re-employment and promotion.[214] More important, perhaps, were the manifold ties that developed even outside the factory floor; the sardar was often the owner of the bustee where the worker lived, the local shopkeeper to cater to his daily needs, a money-lender who would help out with short-term credit. Mill bustees owned by sardars would often be organized on caste lines where he would also be the caste 'panch' or leader, judge and

[212] Ranajit Das Gupta. 'Structure of the Labour Market in Colonial India', *Economic and Political Weekly*, Special Number 1981.

[213] Dipesh Chakravarty, *Bengal Jute Mill Labour.*

[214] Saroj Bandopadhyay, *Bikikinir Hat* (Calcutta, n.d.).

final arbiter, deciding on codes of moral behaviour and punishing transgression.[215]

The state and the management referred approvingly to the possibility of a warm and human relationship between the sardar and the worker. What they preferred to ignore, however, was the element of corruption and coercion structured within such absolute domination and control. For employment, re-employment, leave and promotion the worker had to pay a regular bribe which was generally extortionate. 'I had to pay Rs 4 as bakshish to the sardar who appointed me. Each time I return back from the village I have to pay the same amount. I also pay him 2 annas every week. If we refuse to pay to the sardars we will not get work. Every worker pays a similar amount to the sardar'. These comments came from Babuniyah, the woman worker from a jute mill with a weekly income of Rs 3. Her husband, who had a slightly higher income of Rs 5.7 as. 6p, had to pay a somewhat higher rate of bribes. Even where the factory did provide accommodation, workers were forced to rent rooms at bustees owned by the sardars which were filthy, insanitary and even more expensive.[216] The discipline that they imposed upon the workers was harsh in the extreme and was enforced through foul, abusive language and physical assaults.[217] Sardari corruption and oppression were frequently included in lists of grievances during strikes; Calcutta scavengers, for instance, demanded the punishment of Block Sardars for bribery.[218]

In spite of all the resentment and even the occasional resistance to it, the sardari system was integrated into the moral universe of the workers in a way in which the authority of the European managers and capitalists could never be. The very oppression which the sardars embodied was not only far more personalized but was also deeply familiar to the worker. With his patronage functions, his caste and kinship connections, with his ownership of land and bustees and his control over the caste panch, the sardar and the system based on his control in several significant ways replicated the village authority structure within Bengali industrial suburbs while, at the same time, subtly modifying the known aspects, through the additional new functions that were tied to the factory floor/urban

[215] Babuniyah's evidence, RCLI.

[216] IJMA representative, RCLI; Ranajit Das Gupta, 'Structure of the Labour Market'.

[217] Dharani Goswami's speech, *Meerut Conspiracy Case Progs*. P. 1938.

[218] Evidence of IJMA representative, RCLI.

slum control. Even oppression and domination, therefore, would be muted through a sense of continuity and familiarity.

The ambivalence of the relationship and the elements of symbiosis within it were reflected sometimes in the role that the sardars played in the strike wave. The 1929 transition to a single-shift system of work in the jute mills meant a reduced scope for manipulation of the reserve or 'badli' labour force. That provided far less opportunities for bribery and corruption. The sardars were now pushed down to 'the position of technical overseer'.[219] The conjuncture of grievances of workers and sardars made for a particularly intense and powerful general strike in almost all jute mills in Bengal between July and September. Individual sardars extended their leadership into labour organizations as well; Santiram Mondol, the very important leader of the Lillooah workshop, was a sardar and so was Mahadeo whose encounter with the jute mill managers was a crucial factor in the 1929 strike wave.

The persistence, with important modifications, of traditional behaviour patterns and authority structures, related, as it was, to certain structural peculiarities of the working class, affected ultimately the formation and development of unions as well. The strikes in this period are something of a paradox in working-class organization—the absence of regular unions and workers' indifference to long-standing organized fronts on the one hand and the remarkable discipline and constructive ability of the short-term strike committees on the other. The paradox reflected at the same time the strength of working class militancy at crisis points as well as an immaturity that failed to sustain this experience in an enduring and organized way.

The very nature of the overwhelmingly migrant labour-force posed serious problems. Each wave of migrants brought with it traditions and habits of the catchment areas which could not be easily integrated with the political traditions of Bengal. The percentage of elderly workers was very small and the total spell of factory work for each quite limited.[220] Each generation of workers was replaced with a fresh wave of migrants from villages so that at any given moment a large proportion of the total work-force would be entirely raw recruits who would need a lot of time to get their bearings in the new work pattern. Tulsi Chamar, a mill-hand of the Anglo-India Jute Mill Company, was an agricultural labourer

[219] Gilchrist's report.

[220] C. Revri, *The Indian Trade Union Movement* (Delhi. 1976), 118–9.

who had joined the mill a year before the strike wave began. Prakash, a worker at the Titagarh No. 11 mill used to tend cattle in his village before he joined the mill. Adjustment to an urban industrial rhythm of life often took years and even then the moorings of the earlier existence would not be entirely broken. Karu, a jute mill spinner, had left his village Mungeli ten years before the strikes began. In the middle of a description of his present living conditions in the mill bustee he suddenly and unexpectedly announced: 'I have no cattle here.'[221] Organization among such an amorphous, undefined and generally unskilled labour-force was a major problem. Unlike their counterparts in England or France this working class did not possess any longstanding artisan origins with its own radical-democratic traditions or norms of corporate organization, which could be absorbed by the newly-emergent industrial working class. Artisans in India were displaced not by industrialization but by de-industrialization which threw them back upon land from where gradually a labour reserve was recruited.

There were serious external constraints as well. The Indian Trade Union Act of 1926—far more stringent than its counterpart in Britain—made registration and audit obligatory, fund collection by unregistered unions illegal and restricted entry of outsiders into union executives.[222] The restrictions saw to it that very few organizations could apply for registration. In 1928 only 10 unions applied for registration. But a total of 140 unions functioned 'unofficially'. Of the registered unions not one was really active in the labour upsurge.[223] Dain, the Agent of the Calcutta Tramways Company, found even the registered unions offensive. He admitted that he kept confidential reports on union meetings and summed up his attitude: 'I never consult the union about anything. There is only one way in which I can make the union flourish and that would be by running it myself.'[224] In 1929 two very repressive pieces of legislation were passed to contain labour militancy. The Trade Disputes Act of April 1929 provided for the appointment of courts of enquiry and conciliation boards for settling disputes, for punishing lightning strikes in public utility services, and for a general restriction on strikes. The Public Safety Ordinance empowered the Government to deport British agitators who helped Indian

[221] Evidence of Karu, RCLI, Vol. V, Part II.

[222] RCLI, Vol. V, Part II.

[223] Davis' Evidence, RCLI.

[224] Revri, *Indian Trade Union Movement*, pp. 157–63.

Communists in trade unions and to confiscate funds sent from abroad to Indian workers.[225] Large-scale arrests of Communists and other militant labour leaders for the Meerut Conspiracy Case in March 1929 also reduced the possibility of building stable organizations on the basis of past struggles and victories.

The nature and limits of the external political leadership remained of much deeper significance and importance.[226] An analysis of speeches and writings by labour leaders shows that most of them centred on elementary lessons in discipline, union-functioning and responsibility and on strike demands. As far as broader issues are concerned, there were assurances about solidarity from other sections of the working class at home and abroad and accounts of labour struggles elsewhere. Occasionally the French and the Russian revolutions were touched upon and the electoral victory of the Labour Party in Britain was most misleadingly described as an instance of the workers' Raj.[227] But the stray historical references were not expanded at length and practically nothing was conveyed to them by way of ideological/cultural education. Nor was there a systematic effort on the part of the leaders to study in depth the conditions of the working class they were organizing, to learn from the 'lived experience' of the workers. Part of the reason lay in the very nature of the worker-leader contact. In the absence of stable unions this contact was very hastily made only when the need for strikes became urgent; and then the immediate, all-engrossing responsibility would be to impart training in the conduct of the strike. So the only political education really consisted of economism of a very elementary, though of an extremely militant, variety.

The working class in Bengal was a heterogenous and multi-religious one. There was, therefore, little scope for making use of traditional symbols or habits of thought for propaganda or education. Sections of Calcutta workers had been quite active in the riots of 1926. After that leaders would take particular care to avoid all references to sectional symbols or concepts. But a composite, secular and independent working-class culture had not yet emerged

[225] *Meerut Conspiracy Case Progs.* 1930 (11A) (f). p. 1893 (3) (T), P 2172.

[226] For a stimulating, if controversial, discussion on the nature of the relationship between bhadralok union leaders and workers and the feudal ties of deference that underlay it see Dipesh Chakravarty, 'Trade Unions in a Hierarchical Culture: The Jute Workers of Calcutta, 1920–50', in R. Guha, (ed.), *Subaltern Studies III* (New Delhi, 1948).

[227] Gautam Chattopadhyay, *Communism*.

and the pull of traditional rituals and values remained as strong as ever. This unavoidable omission left large and vital areas of their imagination and life untouched and unutilized in the economic struggles. The experience of these struggles could not significantly remould a consciousness that was as yet insufficiently geared to industrial work discipline and one that constantly recharged itself with peasant values—a consciousness that combined heroic, anti-capitalist demonstrations with slogans of 'Ganga Mai Ki Jai', an insistence on caste-divisions and even communal rioting. The very organization of industry and the structure of the work-force then shaped an existence that could encompass with almost equal persistence, defiance and class solidarity with traditional community consciousness and deference patterns.

Such basic constraints on mobilization notwithstanding the experience of 1928–9 had not been just a flash in the pan. Around the mid-1930s there was another round of movement, accompanied this time, by a spate of more enduring organization work—a definite advance, built on the firm ground of the 1928–9 achievements. But the old constraints and limits remained structured into the new organizations. Also, if workers had learned how to mobilize better, so had the state and the capitalists. The Government armed itself with a battery of permanent anti-labour legislations and deterrents. It also began to intervene far more decisively in labour-capitalist relations. The compromise settlement which concluded the jute general strike in 1929 was the first instance of State arbitration in jute mill disputes as 'hitherto the jute mills had upheld a strenuous individualism'.[228] The employers too strengthened their fronts: the Indian Jute Millowners Association began to take common stands on wages and work conditions—an important departure from their former practice of making purely commercial decisions. Working class solidarity therefore had its corollary in a more unified capitalist front.

The Workers' and Peasants' Party

'The worst aspect of the strike movement', Jackson had remarked at the beginning of the industrial strike wave, 'has been the part played by the outsider and the Communists.'[229] Communists operated not in their own name but through a broad-based open

[228] RCLI, Vol. V, Part II.
[229] Jackson, 14 March 1928, *Birkenhead Collection,* MSS EUR/D 703/22 IOL.

front—the Workers' and Peasants' Party. By 1928, however, there was not the least ambiguity about its ideological affiliation. David Petrie, Director of the Intelligence Bureau, saw the Indian Left movement entirely as an offshoot of a Bolshevik conspiracy to attack the British Empire at its weakest point. Comintern agents, V. Chattopadhyay from Berlin and M.N. Roy from Moscow, had sent their emissaries Abani Mukherji and Nalini Gupta in the early 1920s to get in touch with Bengal terrorists. Some important contacts were made within the Anushilan and Gopen Chakravarty was sent to Moscow. After his return he began to discuss Communistic ideas with his Anushilan comrades and convinced Dharani Goswami with his arguments. Goswami, in his turn, broke away from the Anushilan with a group of young terrorists in early 1927. The group came together with the WPP whose strength was thus crucially augmented on the eve of the industrial unrest.[230]

The British official mind invariably moved along the well-worn grooves of an international conspiracy theory which saw Moscow pouring in Bolshevik gold and agents which, in their turn, created a Left-wing movement in India. The importance of the early Comintern agents and their contacts is no doubt quite substantial. While such linkages were as yet on an extremely limited and purely individual level, the WPP itself had strong indigenous roots. The Bengal wing of the Party was originally formed as a group within the Congress by men who were disenchanted with the pro-landlord affiliations of the Swarajists. A Sramik-Proja-Swaraj Sampraday or a Labour Swaraj Party was set up at Bogra on 1 November 1925 with a provisional constitution and policy statement drawn up by the radical nationalist poet, Qazi Nazrul Islam. It proposed to work among peasants and workers while remaining within the Congress and to send up representatives to the Legislative Assembly. It began to bring out a weekly mouthpiece, *Langal* (The Plough) from December 1925. The journal was financed by Qutbuddin Ahmad and edited by Nazrul.[231]

Early issues of the *Langal* reflect a somewhat curious amalgam of a peasant-oriented populism, rather conservative social themes and nationalist sentiments. The editorial of 13 December 1925 described the caste system as 'based on scientific thought'. It quoted Aurobindo to condemn the competitive spirit generated by modern

[230] Sir David Petrie, *Communism in India* (reprinted, Calcutta, 1972), pp. 122–33.

[231] *Meerut Conspiracy Case Progs.* Sl. No. 459–62: Report of the WPP Bengal Executive Committee 1927–8.

industrial civilization. It postulated a self-sufficient and self-governing village community (Pallitantra) composed of all classes and castes and functioning as an integrated, harmonious whole. It criticized Swarajists and terrorists for their indifference to mass action and interests. Later issues, however, increasingly assumed a strongly-defined radical note.[232]

The Party merged itself with the newly-formed Peasants' and Workers' Party at the All-Bengal Tenants' Conference at Krishnagore on 6 February 1926. A Committee was elected with Naresh Sen Gupta as Chairman and Hemanta Sarkar, Qutbuddin, Rajibuddin Tarafdar, Atul Gupta and Maulvi Shamsuddin Hussain as members. At least two of the Party members were convinced Communists (Soumyendranath Tagore and Muzaffar Ahmad) and they were to set the tone in future. Of the sixteen names mentioned in the membership list (which excluded office bearers) as many as twelve were Muslims. The joint platform was formed at a time of violent communal clashes when many such fronts were breaking down elsewhere. Though early issues of the *Langal* (as the name itself indicates) were preoccupied with peasant problems the Party eventually would be confined to the Calcutta industrial areas for a long time.[233]

In the course of 1926 about forty new members were recruited; almost all of them came from the educated middle class. The *Ganavani* (Voice of the People), edited by Muzaffar Ahmad, which replaced the *Langal* as the Party mouthpiece from August 1926, was a journal obviously meant for the intelligentsia. A lack of definition and an ambivalence about Party purposes persisted under these conditions. Naresh Sen Gupta, in his Presidential address at the Krishnagore Conference, declared that the struggle on peasant issues had to remain subordinate to the national movement; depending upon the requirements of the freedom struggle, it might even be abandoned at times.[234]

The Party broke out of its 'bhadralok' confines and moved into working-class centres once the worst phase of the communal crisis was over and the first stirrings of industrial unrest began. The record of 1927 showed impressive gains. Work in the jute mill belt had begun and the Bengal Jute Workers' Association had affiliated itself to the Party. The Dhakeswari Cotton Mill Workers' Union

232 *Langal*, 13 December 1925, *Meerut Progs.*, Sl. 456, Ext. No. 1, 49.
233 WPP Executive Committee Report, *Meerut Progs.*, 19.
234 *Langal*, 28 February 1926, *Meerut Progs.*

was reorganized at Dacca and the Scavengers' Union of Bengal was formed towards the end of the year. It was active in the dock workers' strike in Calcutta in December 1927 and some members participated in the Kharagpur railway strike. Three members were elected for the BPCC in 1927 and two became AICC members.[235]

By 1928 the WPP (the name was changed to Workers' and Peasants' Party in 1926) had undoubtedly emerged as the dominant influence on the Calcutta industrial belt. Apart from the somewhat highbrow *Ganavani* it also brought out the *Lal Paltan* for the Lillooah railway workshop labourers. It was preparing to issue two Hindi weeklies for mill-hands—*Lal Nishan* (Red Flag) and *Jangi Mazdur* (Militant Worker). It controlled twenty-eight unions—twenty-four in Calcutta and adjacent districts, two in Dacca and two in Mymensingh.[236] It had formed its own youth front, the Young Comrades' League, which was a breakaway group[237] from revolutionary terrorist organizations. While Gopal Basak was the main organizer at Dacca, Calcutta achievements were attributed to Muzaffar Ahmad and the British Communist Philip Spratt. The peasant front remained neglected even though these years saw important developments in their struggles. Part of the lapse was ideologically governed; the industrial working-class was seen as the true base of the revolution. In any case a spatially-concentrated, relatively little stratified working class, a large part of which was located in Calcutta, was rather easier to mobilize and organize. Being a cadre-based Party it was quite a small one still and all members had to be pulled in, to work on the industrial strike wave in the first few years. A few tentative efforts were made to mobilize groups of Tangail peasants where the management of a private forest by the Forest Department had brought cultivators into conflict with the Government. Some meetings were organized in the 24 Parganas to incite local tenants against landlords. Attempts remained sporadic and a sustained peasant movement did not develop.[238]

A comparison between the *Langal* and the *Ganavani* indicates the distance that had been covered between the days of the Labour Swaraj Party and the WPP. The former combined discussions of an

[235] WPP Executive Committee Report, *Meerut Progs.*

[236] Letter from GOB No. 1169–P.S., 19/12/28 GOI. Home Poll 18/XVI/1928.

[237] Statement of Programme and Policy, Young Comrades' League 1927–8—Sl No. 416, *Meerut Progs.*

[238] GOI, Home Poll 18/XVI/1928.

ideal village community that accepted basic caste distinctions with emotional effusion about a somewhat vague concept of socialism. The front page carried a rather uninspired poem on peasant virtues by Rabindranath. The *Ganavani*, in contrast, carried fairly detailed reports on developments on the international Communist scene, articles on Marxism and the Bolshevik revolution. Neither the earlier journal nor the politically more mature *Ganavani*, however, went in for a systematic analysis of social institutions or economic developments within India or Bengal. They showed little interest in learning from the lived experience of peasants and workers. The lapse is striking since earlier recruitment was done exclusively from among intellectuals. The absence of serious empirical research into, or theoretical grasp of the Indian social reality, or the functioning of imperialism on the basis of their new Marxist understanding was a surprising intellectual failure on the part of a sophisticated intelligentsia.

The main polemical exercise centred around a debate with the Congress that grew more and more acrimonious. It reflected a major shift in the Comintern line on the question of national bourgeois leadership. Up to 1927 Communists all over the world were advised to follow a broad-front strategy, based on unity and struggle from within. A Party policy statement filled out this concept in 1927: 'We must support the Congress while it fights Imperialism but must not hesitate to criticize the compromising tendencies of the Congress leaders, however prominent'.[239] The disaster experienced by Chinese Communists in 1927, however, resulted in a radical break with this line. The new Comintern approach veered round to a completely different strategy advocating a total dissociation from the mainstream of the national movement and a sectarian struggle under exclusively Communist Party leadership.

The new strategy, no doubt, was formulated and imposed by the Comintern (now ruled entirely by the Soviet Party). It was not a decision that had been reached independently by Indian Communists themselves. Yet, in Bengal at least, the new instructions fell on fertile and prepared soil.

Swarajist leadership, with its radical demagogy so blatantly contradicting its actual performance, had provoked deep dissatisfaction even in Congress circles. The Gandhian alternative

[239] A call to action, Report on Annual Bengal WPP Conference, Bhatpara, 1928, *Meerut Progs.*

at the moment looked like an exhausted force, incapable of generating new movements. The terrorist creed seemed doomed by its indifference to wider social issues and mass action. In contrast, the recent work of the Communists themselves seemed to vindicate their self-confidence. There was some real possibility of going it alone.

The decision to sever relations with the Congress organization cannot be construed (as it has been done again and again by anti-Communists) as a dissociation from the national movement itself. The major criticism that Communists made about the Congress leadership was that its anti-imperialism was not adequately uncompromising or unambiguous. The All Parties' Conference and the adoption of the Dominion Status goal were bitterly criticized as tame and moderate.[240] The Government itself was fully alive to this. 'It is common knowledge', wrote Jackson, 'that the encouragement of this anti-British propaganda is the main work of the Communists and Extremists'.[241] Elaborate conspiracy charges brought against Communist leaders at Meerut constitute clear evidence of this role.

The critique of the Congress focussed equally on the social anomalies in the Swarajist programme. 'The despicable selfishness displayed in Council over the Bengal Tenancy Act by Congress members—is that also to be counted as part of the Congress propaganda for equality? The Congress is an institution for the higher classes of society.'[242]

Differences were stated clearly enough in the report of the Executive Committee of 1927–8. They were still contained within a broad framework of unity and struggle. The report instructed Communists to work as much as possible with other nationalist bodies. 'The WPP ought to be careful not to oppose the Congress except on well-defined, individual issues, otherwise we shall enable our opponents to claim that we are anti-Congress or even anti-national and that we stand merely for the sectional claims of labour.... Recent developments in the policy of Congress leaders, their action in connection with the Scavengers' strike, etc. show that there is a tendency to mobilize nationalist sentiments against us in a fascist manner.'[243]

[240] *Ganavani*, 23 August 1927. *Meerut Progs.*, P 577 (T)
[241] Jackson, 8 April 1929. *Halifax Collection*, op. cit.
[242] *Ganavani*, 27 September 1929, *Meerut Progs.*, P. 553(T).
[243] *Meerut Progs.*, WPP Executive Committee Report.

The Sixth Comintern line put paid to all willingness to accommodate and widened, to a great extent, already existing areas of disagreement. The final Political Resolution, submitted to the All India WPP Conference in December 1928, affirmed that as long as the Congress remained a general platform, the policy of forming Left-factions within it was to be continued. Emphasis, however, had shifted much more to the purely temporary nature of the arrangements; the ultimate aim of separation and independent Communist initiative had come to be recognized. Although the old WPP connections would still be used, the new Party was to be a strongly-centralized, cadre-based and openly Marxist one. It 'must mercilessly expose the National reformist leaders and carry on a decisive struggle for the conversion of trade unions into genuine class organizations of the proletariat.'[244]

The new Party had overreached itself by exaggerating its own strength. It also confused the distinction between the Congress leadership and its pronouncements on a number of socio-political issues, and the radical militancy of the peasant masses who provided the manpower behind Congress movements and who perceived and translated Congress messages in their own very different ways. Faced with determined persecution the small Party went almost entirely under precisely at a time when it had decided to forsake the broad, united front. When Civil Disobedience swept through the country it could not improve its position by joining and widening the process of mobilization. Nor was it in a position to lead a mass movement on its own as it had so optimistically planned earlier. Repression and the downswing in the labour movement eroded its bases and almost broke its back.

[244] 'The Immediate Task of the Communists', 1929. *Meerut Progs.*

CHAPTER 2

1930

Civil Disobedience: Official Prognostications

On the basis of the assessment of the 1928–9 agitation, the Government made a number of predictions about the prospects for Civil Disobedience in Bengal. These give us an idea of the relative strength of the different forces within the movement. With the beginning of Civil Disobedience, however, the pattern of political involvement and activity shifted.

In October 1929 the Government of Bengal decided that a re-enactment of the Bengal Criminal Law Amendment Act may not be necessary. A draft Ordinance nevertheless had to be kept in readiness, not because of the terrorists but because 'there is a real danger of widespread disturbances, especially in the industrial area in and around Calcutta'. The strength of the youth and volunteer movement was recognized but officials did not pay serious attention to it. Possibilities of a mass upsurge were sought to be gauged from the current state of boycott and anti-Union Board agitations; they did not seem to be particularly ominous. The Permanent Settlement with the zamindars protected Bengal from Bardoli-type no-revenue agitations, which Gandhi had launched so successfully. If Muslims, low caste or untouchable peasants did harbour ideas that challenged the existing colonial property relations, they had fewer illusions still about Swarajists. The growing affinity between Congress leaders and members of the Hindu Sabhas made the Muslim community more anti-Congress than anti-Government. 'Briefly, the situation is better than in 1921', summed up Hopkyns, Chief Secretary to the Government of Bengal: 'there is no Khilafat movement and there is nobody to sway the masses as Mr Gandhi swayed them in 1921.'[1]

[1] Hopkyns to Home Dept. 24/10/1929-GOB, Poll No. 1503 PSD; GOI, Home Poll 2 9 1930.

Not all officers shared such unqualified optimism. David Petrie, Director, Intelligence Bureau, was seriously disturbed about terrorists, volunteers and extremist Congress leaders. He referred to 'the almost indefinite widening of the field of recruitment' among educated middle class Hindus.[2] Emerson, Chief Secretary to the Government of India, however, refused to worry himself unduly about Petrie's estimate. 'I am doubtful whether more than a small minority remains at white heat for very long'.[3] He pointed out sources of comfort. 'The prevalence of communal rancour inevitably tends to mitigate the area and intensity of racial hatred', and in this respect the Government had much to be thankful about. Muslims and Sikhs were largely indifferent, a number of political groups had opposed the Nehru Report and economic conditions in general, were far better than they had been in 1919. No single, decisive issue provided a general rallying-point like Jalianwallabagh or Khilafat. At the same time it could be expected that 'within it's (the movement's) circumscribed area it will be more intense and more violent.'[4]

District reports, too, gave top priority to prospects of renewed industrial unrest. In this respect comments from Chittagong and Midnapur—the two most dangerous districts in 1930—make particularly interesting reading. The Chittagong Divisional Commissioner was confident that the political situation was 'not at all unsatisfactory'. The Midnapur District Magistrate feared, above all, trouble among Kharagpur workers. In the rest of the district, the youth movement was not very significant, boycott had been a failure and the no-tax propaganda affected just some parts of Contai. 'In this district serious trouble is not likely as the people are little affected by propaganda.'[5]

Some of the predictions did indeed come true. Muslim participation was extremely fragmentary and sporadic. Youth, urban students and volunteers were not a very serious threat except at moments of hartal. Some of the actual fears of officials did not materialize. Industrial labour remained passive on the whole, except during the Calcutta carters' strike on the eve of Civil Disobedience. Revolutionary terrorism, however, definitely surpassed the most pessimistic prognostications. Its coincidence with the Con-

[2] Note by Petrie 19/6/1929, GOI, Home Poll 133 1930.

[3] Comments by Emerson, 21/6/1929.

[4] Ibid.

[5] GOB, Home Confidential, Poll 403 (Sl. No. 1–16) of 1929.

gress movement and an upswing in rural resistance and violence made for a major crisis. Totally unexpected Congress success at places like Midnapur upset all calculations. The key to the change may be found in the appearance of the two elements that Emerson had earlier thought were missing. The economic situation took a definite turn for the worse around the middle of 1930 with the onset of the depression; a unifying rallying cry was heard when Gandhi hit upon the strategy of Salt Satyagraha.

The Movement

At midnight on 31 December 1929, Jawaharlal Nehru closed the Lahore Congress session with the Purna Swaraj (Complete Independence) resolution. Another phase of confrontation began. The new movement, however, had yet to choose—or, rather, wait for Gandhi to choose—its forms of action, the issues around which mobilization and resistance could develop. Gandhi began the march from his Sabarmati Ashram to the Dandi sea coast on 12 March and the call for a nationwide violation of the Salt Act—the Salt Satyagraha—was issued on 6 April. The first decisive direction came thus in April. Till then the movement remained in suspended animation. The only new developments were the resignation of Congress Council members—an issue affecting just a handful of Swarajist MLCs—and the Independence Day celebrations which created some impact in Calcutta and Dacca among students, lawyers and middle class women volunteers.[6] Only six districts in Bengal had fulfilled the membership recruitment quota.[7] Work for Civil Disobedience, in fact, was very much of a secondary priority for Bengal Congress leaders. They dissipated all their energies in factional quarrels over Corporation elections. 'A pretty quarrel is developing between the Bengal Provincial Congress Committee and the various Calcutta District Congress Committees', noted an official gleefully, 'each claiming the right to nominate the Congress candidates'[8]. At a public meeting, held at the Shraddhananda Park

[6] *Fortnightly Reports on Bengal* 1st and 2nd halves of January 1930, GOI, Home Poll 18-11/1930.

[7] Bankura, Chittagong, Faridpur, Hooghly, Howrah and Jessore. Midnapur, interestingly is not included. Chittagong's performance really indicated the activities of the young terrorists in the District Congress Committee who soon launched their own struggle. Civil Disobedience itself never prospered there. *AICC Papers*–P30 (ii) of 1929.

[8] *Fortnightly Reports on Bengal*, 1st half of February, 1930, GOI, Home Poll 18 3/1930.

in Calcutta in March 1930 quite a lot of BPCC dirty linen was washed openly amidst noisy and violent mutual abuse.[9] When the Dandi March began and preparations became increasingly urgent, the two groups formed rival bodies to conduct the campaign.[10] Up to the first week of April the only serious political development was the carters' strike which had nothing to do with the Congress. Official prognostications seemed to be perfectly valid. On the eve of Gandhi's arrest, after Civil Disobedience was well on its way, Jackson considered the mill areas to be the likeliest trouble spots. 'I have borrowed a battalion of Assam Frontier Rifles . . . to reinforce our Police in the industrial areas in Calcutta.'[11]

The subsequent spread and intensity of the movement then had little to do with organization from above. Some of the roots of post-April developments, however, had already existed in some of the earlier agitations, in a few Gandhian rural ashrams and, as we have seen, in the fairly prolonged boycott campaign in Calcutta and mofussil towns. Gandhian ashrams became centres of training and propaganda and provided the initial organization for the salt campaign. The first training camp for Satyagrahis was opened at Sodepur. First violations of the salt law were organized by prominent Gandhians like Satish Dasgupta and Dr Suresh Bannerji.[12] The alliance of rural Gandhians with Sen Gupta was embodied in the Bengal Council of Civil Disobedience (BCCD) which was set up on 11 March in Calcutta under Sen Gupta. Satish Dasgupta became its leader after Sen Gupta's arrest.[13]

Another point of continuity may be found in the anti-Union Board agitations at Bandabilla in Jessore, at Mahishbathan in the 24 Parganas and in parts of Bankura. Villagers were extremely active in resistance against chowkidars even while their cattle and other goods were being seized and auctioned off by the police.[14] Low caste and untouchable peasants (Bagdis, Keoras, Naskars and Mondols) and Muslim villagers joined the Mahishbathan agitation and as a result, lost a lot of their property.[15] The struggle prepared

[9] H.W. Hale, *Political Trouble in India, 1917–37* (Calcutta, 1937).

[10] *Fortnightly Reports on Bengal,* 1st half of March, GOI, Home Poll 18/4/1930.

[11] Jackson 170 B of 28/4/1930. *Halifax Collection.*

[12] Birendranath Guha, Secretary BCCD to AICC, 6/11/1930. *AICC Papers* G 86/1930.

[13] *Laban Satyagraha, Ananda Bazar Patrika*, Annual Number, 1931.

[14] *Bangabani*, 24 February 1930.

[15] *Laban Satyagraha.*

the ground for a powerful Civil Disobedience movement at Bankura and Mahishbathan.

The issue of salt, around which the first phase of the movement was woven, implied the selection of one of the extremely rare items of consumption that was literally shared by all. The Government's monopoly over salt manufacture could symbolize the denial of a very fundamental right. The appeal of the agitation was heightened by the emotive content of salt; the essential food, the universal property in diet with implications of trust, hospitality, reciprocity and mutual obligations—associations which have been powerfully expressed in folklore. Refusal to consume salt provided by the Government probably denoted the rejection of its claims on the allegiance and loyalty of Indians. We no longer 'eat their salt', so we can legitimately resist them. The alienation of the salt-making right thus provided a number of highly emotional overtones which could be very skilfully woven into effective propaganda; a nationalist song compared the salt-earth to the mother's breasts from which no one had the right to take the child away.[16] At the same time, its role as a unifying rallying cry was perhaps less important than its corollary—the complete absence in this slogan of any socially divisive potential, of any implication that could be extended to refer to internal class contradictions.

Apart from the symbolic value of the theme, salt had a very immediate message for a number of coastal districts like Midnapur. These districts had a rich tradition of salt manufacture till as late as the nineteenth century. Its extinction during the process of colonial de-industrialization had left bitter traces in popular memory. Midnapur still had a large body of illicit salt manufacturers who could relate very directly to the Congress slogan. Officials worried about the fact that salt camps were located in areas where illicit manufacture was quite strong; 'the sympathies of the villagers are rather on the side of volunteers than on the side of Government officials'.[17] As soon as the news of Gandhi's Dandi march began to spread, villagers of Bhangar and Matla in the 24 Parganas began to openly manufacture salt. They possibly were already making it for personal consumption and also for local sales at less than market rates. The Satyagraha transformed the nature of the operations, making it an act of open and proud rebellion rather than a secret,

[16] Prabhat Chandra Maity, *Swaraj Sangeet* (Calcutta, 1931).

[17] *Fortnightly Reports on Bengal*, 1st half of April 1930. GOI, Home Poll 18/5/1930.

petty crime. The villagers told the Sub-Divisional Magistrate very boldly: 'We are so poor that we do not have even the money to buy salt, so we have made salt for our consumption. We are ready for whatever punishment this calls for.'[18]

The Sub-Divisional Officer at Contai had tried a number of cases of illegal salt manufacture before the Civil Disobedience. He was used to a body of frightened villagers who would meekly plead guilty. But the beginning of the salt campaign changed his entire experience. The very next batch hauled up before his court after the Satyagraha began, refused to plead guilty and defiantly claimed a right to salt-making.[19] The sudden transformation of the self-image of men who had long perceived themselves as petty criminals, a new access to self-confidence and self-respect, a reinterpretation and new understanding of their own gestures and actions—all this stemmed from the inversion of the concepts of legality and criminality in the course of the national movement. There could be, for these marginal groups, no limited concept of Swaraj in terms of a simple transfer of state power. The very process of struggle necessarily had to imply a new world order, a new set of values, a redefinition of the boundaries of possibilities.

A plethora of local cyclostyled newspapers proliferated in defiance of the Press Ordinance. These circulated detailed news of the movement at district towns and even among villages in Midnapur, Dacca, Sylhet, Bankura and Burdwan. Police torture, the courage of volunteers, non-violence, and martyrdom were the main items of Satyagraha news.[20] Congress messages and instructions were also conveyed through village meetings (usually held at *hats* or weekly bazars) or nationalist songs, plays performed by roving jatras (play groups), and magic lantern shows.[21] The blend of visual effects in these shows with stirring music and emotional words strung up in songs and plays (which made very extensive use of music) captured the imagination of unlettered peasants and women who attended in large numbers. Composed largely on the lines of religious festivals, ceremonies and the 'Kathakata' tradition (recitation, translation and expounding of religious texts by professional Kathaks on ceremonial and ritual occasions) and using very similar images and

[18] *Bangabani*, 16 March 1930.

[19] The author's interview with Shri Saibal Gupta (Contai SDO in 1930), 20 July 1978.

[20] Report by Guha, *AICC Papers*, G 86/1930.

[21] *Bangabani*, 3 March 1930. See also Report by Guha, *AICC Papers*.

emotions, the movement of nationalism thus added a new dimension in the organization of leisure in villages. These folk-shows combined entertainment with moral and religious education.

Nationalist pamphlets were shown to villagers and read out in large gatherings. Messages usually carried with them illustrations with bold captions. One showed Government credit facilities as traps to ensnare peasants. 'Beware!' warned the caption, 'Do not let them trap you so easily'. It also depicted the Union Board as a huge scorpion with widely extended tentacles to capture innocent villagers. The caption below said. 'Take care! Do not let this strange monster enter your locality'.[22] A wide range of songs and verses were printed to celebrate Swadeshi salt-making; repression and self-sacrifice constituted the two dominant motifs in such literature.[23] Drain of wealth, very literally interpreted, remained the central economic criticism; illustrations evoked a vision of Mother India in chains and tatters with white men dragging off her rich attire and jewels across the seas.[24]

Popular consent to Civil Disobedience was signified in a very forceful way through social boycott of police and administrative officers. Replacement of customary fear and obedience to the Government through fraternization with Congress volunteers—political outlaws in official definition—deeply demoralized and depressed loyalists and officers. A report by the Government of Bengal described its repercussions in mid-April: 'The situation in Calcutta is threatening. Police are openly, filthily, abused, hustled and threatened in social boycott. Reporters are unable to take notes'.[25] At Contai (Midnapur) shopkeepers refused to sell provisions to police and Government officers; bus owners would not take in their servants or luggage and when a police officer requisitioned a boat, villagers sank it.[26] Taxi drivers, on the other hand, drove around volunteers from the Comilla Abhoy Ashram free of charge. When the properties of Jhareswar Majhi, a pro-Congress rich peasant at Pichhaboni (Contai) were auctioned off, no Hindu or Muslim coolie would agree to carry the goods away. At Kalikapur, in the 24

[22] *Desher Dak* (Call of the Nation) (Calcutta, 1931). Proscribed pamphlet, PP BEN B 20 IOL.

[23] See for instance Maity, *Swaraj Sangeet*.

[24] Hemendralal Ray, *Rikta Bharat* (Bankrupt India), (Calcutta, 1932). Proscribed book PP BEN B 22.

[25] Teldgram P. 15 April 1930 No. 1130 P.S. to Secretary of State, *Halifax Collection*.

[26] Narendra Nath Das, *History of Midnapur*, Part II (Calcutta, 1962), p. 137.

Parganas, fish and milk sellers donated their wares freely to Congress volunteers.[27] Social boycott has been the traditional mode of enforcing community sanctions and prohibitions to punish transgressions against the established moral code. An adaptation of this device helped to define a new community—that of patriots. It marked the boundary between this community of believers and that of the godless—the loyalists and collaborators. The distinctions that the boycott concretized helped to draw members of the patriotic community closer to one another through a constant affirmation of solidarity among themselves.

As the salt and the no-tax movement developed, passive boycott too hardened into open abuse, defiance and mockery which came to constitute a new form of resistance. The District Magistrate and the Additional District Magistrate of Midnapur 'were insulted by the cultivators in the worst manner possible...'. District Magistrate Peddie went through a traumatic experience. 'When I personally went out to Panskura (Tamluk subdivision) I was first insulted and then informed that arrangements had been made to attack me the following day'.[28] The Additional District Magistrate had an even more harrowing time in November at Moyna in Tamluk, 'Reasoning was looked upon as a sign of weakness and even the old men had begun to swagger about truculently and talk insolently . . . . I even had a Kayastha spitting at me. The ordinary cultivator simply squatted on his haunches and laughing sarcastically said, "We know how powerful the Sarkar is"'.[29] When the District Magistrate personally went around to the villagers to persuade them to pay the chowkidari tax, they laughed and mocked him. Zamindars had waited deferentially before such dignitaries in the past and now mere peasants scorned their requests! Sarcasm and derisive laughter played a significant political role. They liberated whole areas from fear, they struck the Empire off from the hearts of people. Considering the splendour that surrounded their status, the deference and wonder with which they used to be treated, at least outwardly, officials found the change a traumatic one. Peddie had a reputation as a conscientious and concerned district administrator. Common people in his districts on the whole trusted him and depended on him. Villagers used to make daily trips to his residence

[27] *Bangabani*, 10 April, 14 April and 29 April, 1930.

[28] *Fortnightly Reports on Bengal*, 2nd half of July. GOB, Home Confidential, Poll 249/30 (1–3) of 1930.

[29] GOI, Home Poll 18 VIII of 1930.

to get a 'darshan'.[30] Not only was it important for self-esteem, it sustained the illusion of being in *loco parentis*, 'Sarkar-ma-baap', to simple common folk. Such assurance had long been the basis of a strongly-rooted necessary conviction; peasants needed the Government, Congress slogans moved only a 'microscopic minority'; officials were in India to protect Indians. Since the movement put paid to this conviction and stripped the basis of power bare of everything else except force, force was then exercised with a bitterness and brutality that matched the collapse of a much-needed self-image.

Such rejection was hammered home when the movement moved to villages. A contrast between first batches of Satyagrahis and later recruits (enlisted after the salt campaign began) indicates a significant shift to new areas of support. In the first week of April a group of twenty-nine satyagrahis went to Mahishbathan to work under Satish Dasgupta. Seven were non-Bengalis: traders, students, a Khadi worker from Burra Bazar and a shopowner from Jiyaganj. The rest included a trader, a tailor, an agent, two contractors, a mine-owner, a Calcutta businessman, two photographers, a Congress worker, two school teachers, a doctor's assistant, a shopkeeper, a few students and clerks. All were men between twenty and thirty years of age and two were below forty. All came from the three upper castes.[31] It was a group of fairly young (though not extremely young), urban, professional men, traders and petty traders with a sprinkling of students and one or two wholetime Congress workers.

By mid-April arrests of top level leaders left the movement open to local initiative and leadership. The change that this brought about was felt most dramatically in Midnapur, a district which had earlier failed even to fulfil the quota of member enlistment. The Contai Congress had long been riddled with factional squabbles and the local National School was practically defunct. Yet, on 20 April, Peddie told the Contai Sub-Divisional Officer: 'Do you realize that this is the worst thing we have faced after the mutiny?'[32] Volunteers and villagers seemed to have an instant rapport. When a BPCC band arrived at Mushir Hat they found a large group of villagers (about a hundred of whom were Muslims) ready to welcome them. At Pichhaboni, as soon as volunteers arrived, fifty

[30] Interview with Ashok Mitra, ICS Officer, 12/10/1978.
[31] *Bangabani*, 7 April 1930.
[32] Interview with Saibal Gupta.

villagers enlisted on the spot, of whom two were over eighty.[33] The first batch of Satyagrahis to the 24 Parganas was warmly greeted by villagers from Adhata. After the first meeting thirty-three enlisted: twenty-two of them were Muslims, ten were low caste Hindus, and there was only one Brahmin in the group.[34] Bankura villagers not only welcomed volunteers warmly, but from the beginning they also displayed a marked contempt for the police. At Dhansimla village the police melted away from the Congress meeting as soon as they attracted notice. At Bhagawanbati nobody was willing to arrange their transport. At Balshi, 'they stood with melancholy faces far away from the meeting'.[35] The police had always been the immediate, tangible and most fearful expression of colonial authority at the local level; the more arbitrary its exercise of power, the greater the awe it inspired. Defiance of the police therefore signified a major step in political involvement and consciousness.

After the first Congress meeting at Neela thirty-eight men joined as volunteers: one was a Muslim and the rest came from Mahisya and low agricultural castes.[36] Tamluk subdivision in Midnapur gave officials the worst trouble in this respect. Unlike Contai, which had two quite influential Gandhian ashrams, the Tamluk campaign was an autonomous effort from the beginning. Volunteers organized the first round of salt-making but villagers immediately took it up and continued it on their own.[37]

Arrests of leaders started from about 12 April. Instead of killing the campaign they widened its scope enormously. Waves of volunteers poured in without a break. Local people were always ready with a welcome and provided sustenance. The authorities responded with a variety of torture: volunteers were dipped into boiling salt, there were frequent floggings, arrests, caning, assaults (even of women) and firing.[38] Gandhi's logic behind the use of non-violence as a strategy for struggle was indicated in day-to-day encounters between police and volunteers. The spectacle of unar-

[33] *Bangabani*, 6 April 1930.

[34] Ibid, 8 April 1930.

[35] Ibid, 5 April 1930.

[36] *Fortnightly Reports on Bengal*, 1st half of April 1930, GOI, Home Poll 18–V/1930.

[37] Contai Civil Disobedience Report to AICC Press 6/11/193, *AICC Papers G* 86/1930.

[38] Report by Birendranath Guha, *AICC Papers*, G 86/1930. See also *Law and Order in Midnapur—Report of the Non-Official Enquiry Committee* (Calcutta, 1930). Proscribed book PIB 9/32.

med, unresisting Satyagrahis standing up to abominable torture aroused local sympathy, respect and involvement as nothing else would ever have done. Bodies of volunteers provided the stage on which morality plays were performed; everyday one witnessed the struggle between Good and Evil, moral power and brute force, spiritual courage and physical coercion. The process of martyrdom was enacted at a pitch of such emotional intensity that the very act of watching it became an act of participation. The distance between emotional involvement and actual physical engagement could be leaped in no time at all. Fraternization and participation spread in concentric circles from each such incident. At Basudebpur village in Sutahata (Tamluk) there was a fierce lathi charge on satyagrahis in May. The next day men poured in from distant villages to break the salt law. At Babupur (also at Sutahata) again a batch of volunteers was beaten up. A huge crowd of angry villagers arrived the next day, stoned the police and smashed the police camp.[39] Whenever there were police raids on salt centres at Contai, villagers blew conchshells to warn others and pass the message on to other villages—an interesting reversion to old *thuggi* customs.[40]

The salt satyagraha was rather short-lived. It slackened off by early May and in the second week of June it had to be given up since the arrival of the monsoon made work impossible. In any case it had been able to significantly involve the coastal districts only. Other districts did send in volunteers and contraband salt was sold in distant markets. Even before the rains had started, however, other forms of resistance had begun to eclipse it.[41] The no-chowkidari tax movement began in July and persisted until the close of the year.[42] Each thana area in Bengal was subdivided into ten to twenty unions, each of which employed about ten to twenty chowkidars who were an essential part of the district administration and who supplemented the meagre police force at Union level. Their pay came from the chowkidari tax collected by Union Board officials from villagers. The Congress attempted to paralyse police and Union level administration by withholding this tax. The issue, like salt, had the additional virtue that it was socially a safe one.

[39] Bankim Brahmachari, *Swadhinata Sangrame Sutahata*, (Midnapur, 1977), pp. 39–40.

[40] Interview with Saibal Gupta.

[41] GOB, *Report on the Administration of Bengal 1929–30*.

[42] *Fortnightly Reports on Bengal*, Ist half of December, GOI, Home Poll 18/III/1930.

More than salt, the no-tax agitation was a grassroots demand, developed through local initiative. At Bankura for instance, a movement was growing from late January when the salt campaign intervened. After arrests of senior leaders, Congress workers at Bishnupur decided to launch it on their own in June and then asked the Bankura Dictator's permission to start it at Indas and Patrasayar thanas. After some hesitation it was finally allowed from July.[43] Preparations for no-tax had started before Congress instructions came from above at Arambagh in Hooghly, Balurghat in Dinajpur, Contai in Midnapur, Nawabganj and Vikrampur in Dacca, Maju in Howrah and parts of Sunamganj subdivision in Sylhet. At all these places "the Congress mandate on the no-tax campaign came not a moment too soon.'[44]

Large numbers of village women were activated through this form of resistance. At Arambagh they impeded tax collection efforts in large groups. At Indas in Bankura, as many as two hundred and fifty women lay down on the road and barred the exit of distrained property for three days.[45] As resistance and repression reached new heights in Midnapur, women became increasingly important as fully politicized and active members in the movement. In June a number of men and women were severely hurt during a case of police thrashing at Keshpur Thana. The first woman martyr from the district which produced Matangini Hazra in 1942 was Urmilabala Paria, a young woman from the Mahisya peasant caste.[46] At Contai where punitive police were posted in disturbed areas to force tax payments, there were frequent detentions and flogging of women from families that had refused payment. There were police raids on 500 villages in four months, and men and women of whole hamlets fled to nearby forests to avoid payment.[47] Property, far in excess of the taxes that were due, was wantonly destroyed. Satya Manna of Gokulnagar village (Moyna in Tamluk) had three houses and a granary gutted and suffered a total loss of Rs 350 for non payment of an annual tax of Rs 1-8 as.[48] It was expected that in the course of the movement all adult members of a family might be arrested, crops burnt down, granaries and houses looted and all moveable property

[43] *Laban Satyagraha*.

[44] Report by Guha, *AICC Papers*, G 86/1930.

[45] *Laban Satyagraha*.

[46] Gopinandan Goswami, *Medinipurer Shahid Parichay*, (Midnapur, 1977) p. 24.

[47] Contai Civil Disobedience Report, *AICC Papers* G 86/1930.

[48] Guha's report.

distrained.[49] Such large-scale risks needed the full consent of all family members.

The apparently smooth, painless politicization of women—including volunteers from non-Bengali trading families in Calcutta—who belonged to a milieu which had traditionally restricted their role within well-defined domestic confines, was a process that met with applause rather than resistance from male guardians. This would be, for most women, the first instance when they were allowed to share an activity outside the household. There can be no denying that this step must have been preceded by an acute, indeed revolutionary, struggle with their own sensibilities and inhibitions. Even that would be mitigated considerably, however, by the sure knowledge of social approval. What may explain such sanction? To a certain extent an important precedent was set by the example of immediate social superiors. Locally dominant peasants, like Jhareswar Majhi at Pichhaboni in Contai or zamindars like Lakshmikanta Pramanik would set the pattern by bringing out their women into the movement which encouraged lesser peasant nationalists.[50] A more serious explanation would relate to the nature of the Gandhian movement itself and its implications for socially-accepted, prescribed roles of women. Participation was intended for non-violent modes of action and would not entail the drastic violation of the feminine image that a violent struggle would have involved. Again, since in Congress strongholds like Midnapur the Congress itself had become something like a parallel authority, involvement in its movement could become, by extension, obedience to the properly-constituted authority and not its defiance. This, too, was more in keeping with womanly attributes.

The crucial element in dovetailing the feminine role with nationalist politics was perhaps the image of Gandhi as a saint or even a divine figure, and the perception of the patriotic struggle as an essentially religious duty. Joining the Congress agitation then would not really be politicization, a novel and doubtful role for women but sharing a religious mission. A subtle symbiosis between the religious and the political, enabled nationalism to transcend the

[49] *Laban Satyagraha*, 14 June 1932. See also *Law and Order in Midnapur*.

[50] *Ananda Bazar Patrika* Annual Number, 1931. Also interview with Saibal Gupta. On this problem see Tanika Sarkar. 'Politics and Women in Bengal: The Conditions and Meaning of Participation;' *Indian Economic and Social History Review*. v. 21 1, 1984.

realm of politics and elevate itself to a religious domain. The special implications of all this for women, held to be aspects of Shakti themselves, were not left unexploited. This mode of appeal, however, had a fundamental problem which we shall explore in the context of revolutionary terrorism. It seemed to be an evocation of the latent strength, even violence, in feminine psyche which tradition strives to contain. The Gandhian movement resolved the tension beautifully by retaining the religious content of nationalism while keeping the movement non-violent and imparting to it a gentle, patient, sacrificial ambience, particularly appropriate for women.

Apart from local women the no-tax agitation involved even union officials and chowkidars themselves. Eight Union Board members and five chowkidars resigned at Arambagh.[51] At Sabong in Midnapur only 432 ratepayers out of 15536 paid taxes and 101 chowkidars out of a total of 133 resigned.[52] 'At the worst period', Peddie remarked later, 'practically the whole of Tamluk and Contai . . . plus the thanas of Mohanpur, Danton, Naraingarh and Sabong in Sadar subdivision were out of hand. There were no chowkidars, dafadars, Presidents, Panchayats'.[53] At Itahar in Dinajpur large bodies of low class people including Santals, resisted tax collection with bows and arrows.[54]

A remarkable variety of techniques and collective initiative was developed by villagers on their own, since there were few pre-decided norms of resistance imposed from above. Many local traditions of struggle were no doubt revived to enrich the movement. The effects are best described by the panic-filled words of the Sub-Divisional Officer, Midnapur Sadar: 'I never expected an organization which seemed to have been worked with the greatest care and caution . . . the entire thana was not willing to pay a single pice. I was informed that all the villages had been converted into good forts—cutting up village paths, filling them with loose earth, thorns and rough sharp shells . . . also barricades of huge bamboo trees and houses barricaded with thorns, removal of bamboo bridges and trenches dug in the middle of fields.'[55]

[51] *Ananda Bazar Patrika* Annual Number, 1931.

[52] *The Challenge,* Calcutta, 11 August, 1930. *AICC Papers* G 86/1930.

[53] Peddie's report, January 1931, GOB, Home Confidential, Poll Poll 249/30 (1–3) of 1930.

[54] *Fortnightly Reports on Bengal,* 2nd half of October, 1930. GOI, Home Poll 18/XI/1930.

[55] Report by Sadar SDO, August 1930.

The groundswell that developed with arrests of more established leaders reached its height around June and was most powerfully expressed through a series of violent confrontations with the police; very often villagers retaliated with violence, flouting Gandhian injunctions and thus appropriating the movement entirely for themselves. While firm Gandhian centres like Arambagh and Mahishbathan remained consistently non-violent, Gandhian discipline was far more loosely exercised at BPCC centres like Neela in the 24 Parganas or at Ghatal in Midnapur. The incidents clustered around three main types of developments: during picketing and boycott which would often turn aggressive; in villages as a form of popular revenge against the police for atrocities against Congress volunteers; in cities and district towns during hartals.

Picketing often involved intimidation of shopkeepers and consumers dealing in foreign goods. It led to fairly large-scale clashes with the police on the one hand and volunteers and crowds of local sympathizers on the other. A riot occurred at Mymensingh in late May when a large crowd blocked the exit of liquor stocks from an excise godown. There were secret attacks on liquor shops at Bankura,[56] telegraph wires were cut at Munshiganj (Dacca) and a bomb was thrown into a Nalchiti ganja shop at Barisal.[57] A convergence of terrorist methods and Congress issues characterized such attacks which were secretive rather than open confrontations.

Rural violence in sharp contrast seemed to be deliberately open and in public. The incidents were something of a public trial, an open implementation of collective justice. The first major episode occurred at the BPCC camp at Neela in late April. The police attacked a band of satyagrahis and suddenly found themselves surrounded on three sides by a large party of villagers brandishing clods of earth and branches of 'babul' trees. In the ensuing scuffle police firing killed one and wounded three while all policemen were hurt.[58] Midnapur witnessed what was described by Acting Governor Stephenson as 'practically a rising'. 'The district was honeycombed with volunteers who had organized the villagers to blow conchshells wherever a police force appeared upon which signal two

[56] *Fortnightly Reports on Bengal*, 2nd half of May 1930, GOI, Home Poll 18/VI/1930.

[57] *Fortnightly Reports on Bengal*, 2nd half of June 1930, GOI, Home Poll 18/VII/1930.

[58] *Fortnightly Reports on Bengal*, 2nd half of April 1930, GOI, Home Poll 18/5/1930.

villagers from every household were to come out with whatever weapons they could get and attack the police. We poured about 400 police into the district and got a Company of Indian regiment to move in'.[59] The police beat up a band of volunteers on 20 May at the local *hat* at Gopinathpur in Contai. Villagers who were at the *hat* grew furious at the sight. A crowd which included Muslim villagers from Kulapara, rounded up the Sub-Inspector, Lalit Ghosh, locked him up in a room and set fire to it. He had to be rescued by Congress volunteers.[60] At Chaulkhola in Sutahata (Tamluk) the police attacked the house of a Congress sympathizer in November. As soon as they entered the village, conch shells were heard in all directions and men and women of the village poured in with cudgels, brooms, axes and knives, and surrounded the police who fired injuring five of them.[61] At Tamluk 'the temper of the people was such that it was impossible for small or unarmed bodies of police to go into the villages without running the risk of being surrounded, assaulted or even killed'.[62] Large scale attacks on police parties occurred in late June at Pratapdighi and Balisai in Contai and at Khirai in Sadar; the crowd refused to let the police arrest volunteers and retaliated against their lathi charge with axes and earth clods.[63]

Each such incident was followed by months of systematic repression including the deployment of punitive police.[64] The trend, however, survived even after organized Civil Disobedience had more or less waned. As late as January 1931 a 'distinct increase in the number of cases of violence' was reported. A crowd rescued volunteers from two chowkidars at Contai and beat the latter to death. Severe assaults on police constables were reported from Dinajpur, Dacca, Faridpur and Mymensingh. Rumours were heard, particularly at Midnapur, that the British Raj was coming to an end.[65] There was almost an apocalyptic note in the extreme character that the Congress campaign, social boycott and popular resistance, as-

[59] Stephenson's letter 347, 25 June, 1930, *Halifax Collection*.

[60] Probodh Chandra Basu, *Medinipura Jelar Bhagawanpur Thanar Itibritta* (Calcutta, 1976), pp. 127–8.

[61] Bankim Brahmachari, *Swadhinata Sangrame Sutahata*, (Midnapur, 1977), p. 63.

[62] GOB, *Report on the Administration of Bengal 1929 30*, p. 12.

[63] *Fortnightly Reports on Bengal*, second half of June, 1930, GOI, Home Poll 18/VII/1930.

[64] Weekly Appreciation Report on the Political Situation in India up to 21 June 1930. GOI, Home Poll 483/1930.

[65] *Fortnightly Reports on Bengal*, January 1931, GOI, Home Poll 18/1/1931.

sumed in this area. Rumours of this sort usually circulated when the British Government had just faced, or was still facing, some kind of a wider external crisis as well; the two World Wars, for instance, gave rise to a very similar body of rumours. Civil Disobedience, however, remained a purely internal matter. The growth and spread of such rumours at this point probably indicated a greater certainty and self-confidence of the movement itself.

The high point in grassroots resistance and violence occurred in the first week of June at Chechuahat under Daspur thana in Ghatal subdivision (Midnapur). Officials claimed that BPCC volunteers, connected with the Jugantar terrorists under Purna Das, had masterminded the entire operation. The prosecution in the Chechuahat cases made extensive use of a letter that was found with the volunteers; it carried Purna Das's stamp and was accompanied with a document containing a formula for making bombs. Ghatal volunteers themselves might well have had Jugantar links. But the Chechuahat episode concerned primarily local villagers who had no contact with the BPCC headquarters or with the Jugantar. The pattern of events coincided with crowd action elsewhere in Midnapur and reflected no influence of terrorist methods. Of the forty-five men arrested in connection with the cases, only four were volunteers from outside—the rest were overwhelmingly Mahisya peasants with a sprinkling of low castes.[66]

Antecedents behind the Chechuahat-Daspur incidents encapsulate the entire process of widening fraternization which grew out of official repression. Since early April the Sub-Inspector of Daspur Thana had kept the BPCC camp under observation, organized counter propaganda and intimidated villagers against any contact with volunteers. On 13 April the police attacked the camp at Shyamganj and severely injured several volunteers. A large crowd gathered around and silently watched the torture. On 28 April the police came back to beat up volunteers. This time the spectacle drew a much larger crowd of several thousand men and women. It was the largest crowd that had so far gathered in the locality. They watched once again in silence but later no one would sell provisions to the police. Three chowkidars resigned in protest. After the attack was over, the crowd rushed in and fed volunteers free of charge.[67] The police were especially incensed with the Shyamganj volunteers since they used to train 'Bagdis, and other low classes' in lathi-

[66] GOI, Home Poll 481/1930.

[67] *Bangabani*, 10, 14, 29 April 1930.

play.[68] In May Ghatal volunteers had organized a huge procession which many Bagdis and 'low class' people joined with lathis.[69]

The Ghatal CDC was declared illegal around 13 May and volunteers were expelled from the Shyamganj Camp. They took shelter in the Bandar village in Hooghly, about five miles away from Ghatal, and continued to send out batches of volunteers. On 2 June the Daspur Sub-Inspector Bholanath Ghosh and his assistant Aniruddha Samanta went to Chechuahat to arrest volunteers who were making speeches at the *hat*. There was a scuffle with volunteers. As soon as the news spread, villagers from within a radius of four miles began to pour in. Whistles blew and the crowd rushed straight towards the police shouting Bande Mataram and Maro Maro (Kill, Kill). Volunteers were freed, the Sub-Inspector was dragged out from his hiding-place and lynched to death. Before he died he begged for mercy and promised to give up his job—'The people said that he had assaulted them very severely at Shyamganj and then declared that they would take vengeance that day'. Someone from the crowd asked them to stop but one Lachhman Singh 'poked him saying that he was helping the man who had poured salt water into their nostrils at Shyamganj'. Of the forty-five men charged with offences 'in pursuance of a conspiracy to commit murder of public servants engaged in the suppression of Civil Disobedience' eleven were found guilty of murder and were given life-transportation sentences. They were the only non-terrorist prisoners, convicted from Bengal in connection with Civil Disobedience, who remained in the Andamans with terrorists up to 1945.[70]

The sequel was equally dramatic. On 5 June the Midnapur Additional District Magistrate and Additional Police Superintendent went to Daspur to investigate into the incidents of 2 June. A large police party with British sergeants, sixteen armed constables and sixteen ordinary constables went with them. On 6 June there was an encounter with a massive crowd of villagers; the police fired twenty-two rounds even though the crowd had not actually attacked it. 'As the crowd was prevented from actually using physical force or violence there is no charge of rioting...'. Obviously, the police panicked even before clashes could begin. The police party had found villages deserted and ominously silent all along the way. As

[68] Report by Midnapur ASP to ADM, sent by Bengal Chief Secretary to GOI, Home 19 June 1930, GOI, Home Poll 248/30 of 1930.

[69] GOI, Home Poll 14 20 of 1931.

[70] Niranjan Sen, *Bengal's Forgotten Warriors* (Bombay 1945), p. 1.

evening approached and darkness began to gather, they saw an enormous crowd, several thousands strong, approaching them from the other side of the Kangshabati river bed. It seemed to be 'in a state of frenzied excitement'.[71] As they drew near 'conchshells and whistles (were) blowing in all the surrounding villages and fields and men running with lathis . . . and shouting and dancing and almost frenetic and wild'.[72] The police ordered them to disperse at gunpoint but they kept pressing on closer with derisive shouts. Three men from among them then crossed the dry river bed and, in their turn, ordered the police to leave at once. The ADM told them that the police would go away if the assailant of Bholanath Ghosh was surrendered to them. The men returned to the crowd which discussed the proposal and then sent over messengers to convey their refusal (note the battleground-like aspect of the negotiations). An elderly Mahisya peasant, Pran Krishna Guchait from Jot Gauranga, came up to the police and said, 'How would you like to be beaten with broomsticks and stones'. He also said that the British had fleeced the country for a hundred and fifty years and had ruined her completely. More and more people seemed to join the crowd on the other bank every minute while darkness deepened. In sheer terror the police kept up a barrage of shots and escaped from behind it.[73] Fourteen men were killed from the crowd in the firing, all of them local Mahisyas.[74]

Such violence and the popular consensus that lay behind it so demoralized the police in general that in June at Pabna a group of them ran berserk one night, assaulting passersby. Twenty constables refused duty at Pabna.[75] Officials were dumbfounded. 'The manufacture of salt does not appear to have created much excitement among the populace', Governor Jackson had written, rather smugly, in April. In June, he was writing in utter panic: 'The spirit of disobedience and defiance is much too rife . . . We certainly need another battalion in Bengal . . . I feel that another British Division and a warship off the main ports would prove an assistance'.[76] Peddie, the Midnapur District Magistrate, was hysterical. 'I feel

[71] GOI, Home Poll 481 of 1930.

[72] GOI, Home Poll 248/30 of 1930.

[73] GOI, Home Poll 481 of 1930.

[74] Gopinandan Goswami, *Medinipurer Shahid Parichay*, p. 24.

[75] *Fortnightly Reports on Bengal*, 2nd half of June, GOI, Home Poll 18 VII of 1930.

[76] Jackson's letter 164 of 26 April 1930 and 270 of 1 June, 1930, *Halifax Papers*.

very little hope of any measure of peace until we have a few more shootings . . . I am issuing orders to say that there should be no hesitation whatsoever in using guns . . . the best thing that could happen would be to have more shootings'.[77] Lowman, Inspector General of Police, drew a deeply melancholy lesson from all this. 'I had no idea that the Congress organization could enlist the support of such ignorant and uncultivated people.'[78]

The lightning strike of 15 April after Jawaharlal's arrest brought Calcutta crowds out into violent action. Students clashed with the police on College Square, tramcars were burnt, fire brigades attacked, cars stoned and Europeans assaulted. Transport workers, especially Sikhs, were extremely militant at Bhowanipur and Chitpur and eight hundred Budge Budge mill-hands observed hartal.[79] The protest hartal after Gandhi's arrest in early May saw buses and trams burning again at Bhowanipur and fierce attacks on police parties at Ramkrishtopur ferry pontoon at Howrah. Howrah carters, who had paralysed the city through a strike of their own in early April, took a leading part in this hartal as well; they attacked the police and mobbed the District Magistrate.[80] Whether in rural violence or during urban street fights, a breakdown of Gandhian restraint on violence seems to be invariably associated with a widening (however momentary) of participation. Regions like Barisal and Mymensingh and groups like Budge Budge mill-hands, Sikh transport workers, carters, Bagdis, Santals and low classes in Ghatal and Muslims in Midnapur villages would be activated through these encounters though they had not participated in the Civil Disobedience movement.

Except at moments like these, urban youth and students generally stayed aloof from the movement. The most militant of them associated themselves with resurgent terrorism. Picketing in cities and towns, was largely the work of 'Banar Senas' of schoolboys and of middle class women. This created serious problems for the police. They could not use the usual harsh methods of dispersal with them for fear of critically outraging middle class Hindu sensibilities. This calculation probably inspired the strategy behind the despatch of women to such encounters. The Comilla District Magistrate

77 Peddie's letter, 12 June 1930, GOI, Home Poll 248/30 of 1930.

78 Ibid, letter 446 J of 12 June 1930.

79 *Fortnightly Reports on Bengal,* 1st half of April 1930, GOI, Home Poll 18/5/1930.

80 *Fortnightly Reports on Bengal,* 2nd half of May 1930, GOI, Home Poll 18/6/1930.

pointed out another motive. 'They [the women] are jumping at the chance of coming out of the Purdah'.[81] Occasionally support came, unsolicited and unexpected, from unusual quarters. Oriya coolies at Burrabazar observed hartals faithfully and refused to carry bales of foreign cloth.[82] Malaviya achieved a notable success in Calcutta when in April he persuaded the Marwari Association not to import foreign cloth for the rest of the year.[83] The Association, however, went back on its pledge quite soon and in May issued a statement to condemn picketing.

Birla and his Indian Chamber of Commerce did remain steadfast and became the 'guiding spirit' behind the boycott of foreign cloth.[84] Laird. President of the Bengal Chamber of Commerce reported on 3 July: 'It cannot be denied that the campaign against British piece-goods, cigarettes and other commodities had met with considerable success'. He requested Ainscough, the Senior Trade Commissioner, to invest Rs 50,000 on counter-propaganda without delay.[85] Trade figures for 1930 show that the import of tobacco and cotton goods did decline noticeably though that of liquors, sugar and salt had gone up.[86] A boycott of football matches and film shows was also planned so as not to distract attention from Civil Disobedience. The Aryans and the Mohun Bagan Club stopped two matches on 24 May when the Nari Satyagraha Samiti asked them not to play. Indian football players later agreed not to play any matches at all for the rest of the year.[87]

Salt, no-Chowkidari tax and boycott had all been carefully chosen as socially safe and non-divisive issues. The militancy, violence and downward spread of the movement, however, made propertied classes increasingly uncomfortable. A process of dissociation began. Marwari traders declared in May that Civil Disobedience had affected trade disastrously. They also protested against picketing and no tax.[88] The Law member B.L. Mitter warned zamindars: 'If Gandhi's no-tax campaign succeeds you zamindars will be the first victims in Bengal'.[89] In June Jawaharlal told the Noakhali DCC, 'I

[81] Ibid.

[82] *Ananda Bazar Patrika*, Annual Number. 1931.

[83] *Fortnightly Reports on Bengal*, 2nd half of April. GOI, Home Poll 18/5/1930.

[84] Note by Sir B.L. Mitter, GOI, Home Poll 248/11/1930.

[85] Laird's Letter of 19 July 1930, GOI, Home Poll 201/40/1930

[86] GOB, *Report on the Administration of Bengal, 1929–30*, pp. 98, 103.

[87] *Ananda Bazar Patrika*, Annual Number, 1931.

[88] *Fortnightly Reports on Bengal*, 2nd half of May 1930. GOI, Home Poll 18/6/1930.

[89] Mitter's letter 19 May 1930. *Private Papers of B.P. Singh Roy*.

will advise you not to declare frequent hartals as that would dislocate business and might even alienate the sympathies of the public at large and particularly tradesmen and professionals'.[90] Intense picketing at Burrabazar was in fact a confession of failure to win over traders. The next phase of Civil Disobedience would extend this dissociation to the bulk of the Hindu middle class. Given the prevailing sensitivity of the Bengal Congress to social tension and issues this might seem difficult to explain. Yet, in the middle of agrarian depression and a potentially explosive situation, the spectacle of uncontrolled rural initiative and violence, even on purely nationalist issues, would inevitably be a most unnerving one. The fears and apprehensions that this aroused were summed up by B.L. Mitter. 'He [Gandhi] is out to undermine the very foundation of social order . . . when Gandhi's volunteers attempt to commit theft or robbery, as the "salt raids" are nothing else.'[91]

The straight equation between defiance and rebellion in any form and threats to the established social order was a deeply-rooted conviction. With all its socially innocuous positions, the Congress could never fully allay such fears or resolve this tension.

Revolutionary Terrorism

The last chapter in the history of revolutionary terrorism opened in 1930 with the sensational Chittagong Armoury Raid of 18 April 1930. This was followed in rapid succession by several major episodes: the 25 August bomb incident at Dalhousie Square by the Calcutta Jugantar, the assassination of Lowman at Dacca by Bengal Volunteers' members on 29 August and another Bengal Volunteers' raid on the Writers' Building—the administrative heart of Calcutta—on 8 December. In the course of the year eleven English officials and ten non-officials were killed, twelve British officers and fourteen non-officials were injured. Four hundred and fifty-four terrorists were held under preventive detention.[92] Lulled into false security by the preceding years of inaction, the Bengal Government had deliberately relaxed vigilance. It was now completely taken aback and the sense of shock and surprise partly accounted for the massive and multi-pronged manhunt that engaged the biggest part of its attention.

[90] Nehru's letter of 4 June 1930. *AICC Papers* P 6 † 1927–31.
[91] *AICC Papers*, Mitter's letter.
[92] D.M. Laushey, *Bengal Terrorism and the Marxist Left*, pp. 76, 67.

The coincidence of this phase with the beginning of Civil Disobedience presents some problems of classification and categorization. Gandhian leadership in the rest of the country dissociated itself sharply from the cult of violence; in Bengal, however, the line of demarcation was never very clear. Organizational links between the Karmi Sangha (the terrorist group within the Congress) and the BPCC leadership, between Bose and Sengupta on the one hand and different terrorist groups on the other, between Congress volunteers and covert terrorist activists in districts, have already been referred to. Bengal Gandhians undoubtedly had a genuine abhorrence for terrorist ideas and actions. They still found it difficult to deny the inspiration that the revolutionary tradition provided for all nationalists. Prabhatmohan Bandopadhyay, a Gandhian poet, captured this mood very sensitively. In a poem called *Hingshabratir Prati* (To a Practitioner of Violence) he humbly acknowledged terrorist contributions before launching into ideological criticism: 'It was you who once taught me to overcome the fear of death, to realize the agony of subjection, to love my country. I have not forgotten that you were the sun at the first dawn of my life, you were my teacher, my ancestor. I still have to declare firmly and mercilessly that I no longer belong to you. Today, when at last the country is realizing itself . . . you have reappeared to dazzle us with illusions... and to stifle the rise of mass power.' The reproach, however, turns into deep love and agony, into even shame at the impossibility of identifying himself with them when the Gandhian prisoner watches from his cell a young terrorist convict who is going to face execution the next day. 'I have to look at you from a distance like a spectator at a play. You must regard me as heartless and shameless. I know that my entire being shudders at your cold, icy glance. I know that even tears cannot flow easily where you stand today...O my friend, how can I console you? I have forgotten the words of comfort. What can I do to give you sustenance? What can I do to express my love?'[93]

Many terrorists considered their own activities an extension of the Gandhian non-violent programme and not as something entirely antithetical to it. Some of them occasionally joined the various Congress satyagrahas. Ananta Singh has described how, at the time of the Chittagong Armoury raid, the takeover of the armoury

[93] Prabhatmohan Bandopadhyay, *Muktipathe* (Mahishbathan, 1931), pp. 96–100, 110.

was celebrated with a cry of 'Gandhiji's Raj has come'.[94] Government officials were often confused. 'The *Swarajists* (italics mine) were in command of the town . . .', wrote Jackson to Irwin, reporting on the Chittagong episode.[95] Tegart, however, perceived and recognized the distinction very clearly. He saw the Congress as an open mass front, its real strength lying in its recruitment of illiterate peasants while terrorists were exclusively urban, educated, middle class youth.[96]

Urban, educated youth remained the standard recruits. Though most officers tried to see this as a function of growing middle class unemployment, a senior official pointed out a basic flaw in the argument. He noted that most of the actual terrorists did have stable jobs which they gave up. Others were recruited at the pre-employment stage, that is, when they were students.[97] Most students were recruited from district towns—Chittagong, Dacca, Faridpur, Midnapur, Rangpur, Dinajpur, Tippera, Barisal, Burdwan, the 24 Parganas and Jessore.[98] Young women from a similar background became increasingly important as 'housekeepers, messengers, custodians of arms and sometimes as comrades'.[99] By this time the last role, too, had become a fairly well-established one. Some of the women comrades were to become as active as any of the men. Kalpana Dutt would abscond later with Surya Sen's group and Suhashini Ganguly took great political and social risk by setting up a house at Chandanagore, pretending to be the wife of another terrorist comrade, to provide shelter for Chittagong absconders. Contemporary nationalist literature reflected and encouraged this trend. An exceedingly romantic collection of short stories, *Chalar Pathey*, which dealt exclusively with this theme, became a favourite reading matter of young terrorists.[100]

Activists continued to band together in small cells and planned localized actions which often verged on the suicidal. The point was to make 'examples by action', to create an inspiring tradition of

94 Ananta Singh. *Chattogram Yuva Vidroha*, Pt. I (Calcutta. 1968), p. 91.

95 Jackson's letter 149–of 21 April 1930. *Halifax Collection.*

96 Tegart's Speech to Royal Empire Society, 1932; *Tegart Papers* (CSASC).

97 Robert Reid, *Note on the History of Terrorism*, 1936, *Robert Reid Papers*. MSS EUR/E/278/ (*a-c*) IOL.

98 See the break-up of Andaman prisoners in Niranjan Sen, p. 2.

99 H.W. Hale, *Political Trouble in India 1917–37* (Calcutta, 1937 ; Indian edn., 1974), p. 8.

100 Bhupendra Kishore Rakshit Ray, *Chalar Pathey* (Calcutta, 1930). Proscribed book. PP. BEN B 74 IOL.

martyrdom. The fantastic daylight attack on the Writers' Building was undertaken by three young men. They rushed into the room of Lt. Colonel Simpson (Inspector General, Prisons), shot him dead and then openly advanced along corridors, firing in all directions and injuring Townsend (Secretary, Agriculture and Industries Department) and Nelson (Legal Remembrancer). At the point of capture all of them attempted suicide and Benoy Ghosh (who had earlier killed Lowman) did die very soon.[101]

Chittagong constituted a remarkable departure from this pattern. It involved an unusually large group of men—about sixty in all.[102] The action was planned out in every minute detail over a long period. A meticulous organization was patiently built up for the ultimate purpose of simultaneous attacks on Police lines, the Telegraph Office and the Volunteer Headquarters so that the town authorities would be paralysed for a while and the terrorists could make away with a good supply of arms.[103] 'They proposed to take by surprise the District Police and capture the District Treasury and Armoury . . . even if they sustain the attack for an hour and then die fighting as the Irish rebels did in their Easter rising in Dublin, they consider it will have a tremendous moral effect.' A copy of their manifesto declared: 'The Indian Republican Army proclaims today its intention of asserting their right in arms in the face of the world and thus put into actual practice the idea of Indian Independence declared by the Indian National Congress.'[104]

Even British officers, shaken and furious as they were, could not withhold a grudging tribute to this 'amazing coup'.[105] A Government of India memorandum crossly asked 'how the insurgents were able to plan and execute a raid of this magnitude without arousing the previous suspicions of the authorities'.[106] The sequel was worthy of the episode; a surprisingly tenacious resistance that began with guerilla warfare with military and police personnel at the Jalalabad hills, escape *en masse* from the tensely vigilant district, development of a superb underground apparatus all over Bengal and finally the amazing success of the most serious of absconders in

[101] *Fortnightly Reports on Bengal*, 2nd half of December 1930, GOI, Home Poll 18–VIII 30 of 1930.

[102] GOI, Home Poll 4 9 1931.

[103] Ananta Singh, *Agnigarbha Chattogram*, Part I.

[104] GOI, Home Poll, 4/9/1931.

[105] Hale, *Political Trouble in India*, p. 14.

[106] GOI, Home Poll, 4 9 1931.

remaining undetected within Chittagong itself for the next three years.

Embattled Ireland remained the most important source of inspiration. Ideas about death, duty and moral mission in life came from the *Gita*. Dan Breen's *My Fight for Irish Freedom* was the main classic for most Indian terrorists.[107] The few tendencies towards ideological self-questioning that had developed earlier, got rather swamped by the spectacular resurgence of terrorist ideas and practices. A simple and uncluttered ideal of dying and killing on an individual scale for the Motherland remained triumphant as the only vision and aim.

The Carters' Strike

Labour movement and organization had suffered a decisive setback after the Meerut arrests. Depression reduced food prices while at the same time it held out the threat of retrenchment and unemployment. Though such a conjuncture was particularly unpropitious for labour action, the year was not entirely free from conflicts. In April a large number of Titagarh jute mill-hands went on strike. In May there was police firing on labourers of a Lilooah workshop over a wage dispute.[108] These remained rather minor affairs which did not add up to a sustained militancy.

The one remarkable exception to this picture of general decline was the Calcutta carters' strike on the eve of Civil Disobedience. The Government, prodded by the Society for Prevention of Cruelty to Animals (SPCA), had imposed a ban on the movement of bullock carts between 12 noon and 3 pm during the hot months of the year. The touching concern for the unfortunate animals ignored the fact that godowns opened quite late in the morning and closed early. If the noon hours could not be used for plying bullock carts, then carters would have no chance of loading up and reaching their destination before closing hours. Forty thousand carters of the city thus faced virtual ruin. A labour leader later alleged that the move was also inspired by pressure from the American Ford Company; there was a glut in the production of their trucks and the elimination of cheap bullock carts would create an Indian market.

A carters' union had come into existence in 1925 under Dr Bhupendranath Dutta. The next year's communal rioting, where

[107] Hale, *Political Trouble in India*.

[108] *The Amrita Bazar Patrika*, 2 April and 30 May 1930.

Calcutta carters were extremely active, had, however, rendered it practically defunct. Faced with the new threat some carters now approached a Congress Corporation Councillor who took them to the WPP office. The Meerut arrests had depleted its organizational strength and its leadership. A very young and inexperienced cadre, Abdul Momin, thus found the leadership of the strike most unexpectedly thrust upon him.

Momin had to learn hurriedly the basic facts about the existence of men whom he was supposed to lead. Calcutta carters were a huge, dispersed group, scattered all over the city. Most of them came from Eastern UP and Bihar. They were controlled by a thin upper-stratum of cart-owners—'chaudhuries' who often combined a subsidiary employment with the Calcutta police force and who would not be expected to be too eager for a confrontation. Some of them still evinced interest in the possibility of a strike after a few dialogues with Momin. The young leader discovered in his very first meetings with the general body of carters, a warm response, a good deal of constructive assistance and evidence of formidable organizational capacity. Carters like Raja Singh, Kishore Singh and Khaleque helped him to build up within six weeks a city-wide intricate strike apparatus, divided into thirty-two zones, each providing sixteen volunteers. Congress and terrorist leaders kept their distance from the strike preparations. Momin recalled how Satish Dasgupta scolded him for creating a diversion on the eve of Civil Disobedience. Anushilan and Jugantar leaders, whom he tried to entice with the possibility of having a go at the dreaded Police Commissioner Tegart during street fights, were not interested. In sharp and significant contrast, carters were so moved by the news of Gandhi's Dandi March on the eve of their own struggle, that they were keen to court arrest, thereby suspending their movement. Momin had considerable difficulty in holding them back.[109]

With the help of carters Momin devised an unusually brilliant and original strategy for the strike. The new traffic law was to come into force from 1 April. Carters were instructed to leave their carts at 12 noon on that day, taking away the bullocks, thus blocking main traffic arteries. This would comply with the new law but would effectively paralyse the city traffic. Wheels were to be removed from the carts which would then be arranged crosswise, setting up barricades. An Intelligence Branch report stated in 1935: 'This was later acclaimed by the official Communist Press as the first bar-

[109] Abdul Momin, *Kalikatar Garoan Dharmaghat, Mulyayan*, Calcutta, 1970.

ricade street fight with the police in India—which indeed it was.'[110]

Clashes spread throughout the city on 1 April. The police charged at the barricades with lathis, firing frequently, and carters resisted them from behind their carts. Tegart wrote to the Chief Secretary: 'The carters, numbering about 25 to 30,000, had entrenched themselves behind barricades of carts, in houses and "gullies" from where they maintained a persistent fusillade of bricks, soda water bottles, iron bars etc., on the police.'[111] Another police officer commented: 'I cannot say on how many occasions the men under me had to fire but it was absolutely ineffective.'[112] The *Amrita Bazar Patrika* came out the next day with two photographs which together constitute a striking study in contrast. In one, a heavily armed and helmeted group of white sergeants is charging at the crowd. In the other a bare-torsoed carter retaliates with a brick.[113]

Pedestrians, in their thousands, spontaneously joined in the fight. They would have known very little about the issues since Momin had no time to spare for advance propaganda. In the College Street-Cornwallis Street area, students 'adopted the same tactics as the carters' and fought a long, pitched battle with the police from behind the shelter of houses or shop awnings. Young Congress volunteers at Burrabazar rushed out from the Congress office to join the fighting, flouting instructions from their leaders'.[114] Ironmongers from Cornwallis Street were very active, the death of an Oriya coolie in the day's firing was followed on 2 April by a strike of all Oriya coolies at Burrabazar and there were rumours about plans for a sympathetic strike by dockers. A protest meeting was held at Tarasundari Park on 2 April. Of the two thousand who attended it, not more than two hundred were carters.[115] Waves of sympathetic involvement and action engulfed the city as a whole and from the first day of the street fights the strike ceased to be just an affair of the carters.

Seven carters died in the first day's firing. Six of them were Hindus and one was a Muslim. About 50,000 Hindus and Muslims joined the mourning procession on 2 April. The Imam of the

[110] H. H. Williamson, *India and Communism, Hallet Collection*, MSS EUR 251—33 IOL.

[111] Tegart's letter, 1/4/1930 GOB, Home Confidential, Police 185 (1–32) 1930.

[112] Note by Bartley, Deputy Commissioner of Police Calcutta, 1/4/1930.

[113] *The Amrita Bazar Patrika*, 2 April 1930.

[114] Tegart's letter.

[115] *The Amrita Bazar Patrika*, 3 April 1930.

Nakhoda mosque came out to bless the martyrs, women from housetops scattered flowers over their shrouds and Muslims indignantly refused to listen to Suhrawardy when he advised them to take out a separate procession.[116] This constituted a moving spectacle of Hindu-Muslim unity, all the more remarkable in a city that had been ravaged by communal riots just four years back in which the same carters had played a major role. Such an expression of unity would seldom be realized within the Civil Disobedience movement. At the same time it also revealed a state of consciousness that moved rather too easily and without any awareness of a break or rupture, between communal conflict and inter-communal solidarity.

As clashes continued on the second day, Governor Jackson wired to Irwin: 'Charles Tegart told me that the attack on the police was the most violent that he had experienced in Calcutta . . . I do not like the idea of retreating from the position we have taken up, but I fear—and Tegart agrees with me—that unless we make some concessions we shall have continuous trouble.'[117] Negotiations with union leaders began very hastily at Tegart's initiative. Eventually the new regulations were tacitly abandoned.[118]

The Government's surrender on the very eve of Civil Disobedience was a tremendous inspiration to all nationalists. 'The Government did not lack in arms, troops or anything of that sort. Yet yesterday they could not hold out to a handful of carters', exulted a Congress leader at a Calcutta meeting on 2 April.[119] The strike in fact was a kind of dress-rehearsal for coming confrontations. 'Persistent efforts have been made for months past—to incite the student community to acts of open rebellion against the Government and I consider this was one of the first fruits of this propaganda', Tegart pondered gloomily.[120] Throughout Civil Disobedience carters would often join hartals and demonstrations quite on their own, without prior Congress mobilization. The nationalist leadership, however, chose not to deepen or strengthen this involvement.

Dacca and Kishoreganj Riots

Muslim participation in Civil Disobedience was not negligible.

[116] Momin, *Kalikatar Garoan Dharmaghat.*

[117] Jackson's letter, 116 d of 2/4/1930. *Halifax Collection.*

[118] Momin, *Kalikatar Garoan Dharmaghat.*

[119] *Bangabani*, 3 April 1930.

[120] Tegart's letter of 3 April 1930.

Jamait-ul-Ulema leaders like Mufti Kefayetullah and Ahmed Syed toured villages in Mymensingh, Chittagong and Comilla and distributed leaflets which stated: 'British are the common enemies of Hindus and Muslims alike, particularly of the Muslims'.[121] There was an ugly communal incident at Dacca town on 26 January. Students of the Dacca Muslim Hall nevertheless illuminated their hostel that night, raised the national flag and paraded the streets chanting, *Bande Mataram, Gandhiji-ki-jai* and *Allah-Ho-Akbar*. They also held public meetings to read out proscribed literature and sent volunteers to Contai. At the predominantly Muslim quarters of Dacca such as Kamartuli, Islampur, Sachibandar, Maulavibazar and Nawabganj, picketing would have been impossible without the assistance of local Muslims. Muslim 'biri' manufacturers were enthusiastic about the boycott of cigarettes. The Dacca DCC organized a meeting which unanimously passed the boycott resolution and which was attended by a large number of Muslim shopkeepers, cloth dealers, tailors and outfitters.[122]

All through the movement the Government generously patronised all manner of anti-Congress Muslim organizations. Police officers at Faridpur instigated Muslims to set up Fauji-i-Islam branches to counteract Civil Disobedience.[123] The Collector of Barisal wrote on 22 July: 'There were about 100 anti-Civil Disobedience Volunteers lined up for review by me....They are all Muhammedans.[124] Muslim policemen and criminals were deliberately deployed in non-Muslim localities to smash salt centres and inflict torture on Salt Satyagrahis.[125] At times the most careful attempts would boomerang. The Sub-Divisional Officer of Madaripur described how he had painstakingly organized a Muslim loyalist meeting in August. 'We had arranged for a very influential local Pir to come and deliver a strong pro-Government speech to his followers but he betrayed us at the last moment and appeared as a Non-Co-operator.'[126]

Two major bouts of communal riots crowned such efforts at Dacca and at Kishoreganj in May and July. An attempt to under-

[121] Note by A.H. Ghuznavi. GOI, Home Poll 190/1930.

[122] Ramananda Chatterji, 'The Political Situation in Dacca Before the Disturbances'. *Modern Review*, July 1930, pp. 61–2.

[123] *Ananda Bazar Patrika*, 3 April 1930.

[124] J.T. Donovan Papers, CSASC.

[125] Contai Civil Disobedience Report, *AICC Papers G-86-1930*. See also Probodh Chandra Basu, *Medinipur Jelar Bhagawanpur Thanas Itibritta*, p. 127.

[126] *E.B.H. Baker Papers*, CSASC.

stand their causes in terms of wider social and political processes, to differentiate them from what was allegedly an innate religious intolerance and fanaticism of Indian people is not to deny the logic that informed the perceptions and actions of most of the actual participants. Communal discord and violence did necessarily stem from a religious world-view: an ordering of experience, a self-recognition and an understanding about the outside world in accordance with fundamentally religious categories. A search for different kinds of motives is not an attempt to discount the culture of common men and women. In Bengal, however, due to the rather peculiar configuration of property relations, social tensions and conflicts did have a marked tendency to correspond to the contours of a communal conflict. Sectionalist politicians and Government officials played upon this peculiarity for all they were worth. The violence that ensued can be partially isolated from the undoubted pressures and strength of a distinctly religious response to a different community.[127]

The first round of trouble erupted in Dacca town on 26 January 1930 when the Bengal Provincial Students' Association insisted on taking out a procession in front of the Narindia mosque at prayer time. The All Bengal Students' Association opposed the move, as since the 1926 riots this had practically been a proven method to provoke rioting. The advice was ignored and a scuffle developed. Volunteers forced their way into the mosque and tore up a copy of the Koran while Muslims stoned the procession from within the mosque. The conflict did not go very far. The city, however, remained in a state of tension which erupted into large-scale riots on 22 May, over what was literally a schoolboys' quarrel.[128]

In the May riots a large number of prosperous Hindu houses and shops were burnt, most of them at the predominantly business area at Kayettuli. Altogether eighty Muslim shops and one hundred and ninety Hindu shops were looted. Hindu losses were estimated to be twelve times bigger than Muslim losses. Twelve Muslims and ten

[127] I have my doubts though, about an uncritical use of the term religious in the context of traditionalist systems of understanding. It would be extremely difficult to define a domain distinctly religious in opposition to a domain that was secular or non-sacral. It is, perhaps, more helpful to think of a unified integrated consciousness that does not differentiate between categories of experience or compartmentalize experience very definitely into spheres of rituals, religiosity, production, art or struggle.

[128] Dacca Disturbances Enquiry Report of 12 August 1930, GOI, Home Poll 4/9/30 of 1930. See also GOI, Home Poll 10/2/1930.

Hindus were killed. Police action was extremely tardy. Four days went by before any action was taken.[129] By that time riots had spread to villages around Dacca. There was a spate of looting of *hats* by Muslims at Matwail, Ati, Jinjira and Rohitpur thanas. Houses of Hindu Sahas and moneylenders were attacked and debt bonds torn up. The Muslim Union Board President at Rohitpur floated a rumour through the agency of village chowkidars: a message had supposedly come from the Nawab of Dacca that the Government had declared a week-long 'hartal' during which Muslims could freely loot Hindu mahajan houses at the cost of only token punishment later. The rumour caught on so much that even chowkidars looted in their uniforms. A massive plunder of the local *hat* took place which was described as 'one of the biggest cases of *hat* looting ever known in Bengal'. Hindu property worth Rs 2,43,182 was destroyed.[130] Rice godowns were attacked and about 20,000 maunds of rice were taken away from the Badamtoli godown. Other forms of rioting, like murder or rape, were completely absent in rural rioting.[131]

In the Kishoreganj subdivision at Mymensingh the Young Comrades' League (the youth organ of the WPP) had been active since 1929 among Muslim poor peasants. An anti-mahajan movement seemed to be in the offing but a spate of arrests after the Chittagong raid removed most of the activists.[132] Mullahs from Dacca and Noakhali immediately rushed to fill in the gap. Villagers accepted their leadership after their miracle-making claims had been established. The District Magistrate had at first wanted simply to scare the rioters off and ordered firing above their heads. The Mullahs claimed that they had eaten up the bullets.[133] Under their guidance there were large-scale and systematic attacks on mahajan houses. About sixty villages participated in the riots.[134]

[129] Report of the Secretary, Bengal Provincial Hindu Sabha; *The Amrita Bazar Patrika*, 3 June 1930.

[130] Bengal Chief Secretary to GOI, Home 26/6 |1930

[131] Statement by Secretary, Bengal Provincial Hindu Sabha, *The Amrita Bazar Patrika*, 3 June 1930.

[132] Pramatha Gupta, *Je Sangramer Sesh Nei* (Calcutta, 1971), pp. 40–7. See also Dharani Goswami, *Ekti Krishak Bidroher Kahini, Parichay* (Calcutta, October 1969), p. 215.

[133] My interview with Shantimoy Ray. He was then a terrorist prisoner at Mymensingh and he met several convicts from Kishoreganj.

[134] *Ganer Bahi—Loter Gan*, (Published by Lakshmikanta Kirtaniya and Kumud Bhattacharya, Mymensingh, 1930) Proscribed book, PP BEN B 24 IOL.

The predominant characteristic of these riots was the snatching of debt bonds; there was very often plunder, loot, arson and sometimes even murder when mahajans resisted very strongly. The police acted very promptly in sharp contrast to Dacca incidents. Gurkha troops were immediately despatched under senior officers, and there was frequent firing at the slightest provocation.[135]

A number of points strike us in this rather bald summary of events. Right at the beginning political agencies of a very different nature had had some success. The Young Comrades' League had developed an important base among poor peasants. A young Muslim peasant, Abdul Jalil, had emerged as an influential orator and singer whose songs moved large numbers of peasants.[136] In Dacca there had been considerable Muslim enthusiasm for Civil Disobedience even among some senior Muslim politicians. A group under Khwajab Atikullah, President of the 22 Panchaits, in particular, 'was inclined to coquette with the Congress Party'.[137] Atikullah had a formidable rival in Syed Abdul Hafeez, President of the Islamia Anjuman. Hafeez issued a notice forbidding Muslims to participate in nationalist demonstrations and hartals. The ban, however, was not really very effective. Hafeez called a meeting at the Ahsan Manzil (the palace of the Dacca Nawab) to decide on future policy. It was attended, curiously enough, by the District Magistrate.[138] The Magistrate then forced Atikullah to resign and his base in the 22 Panchaits was taken over by the Ahsan Manzil group.[139]

Police attitudes and behaviour consolidated the communal rift in a variety of ways. At Dacca they followed a policy of masterly inactivity in sharp contrast to the remarkable vigour and promptness with which unarmed salt Satyagrahis were tortured in remote villages. Four days went by before they could at all mobilize for action. Even then they stood aside and allowed virtually free destruction of Hindu property. When Hindus pleaded for help they were told to go and ask their nationalist leaders to save them.[140] An official report was forced to admit: 'We are not satisfied that better use could not have been made of the forces.'[141]

[135] *The Statesman*, 16 July 1930.
[136] Goswami, *Ekti Krishak Biddroher Kahini*, p. 42.
[137] *Dacca Disturbances Enquiry Report.*
[138] GOI, Home Poll 10/2 pf 1930.
[139] *Dacca Disturbances Enquiry Report.*
[140] *Modern Review*, p. 23.
[141] *Dacca Disturbances Enquiry Committee.*

A calculated purpose behind such non-intervention was to let ugly incidents develop and multiply up to a point and to create an ineradicable legacy of communal bitterness. It would force self-defence efforts on both communities since they would lose all faith in police protection. Such efforts would keep mutual suspicion and tension alive permanently. A remarkable consistency characterized a deliberate suspension of law and order responsibilities at certain points of time. Inaction at early stages of rioting as well as active encouragement to Muslim rioters were evident in the Jamalpur and Comilla riots in March and April 1907.[142] In the Calcutta riots of September 1918 the Bengal Government was 'slow to recognize the gravity of the situation' and took no pre-emptive measures at first.[143] Hindus and Muslims in the Kanpur riot of April 1931 'frequently remarked on the reluctance of the Government to intervene to stop Hindu-Muslim clashes'.[144] The rumours in Dacca villages about the Government's orders about the looting of mahajan houses were not as wildly improbable as they might seem at first glance. It is the logic of police inaction and discrimination carried to an extreme.

The situation was entirely different at Kishoreganj. Official connivance was out of the question and antagonism between the police and rioters was open. At Kaliachopra a crowd seized the Circle Officer, bound him to a cowshed post and thoroughly beat him up. Police was 'hemmed in on all sides' by a threatening crowd at Kodalia village. Maulvis had accompanied the police and they pleaded with the crowd to stop rioting. All their pleading was in vain.[145] The identification between Hindu and nationalist activities which had necessitated a temporary withdrawal of official protection from Hindu property at Dacca did not operate at Kishoreganj at all. Krishna Chandra Ray, who was murdered along with his family at Jangalia village, was the President of the local Union Board.[146] The position carried considerable official approval since the Congress was then leading a movement against Union Boards.

The pattern of rioting makes greater sense when we locate it in

[142] Sumit Sarkar, *The Swadeshi Movement in Bengal, 1903–1908* (New Delhi, 1973), p. 452.

[143] J.H. Broomfield, 'The Forgotten Majority—The Bengal Muslims, September 1918', in D.A. Low (ed.) *Soundings in Modern South Asian History* (London, 1965).

[144] G. Pandey, *The Ascendancy of the Congress in Uttar Pradesh 1926–34* (New Delhi, 1978), p. 139.

[145] *The Statesman*, 16 July 1930.

[146] Stephenson's letter 542 of 27 August 1930. *Halifax Collection*.

the context of the respective communal positions in the broader social milieu. In Dacca district the number of Muslim zamindars was extremely small. A few Muslims did control some trade in jute and hide and invested in small shops. Yet 'they (had) not the capital to enable them to compete with the Hindus in wholesale and quasi-wholesale trade and the cream of commerce passes into Hindu hands'. Due, perhaps, to the Islamic taboo on usury, very few Bengali Muslims were connected at all with money-lending. The Hindu money-lending Saha caste, on the other hand, had waxed richer on profits from trade and usury and were buying up zamindaris.[147] In Dacca town 'the economic position of the Muhammadan population had remained much the same while they have seen the Hindus growing richer and richer'.[148] Hindus carried on considerable small-scale banking and jute trade. They had recently set up a few cotton mills.[149] Their relatively comfortable position is indicated by the fact that economically and socially privileged castes, considerably outnumbered the inferior castes in Dacca town. Not only did the extent of Hindu literacy exceed that of Muslims but a better index is that a far larger number of Hindus had received English education.[150]

Contrast in socio-economic status was marked most obviously in the very different kinds of houses that they inhabited. While Muslim residential areas were fast turning into overpopulated, insanitary slums, a large number of Hindus had recently built 'palatial residences' on the best urban sites.[151] The social envy that this generated decided an important feature of urban rioting: repeated attacks on 'palatial residences', and deliberate, wanton destruction. Loot as a motive cannot entirely explain this away. Photographs in the *Modern Review* show enormous, imposing buildings with their walls torn down, floors dug up and doors and windows hacked to bits.[152] *The Amrita Bazar Patrika* found this important enough to comment on the destruction of 'beautiful buildings' which partially replaced the motif of killing in earlier riots. 'On the above occasions (in 1926 and on 26 January 1930) the rioters were after breaking one

[147] B.C. Allen, *Bengal District Gazeteers, Dacca* (Calcutta, 1912), p. 65.

[148] *Dacca Disturbances Enquiry Report.*

[149] *Report of the Bengal Provincial Banking Enquiry Committee* Vol. I (Calcutta, 1930), p. 31.

[150] Statistics for 1921–22, Tables IV and XXII, *Bengal District Gazeteer, Dacca.*

[151] *Dacca Disturbances Enquiry Report.*

[152] *Modern Review*, July 1930.

another's heads—but no attempt was made to set fire to the houses.'[153]

Kishoreganj was the seat of a large number of established Hindu landowning families. From the time of the Dewanganj communal clashes of 1907, however, Hindu landlords, traders and moneylenders in Mymensingh had been targets of anger and attack rather than objects of awe. This was connected with the position of the ambitious and enterprising Muslim peasantry in Mymensingh. A clear manifestation of their social aspirations was a marked aversion to self-cultivation or strenuous manual labour since 'the Muhammadan peasant considers himself a gentleman'. These groups would find Hindu bhadralok sneer and contempt particularly intolerable. Another interesting characteristic of the Mymensingh Muslim peasant was his propensity to listen and respond to 'the preachings of outside mullas and maulvis (which) are at the bottom of most of their discontent.'[154]

The ratio of moneylenders was exceptionally high at both Dacca and Mymensingh. Dacca's ratio of moneylenders was indeed the highest in Bengal—280 per lakh of persons in the district as compared to 40 in Burdwan or 26 in Bankura. Mymensingh came second with 175 per lakh. The usual rate of interest charged in Dacca was 12 per cent to 192 per cent while at Mymensingh it ranged between 24 per cent and 225 per cent.[155] After the Sarda Act (that raised the minimum age for marriage) was passed in 1929 a spate of hasty weddings immediately occurred so that daughters could be married off before the Act came into force. This immensely increased the total debt burden. Just before 1930 a rumour widely circulated among peasants that after the Act the Government would bear a large part of the wedding costs. This again led to large-scale wedding expenses. So far, however, debt payment had not been such an awesome proposition thanks to rising agricultural prices. The picture changed completely after the onset of the depression.

Dacca and Mymensingh belonged to the heart of the jute belt. The fortunes of their peasants were very closely bound up with fluctuations in jute prices. The worldwide slump in agricultural prices vitally affected the cash reserves of jute growers. The

[153] *The Amrita Bazar Patrika*, 6 June 1930.

[154] F.A. Sachse, *District Gazeteer of Bengal: Mymensingh* (Calçutta, 1917), pp. 43, 68, 39.

[155] *Report of the Bengal Banking Enquiry Committee*, Vol. I, p. 194.

magnitude of the problem becomes clear when we look at the index of jute prices. In 1928 the index number was 107.3 if we take 1929 as 100; in 1930 it went down to 54.9 and came down to 50.4 in 1931. [156] In this context the exceptionally heavy dependence of Dacca and Mymensingh peasants on Hindu mahajans, and the exorbitantly high interest rates extorted by them, help to explain the large-scale destruction of debt bonds. Resentment of high interest rates may be taken to indicate that peasants of some substance and not really very poor peasants were the moving spirits behind the attacks. Indebtedness denotes credit-worthiness and the richer soil of East Bengal which supported a larger density of middle peasants also supported a bigger number of moneylenders than did the arid and depressed district of Bankura, for instance. The slump in jute price and consequent cash famine explains another major characteristic. While the important cash crops were bringing in less and less money there was no parallel decline in prices of manufactured articles. There were frequent rushes on shops at village *hats*. Hindus once again suffered more from this since they almost invariably owned *hats* or set up the largest stalls. These broader socio-economic experiences which conditioned everyday existence tie up together to create the concrete contexts behind encounters. Krishna Chandra Ray, a big mahajan of Jangalia village, who was killed by a band of Muslims, had recenly built himself a house the like of which the village had not seen. He also bought himself a car which Muslims were not even allowed to touch. The account of his murder has an interesting point; at first he opened a volley of fire on attackers who fled. After they had gone a little way, a servant of the house with a Hindu name (Subodh) ran after them and called out that his master's ammunition was exhausted and they could come back. The crowd returned and killed off the entire family. [157]

A fine discrimination in the choice of targets characterized both urban and rural rioting. Only one or two temples were attacked at Dacca, domestic shrines in Hindu houses were not desecrated and the only houses that were destroyed were those that appeared as symbols of wealth and ostentation. Shops, godowns and markets bore the brunt of attacks. It was the Hindus who attacked Muslim slums and small, rather dingy shops in the Ticcatooly area. The

156 B.B. Chaudhuri, 'The Process of De-peasantization in Bengal and Bihar 1885–1947'. *Indian Historical Review*, July 1975, p. 117.

157 *Loter Gan*.

158 *The Amrita Bazar Patrika*, 27 May 1930.

Hindu business area of Kayettuli was the scene of repeated Muslim attacks although Ramna, the seat of the professional middle class, was left alone. At least in one instance caste Hindus, untouchables and Muslims looted a Hindu shop together.[159] Loss of property was the chief Hindu grievance, not so much murder. There was no report of rape although the Hindu press from the mid-twenties had systematically put together a stereotype of the bestial Muslim male lusting after Hindu women. Self-restraint, quite remarkable in a riot situation, was in fact evident when a huge armed Muslim gang attacked a Hindu house where four young girls were alone by themselves. The girls just lost their jewels.[160] More Muslims were killed than Hindus.

There was a very similar pattern in villages around Dacca. The Keraniganj *hat* was entirely looted but except for one incident of arson, no other instance of violence occurred like rape or murder. A Brahmin child-widow was threatened with kidnapping but nothing was actually done.[161] The rumour circulated by the Union Board President was that Muslims could loot Hindu Saha houses with perfect freedom. It did not say that all Hindu houses must be attacked. Rioting started off at Kishoreganj with an attack on the house of a Muslim taluqdar. Even when a Muslim religious organization, the Khadem-ul-mulk, assumed leadership, the set of instructions that it issued did not at all imply a general crusade against all Hindus. It specified that only mahajan houses would be ravaged.[162] Crowds generally snatched away the guns of mahajans, threw them into nearby ponds and then broke open safes and destroyed debt bonds. Violence occurred when the mahajan refused to give in.[163]

In most encounters anger was focused on moneylenders rather than on landlords who were very largely Hindus. The rent burden was not particularly oppressive either at Dacca or at Mymensingh and this partly explains it.[164] Again, landlords were perhaps vested with some amount of customary legitimacy or authority in peasant minds whereas mahajans, often forming a distinct group, external to peasants, and displacing them from their lands, would form no part of their patriarchal moral universe.

159 *The Dacca Disturbances Enquiry Report.*
160 *The Amrita Bazar Patrika,* 4 June 1930.
161 GOI, Home Poll/4 of 1930.
162 Goswami, *Ekti Krishak Bidroher Kahini,* p. 41.
163 *Loter Gan.* See also *The Amrita Bazar Patrika,* 16 July 1930.
164 *District Gazeteer of Bengal: Dacca and Mymensingh.*

There were instances, even at the height of the riots, when crowds tried to push through an alternative concept of fair deal; sheer loot and vandalism were not the only important triggers of crowd action. Disturbances began at Kishoreganj when at Chandipasha 'an unusual number of Mohammedans gathered at Juma... and proceeded to the house of a barber and demanded the return of a bond worth about Rs 250 on payment of Rs 97. The owner refused to part with the document and forthwith his house was looted'. It is remarkable that Rs 250 worth of debt bonds were not simply torn up right at the beginning; the mahajan was asked to take the cash famine into account and lower it to a not unreasonable sum of Rs 97. Some indigenous notion of what constitutes a fair interest rate at times of crisis lay behind their calculations. Mahajans were generally asked to surrender their debt bonds first and not their other valuables.[165] After Muslims more or less took over certain areas in Dacca, looted goods from Hindu shops were sold again at ridiculously low prices and were not simply appropriated. After the worst phase of rioting was over and a few stalls opened in the markets, Muslims imposed a strict system of rationing on the amount of stuff that could be sold to rich Hindus of the locality; they did not completely cut off supplies from them.[166] It seems that the Muslim poor exerted temporary advantages gained during the riots to enforce a crude, primitive form of punitive justice against social superiors and oppressors.

[165] *The Amrita Bazar Patrika*, 16 July 1930.

[166] Glimpses of the Dacca Disturbances, *Modern Review*, July 1930.

CHAPTER 3

1931

The Truce and the Congress

The first phase of Civil Disobedience closed with the Gandhi-Irwin Pact of March 1931. A rather uneasy peace was observed till the end of the year. There was little conviction, however, among either nationalists or officials, that the Pact would pave the way for a durable peace. The entire period was, for both, one of recovery and preparation. The one-year interval therefore has a distinct identity and interest of its own.

The Congress got a breathing-space to recuperate and to formulate, if it saw fit, new goals and tactics. This became all the more urgent in the context of the persistent and intensifying slump in rice and jute prices. The consequent heightening of rural tension opened up fresh possibilities. The U.P. Congress, for instance, could not avoid a no-rent-movement that was to have major consequences for its future struggle. Much of the shape of the next movement in Bengal would depend on how far the provincial leadership was prepared to explore such possibilities.

Throughout the year an apparent contradiction lay at the core of political developments. A decline in the formal Congress movement corresponded with a steady, continuous rising groundswell of resistance, even violence. At one pole lay revolutionary terrorism with its long-standing and well-established violent practices. Elsewhere the manifold consequences of the slump in prices led to heightened tensions. 'Crimes' multiplied with a growing incidence of dacoities and looting of *hats*. Occasionally these would crystallize into organized no-rent or anti-mahajan movements. A few Congressmen tried to link them up with the mainstream of the Congress movement; at other times Muslim politicians tried to develop them along sectional lines. It was the second stream of multifaceted resistance rather than the activities of the Congress leadership itself that agitated officials most and defined Government attitudes towards the next phase of Civil Disobedience.

During the months of the truce, picketing, boycott and demonstrations continued to be brisk and uninhibited whenever they were directed by relatively junior volunteers. But where more established leaders, especially Gandhians were in control, there was an air of caution, of scrupulous observance of truce terms. The Commissioner of the Dacca Division observed: 'The agreement has led to an easing of the situation in those places where organized civil disobedience was going on'—in the Munshiganj or Nawabganj subdivisions in Dacca for instance.[1] The contrast is clear when we compare the post-truce situation in two of the most active areas in the last movement—Arambagh and Midnapur. At Arambagh where a Gandhian leadership retained full control, the year was entirely peaceful. 'The local leaders issued pamphlets asking the people to pay up the taxes and meetings for the same purpose were held'. The Midnapur DCC on the other hand did not have much of a long-standing Gandhian influence or tradition. Its links with terrorists had always been strong. The District Officer reported towards the end of March that the Congress rank and file was displeased with the truce and was ready to start village-level work in defiance of AICC decisions. Volunteers organized a demonstration even though the DCC Secretary disapproved. One of the leaders was Prafulla Tripathi, a revolutionary terrorist.[2]

The most interesting form of Congress activity in this year was the attempt to formulate a parallel system of justice in parts of Midnapur. There were similar plans for Bankura, 24 Parganas and Hooghly as well but these did not materialize.[3] Arbitration courts, run entirely by local Congressmen, were set up to provide an indigenous form of justice. In letter this did not flout settlement terms and British legal theory had always praised arbitration. There seemed to be, however, an increasing possibility that these courts might usurp official functions and authority and firmly entrench Congress positions in villages by making it the fount of local justice. The right to discipline and to punish is an essential aspect of political

[1] *Fortnightly Reports on Bengal*, 2nd half of March 1931, GOI, Home Poll 18/3/1931.

[2] GOI, Home Poll 33/1/1931 and *KW*.

[3] GOI, Home Poll 35/50 of 1931.

authority; its appropriation by the Congress, therefore, gave it a real power-base.

Altogether forty courts were set up, most of them at Tamluk, several at Contai and one at Nandigram. The plan was to create an entire hierarchy of courts at village, union and thana levels with a court of appeal at Tamluk town. Village-level courts, however, were the only ones that actually functioned. The Mahishadal Circle Officer described a three-tier system: 'pratham', run by youths, 'madham' run by the elderly men and 'uttam' run by the old. Courts met once a week but there could be extraordinary sittings for urgent cases. Workload was so heavy that at times they continued through the night. All courts sat together but the 'uttam' enjoyed some special powers. A fee of Re 1 was charged when a complaint was lodged. This went to Congress funds along with fines imposed by courts. The Congress thus acquired an additional source of income.

A large number of cases dealt with violations of Congress discipline. A chowkidar of Rajarampur village in Mahishadal thana was fined Rs 10 when he resumed his duties, having resigned earlier. A wide variety of rural conflicts also came under their purview. A Contai court tried a rent suit and made the tenant pay Rs 36 to the landlord. At Batutakonda village a dacoit submitted to Congress discipline and was fined Rs 50. Hare Krista Dey from Debra thana complained to the Government that he had been forced to pay Rs 125 as fine. His was a double crime: refusing to enroll as a Congress volunteer and refusing to abandon his mistress and return to his wife. He and his mistress were beaten up when he did not pay up the fine. Local officers insisted that a lot of force and coercion underlay such practices. A rough and ready sort of justice was very probably meted out, which bore down more heavily on those who defied the Congress.[4] It still would have been much less of an alien, expensive and cumbersome process than what was provided by the agencies of British law. This explains its popularity at the village level. It spread even among sections which ordinarily had nothing to do with Congress activities. 'Low class Muslims' of Sutahata thana, otherwise indifferent to Civil Disobedience, took their complaints to these courts.[5] An officer pointed out in alarm: 'If these courts spread all over the District a sort of dual Government will be established as soon as the peace breaks down. There will be trouble such as has not been known since the days of the mutiny'.[6] Fears

[4] GOI, Home Poll 14/8/31 of 1931.
[5] GOB, Home Confdl Poll 335 (1–22) of 1931.
[6] GOI, Home Poll 14/8/1931 of 1931.

about a dual authority grew stronger when a band of uniformed volunteers began to openly practise lathi play and regularly patrol village streets at Khejri.[7] This looked ominously like the beginnings of a parallel police force. At Tamluk subdivision two or three cattle pounds were set up under Congress auspices and a Congress police station was planned.[8]

An alternative source of authority began to take shape which seriously threatened a loss of official power even in its coercive aspects. At the same time Congress justice did not try to formulate new social values. The rent suit was treated in a conventional manner and the defaulter was fined. There is no evidence that courts tried to make sympathetic landlords agree to rent reduction by arguing about the slump situation. Perhaps a stricter code of sexual morality was enforced when Hare Krista Dey was pressurized to return to his wife. The beating up of his mistress and the enforced rejection of the woman to make the errant husband return to the wife does not, necessarily, indicate a humanizing of personal relations and codes of conduct. Neither is there any evidence that the cause of deserted wives in general ever became a major concern with these courts. In this particular case, the power and position of the wife's natal family and its relation to the Congress might have made a difference. Courts in any case were administered by men even though women in these parts had a splendid record of militancy in the Congress movement.

Immediately after the truce there was a bout of aggressive picketing in several districts that often turned into violent intimidation. Gandhian leaders tried to control it and conform to the agreement as best as they could. Calcutta picketing, organized by the Burrabazar Congress, tended to be restrained, though the Yuvak Satyagraha Samiti (having for its base younger sons of business families), being closely connected with Bose, was far more difficult to control. Emerson sent Gandhi a copy of a pledge that was circulating in the Calcutta piece-goods market. He complained that it indicated intimidation. Gandhi promised to revise it and Sen Gupta readily agreed.[9] After May, picketing was brought under control and it continued thereafter in a rather spasmodic manner.[10]

[7] GOI, Home Poll 35/50 of 1931.

[8] *Fortnightly Reports on Bengal*, from May to December 1931, GOI, Home Poll 18–5/1931 to 18/12/1931.

[9] GOI, Home Poll 33/13 of 1931.

[10] *Fortnightly Reports on Bengal*, from May to December 1931, GOI, Home Poll 18–5/1931 to 18/12/1931.

in any case, factional squabbles inhibited significant boycott for a major part of the year. Bose and Sen Gupta remained engrossed in an extremely bitter squabble over BPCC elections and Calcutta Corporation seats: it was resolved only in late September through the mediation of Aney, the arbiter appointed by the AICC.[11] Even then the boycott movement left a major impact on trade patterns. Bengal's import trade touched a record low in several years, U.K.'s share in it declined by 7 per cent and sales of foreign liquor, sugar, cotton goods and tobacco fell quite sharply.[12]

Throughout the truce, social boycott of loyalists and officers continued practically unabated. It was effective enough to rack the nerves of village chowkidars as well as District Magistrates in many districts.[13] A Barisal officer reported dolefully: 'Where one lal pugree [red turban, which meant a policeman] was enough to do a job a few years ago, ten are required now. The hitherto docile peasant had learnt that the forces of Government are neither so ubiquitous nor so powerful as he believed'. By its nature it was more effective in a closely-knit, socially cohesive village unit rather than in the more impersonal and socially diffused contexts of cities and towns. Even in villages, however, there was a serious limitation. Rural Muslims were neither co-operative nor interested.[14] In some parts of Tamluk, tenants organized a social boycott of loyalist zamindars who were 'threatened that they would no longer receive the customary services of labourers, barbers and dhobis'.[15] But instances of such coincidence between nationalist protest and class tension remained extremely rare.

Some local Congress leaders tried, on their own, to link up their activities with broad social issues. The Arambagh Congress, with its predominantly poor peasant base, organized Sabhas at Hareet, Bainchapota, Somra, Balagarh and other places. The thrust of these gatherings was to criticize unauthorized cesses that the zamindars extorted. At Rajshahi a few Congressmen were arrested on the charge of inciting tenants not to pay rent.[16] The efforts remained sporadic and localized. The provincial leadership did not

[11] GOB, Home Confdl Poll 345 (1–19) of 1931.

[12] GOB, *Report on the Administration of Bengal 1930–31* (Calcutta 1932), pp. 86–95.

[13] GOB, Home Confdl Poll Poll (1–17) of 1931.

[14] Ibid.

[15] *Report on the Land Revenue Administration of Bengal*, p. 29.

[16] *Bangabani*, 15 October 1931.

try to integrate them into their central programme. On the contrary, it deeply feared these developments. *Bangabani*, a nationalist daily allied with Bose's faction, wrote in January 1931: 'We do not agree that all ryots are unable to pay rents. We have been saying for a long time that due to malicious intentions, obstacles are being placed on realization of rents and debts. In this district (Mymensingh) there was never any attempt to start a movement against payment of Union Board and other taxes as the Congress leaders knew that such agitations will in time lead to no-rent and no-debt movements and bring about a serious destabilization of the district'.[17] A spillover of nationalist protest into social issues was readily assumed and deeply feared. It reveals why even strictly Congress programmes like no-tax had to be initiated in strong and safe bases—Bankura, Midnapur and Arambagh. Mymensingh was a district where agrarian tension coincided rather too easily with sectional ones; a situation which the Congress could not handle at all.

Resolutions at the Bengal Provincial Conference in 1931 at Behrampore involved the formation of arbitration courts, boycott of Union Boards, no-tax and social boycott. Boycott was to extend to British goods, banks, insurance and steamship companies and to Anglo-Indian newspapers. Prohibition was yet another important item.[18] All were old planks, quite irrelevant to the new economic crisis. It seems that the Congress deliberately surrendered the possibilities of its own movements and an extension of its own bases in the interests of social stability.

Revolutionary Terrorism

'Bengal writers', claims Laushey in his study of revolutionary terrorists, 'invariably tend to exaggerate the fear and cowardice of British officials in India'.[19] Even a cursory glance at Home Department records and private papers of Englishmen in Bengal reveals that, on the contrary, the full extent of the impact has never been adequately assessed. In terms of actual attacks the year 1931 was quieter than both 1930 and 1932. Major assassinations, however,

[17] *Bangabani*, 12 January 1931.

[18] *Fortnightly Reports on Bengal*, first half of December 1931, GOI, Home Poll 18–12/1931.

[19] D.M. Laushey, *Bengal Terrorism*, p. 79.

were nicely spaced out to maintain a high level of suspense.[20] The running sore of frequent dacoities, moreover, seemed to threaten preparations for a large-scale rising.[21]

Government retaliation was massive and multi-pronged. The Indian Press (Emergency Powers) Act was passed in October to suppress all publications that looked subversive. Ordinance IX was also passed in October, bestowing on the Government highly arbitrary powers of preventive detention. The Bengal Emergency Powers Ordinance, passed in November empowered the use of wide-ranging repressive measures.[22] By August, five hundred suspects had been detained and action was planned against another five hundred.[23] Detention camps, however, were almost entirely counter-productive. Far from being effective deterrents they grew into centres for future organization.[24] A total sum of Rs 21,50,000 was spent on counter-terrorist work during 1931–2.[25]

Home Member Prentice, confessed that 'terrorism has taken a serious toll of the services and reduced considerably the number of officers available for dealing with it'. He referred not just to the dead and the wounded, but more to those who could not cope with the constant nervous tension. Donovan, a Barisal District official, went on leave for security reasons. Baker, the Governor of Hijli prison, escaped to Calcutta. Armed guards had to be provided for officers in all disturbed districts. 'The strain is telling on the services', wrote Prentice. A judge declared that if he was put on the tribunal that was to try the Peddie assassination case, he would immediately leave the country, with or without leave.[26] Young European circles in Calcutta considered the battery of repressive measures inadequate and thought Jackson to be too gentle in his handling of terrorists. They formed a group called the Royalists to pressurize him. There were even rumours of a plot to kidnap

[20] Peddie, the Midnapur District Magistrate, was killed in April; Garlick (the judge who had sentenced two terrorists to death) in July, and Ashanullah (Police Inspector in charge of the Armoury Raid case) in September. In December, Stevens, the Comilla District Magistrate, was assassinated by two young girls of Shiv Sangha. Laushey, *Bengal Terrorism*, pp. 79–81.

[21] GOI, Home Poll 4 28 of 1931.

[22] Laushey, *Bengal Terrorism*, p. 78.

[23] Jackson to Secretary of State Hoare, 27 August 1931, *Templewood Collection*, MSS EUR E 240 (IOL).

[24] Note by Emerson 5 November 1931, GOI, Home Poll 291/31 of 1931.

[25] *Robert Reid Papers,* MSS EUR E 278/2 (*a-c*), IOL.

[26] Demi-official from Prentice to Home Member GOI, 5 December 1931. GOI, Home Poll 291 31 of 1931.

him.[27] A massive deployment of armed forces and security arrangements at Chittagong failed to yield information about the absconders. An official admitted that 'the authority of the Governments has ceased to function in Chittagong'.[28] Fairweather despaired of planting informers on 'the most active terrorist party in Barisal'.[29] A sudden spurt of threatening, annonymous letters and leaflets led to another round of retaliatory violence. On 16 September a minor scuffle between terrorist personnel and guards at Hijli prison resulted in firing within the gaol. When detenus, trapped within the prison, tried to escape from the firing by attacking the guards, a massive bout of firing ensued within the main building. Even the official inquiry report commented on its indiscriminate nature. Baker, the governor of the prison, wrote to his father: 'Most of the firing is held to be unjustified as indeed it was'.[31] Two young detenus, Tarakeswar Sen Gupta and Santosh Kumar Mitra, died in the firing. Rabindranath echoed the general sense of shock and fury when he wrote a poem to express his anguish over the episode. The poem said, 'Even God would not find it possible to forgive this'.[32] Baker had to be sneaked out of Hijli to escape revenge. He was sent on a year long round-the-world cruise to calm his nerves.[33]

Several new features characterized developments within revolutionary terrorism. There was a constant intermingling of local-level Congress volunteer actions with terrorist techniques. This made it impossible to fix responsibility for certain kinds of activities on either the Congress or terrorists in a definite manner; the cutting of telegraph wires in Contai or Munshiganj subdivision in Dacca for instance.[34] Bombs were found at the Congress office at Gobindpur in Faridpur in August.[35] A large number of districts sent in reports

[27] *Robert Reid Papers.*

[28] GOI, Home Poll 291 31 of 1931.

[29] GOI, Home Poll 163 1931.

[30] *Fortnightly Reports on Bengal*, first half of August 1931, GOI, Home Poll 18–8–1931.

[31] Letter of 2 November 1931. Also Official Enquiry Committee Report by Justices S.C Mallik and J.G. Drummond. *E.B.H. Baker Papers*, CSASC.

[32] *Prashna* (Question), December 1931, *Sanchaita* (4th edn.), (Calcutta 1943), p. 609.

[33] Baker Travel Diaries, *Baker Papers.*

[34] *Fortnightly Reports on Bengal*, second half of April 1931. GOI, Home Poll 18–4/1931.

[35] GOB, Confdl, Poll Poll 345 (1–17) of 1931.

of arson, bomb-throwing and assaults in which young Congress volunteers were implicated.[36]

A major departure occurred in December 1931 when two teenaged schoolgirls assassinated Stevens, the District Magistrate of Comilla. Women had helped terrorists and had been active participants in the Civil Disobedience movement even earlier. Many of these activities still could be seen as extensions of the traditional feminine role of nurture: sheltering terrorist fugitives, for instance. In Gandhian movements conformity to the rule of non-violence did not make political action a very drastic transgression of the feminine role. The action against Stevens implied a radical break with established norms of politicization and with the received wisdom about women's functions.

Internment of detenus in remote rural areas was a startlingly new experience for most of them. Shantimoy Roy, a Jugantar activist, was isolated in the extremely inaccessible Sunderban forests. Forced to spend so much time in a completely new milieu, he began to take night classes in adult literacy among local people.[94] Chittagong villages became the main hiding-place for the Armoury raiders and absconders under Surya Sen. They began to develop unexpectedly close relations with villagers for the first time (see next chapter). Satyendranarayan Majumdar, an Anushilanite of Rajshahi, had already become interested in the possibilities of mass-level work. He began to work among the hill tribes in terai areas on his own and made some contact with young Rajbanshi peasants. Gandhi Singh, a young peasant, was even enrolled into the local secret committee—an extremely unusual development in terrorist circles.[38] Marxist theories began to make greater sense in this situation. An Intelligence Branch report commented on 'a sudden thirst for knowledge of Communist theory and history' among Bengali terrorists.[39] On the whole, however, these developments had yet to be reflected on the level of practice which continued to follow well-worn paths. The major functions of terrorists in this year was to sustain an alternative course of violent resistance when the Congress was formally committed to peace.

[36] *Fortnightly Reports on Bengal*, second half of June, 1931. GOI, Home Poll 18–6/1931.

[37] My interview.

[38] Satyendranarayan Majumdar, *Amar Biplab Jignasha* (Calcutta, 1973) pp. 180–1.

[39] *India and Communism*, confidential report by H. Williamson, Intelligence Bureau, Home GOI, 1933, *Hallet Collection*, MSS EUR 251, 33 (IOL).

Chittagong Riots

The Gandhi–Irwin Pact was popularly interpreted as a Government defeat. This perception created acute anxieties among the police and administrative personnel as did the relentless chain of terrorist actions. Deliberations about the grant of provincial autonomy sapped their sagging morale even further and undermined confidence in the Government's ability to give them adequate protection in the future.[40]

Uncertainties exploded with extraordinary savagery in the Chittagong incidents of 1931. Officially classified as a communal riot, the episode requires a separate analysis for an understanding of its different dimensions. Ashanullah, a police officer, who was notorious for his brutality against political suspects, was assassinated on 30 August by a young boy in Chittagong town. That very evening some senior police officers called a Muslim gathering on the Kotwali (police station) grounds. An eye-witness later recorded that 'two Muslim police officers delivered violently anti-Hindu and instigatory speeches'[41] to stir up the Muslim crowd. A campaign of terror was unleashed that night against all Hindus with nationalist records in the town. Pleaders defending Armoury Raid convicts and men working in the local nationalist press, the *Panchajanya*, were rounded up for torture. Europeans and officials organized the entire campaign quite openly. Hirenderlal Chowdhury, in charge of the press, was beaten up very severely. He recognized Baker, Signalling Engineer in the Assam-Bengal Railways, as one of the assailants. Baker also personally supervised the systematic destruction of the press machinery. Other political suspects were tortured in the presence of Shooter, the Assistant Superintendent of Police, and several other Europeans. An old man, the father of a suspect, later died from the injuries he had sustained. Several Europeans, assisted by armed Gurkha bands, assaulted a woman.[42]

Official investigations (which were never published) entirely bore out nationalist allegations. The enquiry report admitted that sixteen to eighteen European Special Constables went to the press building to 'ensure that it ceased to function as a press'. Whoever was found on the premises was beaten up. Press furniture and machinery were smashed by hammers brought over from the Rail-

[40] GOB, Home Confdl, Poll Poll 345 (1–17) of 1931.

[41] Walliullah, *Yugavachitra*, p. 20.

[42] *Report of the Non-official Enquiry Committee* under Sengupta, Sasmal and others, 29 Sept 1931. *E.B.H. Baker Papers.*

way Store. District Magistrate Kemm admitted that he knew about the raid but had done nothing to prevent it. The official report confessed: 'The truth is, that in beating up the press, they were neither Auxiliary force nor special constables but an unlawful assembly'. It also admitted that young men were rounded up at night and brought to the police station—'It is not denied that they were rounded up and beaten under the orders of the Superintendent of Police.'[43]

The riots that followed this lasted till 2 September. Nur Ahmad, Chairman of the Municipality, described how the District Magistrate and European sergeants refused help to Hindu victims and egged on Muslim crowds. Local Muslims looted Hindu shops on a fairly large scale but attacks on persons were exclusively the work of Europeans. Several raids were carried out in neighbouring villages like Guatoli, Sheroatoli, Kanungopara, Sripur and Popadia. Not a single Muslim villager participated in them. Joint peace committees were set up at Chittagong town and 'well placed and influential' Muslims gave shelter and every assistance to Hindus.[44]

The origin of the violence thus becomes clear. Muslim and European police officers tried to make communal capital out of Ashanullah's assassination by making inflammatory anti-Hindu speeches on police premises. Before a riot could actually get going, these officers themselves went on the rampage under the cover of the night. Acording to the official report the next morning 'the entire police force were preoccupied with the funeral (Ashanullah's) arrangements.' Rioters took advantage of this seemingly innocent preoccupation to move into action. Since the funeral was being held within the town itself, it is exceedingly strange that the police took three whole hours to reach the riot-stricken localities from there. The episode finds a grim parallel with the very similar development of anti-Sikh violence in Delhi in November 1984: the entire police force of the capital remained busy with a funeral, not for several hours, but for several days.

Up to the morning of 31 August, therefore, the so-called communal rioting was entirely a police and European offensive; from the morning of 31 August the police left the scene. The subsequent pattern of events more or less followed the model of Dacca riots of

[43] Letter from Chief Secretary, GOB, No. 4034 PS 23 November 1931, enclosing Report of Enquiry by Commissioner, Chittagong Division on 30/8 Disturbances. GOI, Home Poll 4/49/1932.

[44] *Report of the Non-official Enquiry Committee.*

May 1930. From 11 that morning the city poor moved in to snatch Hindu property from which official protection had been openly removed. Reports made prominent mention of looting by 'mainly Mohammadans of the labouring class, including many from villages on the outskirts of the town'. Looting began at Anderkilla Bazar where Bengali Hindu and Marwari shops were set on fire. It soon spread to other bazars: Chowkbazar, Tamaku Mandi, Bakshir Hat.[45] Altogether 280 shops were looted and two were gutted. Goldsmiths, moneylenders and cloth merchants were the biggest losers. Total damage was estimated to be about Rs 10 lakhs.[46] There were no attacks on people, no murder or rape. Within the town there seemed to be remarkable solidarity among men of property from both communities. The official inquiry report concluded with a strong criticism of the local authorities. The Government, consequently, decided not to publish the report. Even then it had to record 'severe censure against Mr Lewis, Captain Yati and Mr Nangle . . . . It was also decided to issue a general warning to all Magistrates and Police Officers that such excesses must cease'. At the end, however, it was decided to understand and to forgive all. 'Government took into account the special circumstances. Faced by dangerous and elusive gangs of murderers the officers had at a moment of extreme exasperation taken the law into their own hands and committed excess for which the menace of terrorism . . . furnished strong extenuation in a case like this . . . the officers were tried beyond endurance.'[47]

Great fear lay behind such outbursts. Even though official policy towards Civil Disobedience would be dictated in large measure by the change in British Govenment in London, these episodes still go to show that local experiences shaped subsequent decisions to a significant extent.

Peasant Action

Agrarian prices continued to plunge throughout 1931. Some districts suffered more severely than others: Mymensingh, Dacca, Rangpur, Tippera, Faridpur, Rajshahi, Pabna and Bogra. Floods badly damaged crops in August in some of these places and Govern-

[45] GOI, Home Poll 4/49 of 1932.

[46] GOI, Home Poll 4/48 of 1932.

[47] Letter from Chief Secretary GOB, No. 23 January 1932. GOI, Home Poll 4/49/1932.

ment relief measures were woefully meagre.[48] A very slight and temporary price rise around October did not bring about any marked change in the situation.[49] A rapid erosion of peasant property occurred, thanks to distress sales or eviction. 'There is a very real danger that through the operation of the civil laws a large proportion of the cultivators' land will be lost to them.'[50]

The severe shortage of cash led not only to grave problems of rent and debt payments but also to a crisis in peasant purchasing power. They suffered as consumers of articles whose prices had not declined correspondingly while the prices fetched by their own products had crashed. The looting of *hats* or bazars which stocked these relatively expensive articles was thus an expression of a threatened consumer consciousness. These *hats* or weekly bazars were places which knitted together localities, even distant villages, into networks of exchange. They provided the area where the bulk of peasant products would be sold off and most of their consumer necessities would be purchased. These were, therefore, focal points in their existence, in their ordering of weekly time, in the regulation of their economic activities, and in providing space and time for socialization. They were also the windows that opened on to the world outside; a place where information about general price trends could be gathered and strategies of production and consumption discussed. A major dimension of village social life, the *hats* were also centres of dissemination of wider and more general information. When sales and purchases had been made, people would relax, meet others and exchange gossip and news. Within this periodic collectivity, grievances would be aired, joint decisions reached and action decided on and carried out fairly rapidly.

The uneven and unbalanced price structure would have been criticized, *hat* after *hat*, ever since the agrarian depression had begun. Looting very often began after a certain price had been offered and rejected. An outraged sense of fair deal thus motivated such action. A careful discrimination in the choice of targets reflected this. The entire market was very seldom looted. Shops that stocked the more expensive items were selected for attack. Occasionally lootings were large-scale and planned, when armed gangs attacked and

48 *Fortnightly Reports on Bengal*, 1st half of August, 1931, GOI, Home Poll 18–8/1931.

49 *Fortnightly Reports on Bengal*, 1st half of October, 1931, GOI, Home Poll 18–10–1931.

50 *Report on the Land Revenue Administration, (1930–31)*, p. 6.

looted systematically. Unlike ordinary dacoity, however, these were all done in broad daylight with no attempt at concealment. Sporadic violence was sometimes replaced with greater method and organization when buyers banded together to boycott a particular shop or a particularly expensive item for a long stretch of time. Since *hats* would be owned mostly by zamindars or big traders who, in any case, would own the largest stalls, these episodes could form a part of a broader anti-zamindar or anti-trader incident. Religious hostility against *hat* owners-cum-landlords could become an additional contributory reason.

At Gurudaspur village at Natore in Rajshahi in January, the looted *hat* belonged to the Hindu zamindar of Shitalai. The whole village had been in a state of tension since the Pabna communal riots of 1926. Paddy prices had declined very sharply at Agartala in Tippera but the price of fish, a staple in local diet, remained very high. Local people of this hill area had been particularly hard hit when prices of cotton and sesamum products (whose cultivation constituted the main part of their livelihood) were halved. The entire Tripur community began to picket fish shops so successfully that sales of fish in the entire area were stopped. Cossipore fish shops in the 24 Parganas were looted by local Muslims in February after their request to lower fish prices had been turned down. Similar action had already led to a fall in prices in a number of neighbouring *hats*. A spate of *hat* looting occurred in February at Jhenaidah in Jessore and at Ghoraghat and Atwari thanas in Dinajpur: all of them related to the price of fish.[51] It is significant that such a large number of incidents should centre around the price of fish. Next to rice, fish is, or used to be, a standard item in Bengali meals. It was valued as the main source of protein nutrition, for ritual purposes and as an index to the family's economic viability. Access to it could therefore be seen as a right, a legitimate claim whose denial justified violence.

It is possible to identify faces among the seemingly anonymous mob of looters—not thugs but 'low class' local people at Narua, Senapur and Baharpur in Faridpur openly looted *hats*, particularly fish stalls in February as part of a general protest against the high prices of ghee, fish, betel leaves and earthen pots. At Tangail in Mymensingh, peasants organized themselves in bands and roamed around, looting stalls that sold salt, kerosene and jaggery. Local money lenders had stopped all credit operations at Comilla. In late

[51] *Bangabani*, 4 January, 8 February, 16 February and 25 February 1931.

February there were large-scale attacks on shops over high kerosene prices. At Munshiganj subdivision in Dacca, a band of fifty peasants, acutely affected by the lack of credit facilities, attacked a *hat* at Tangibari in late March and looted clothes and certain food items.[52] *Hat* looting declined, as a widely-used form of action, over the later part of the year. More organized forms of protest emerged, subsuming these sporadic outbursts.

Rents and loans were difficult to pay up under conditions of distress. Rajshahi peasants refused to pay back agricultural loans in late April.[53] A large and furious crowd gathered at Shahghata in Gaibandha (Rangpur district) in June and demanded a more equitable distribution of Government loans. Gurkha troops had to be brought out to disperse the crowd.[54] Donovan, the Barisal Collector, commented on the trend in his travel diary: 'There is a combination here not to pay rents this year.'[55]

Refusal to pay rent was not simply a blind, instinctive reflex action, triggered off by economic difficulties. Peasants sought to articulate the meaning of such actions. They made certain departures in the very concept of rent, and in their understanding of rural power relations. Falling prices usually lead to customary pleas for rent reduction and relief. These pleas are tied to a recognition and acceptance of the absolute rights of the zamindar to peasant rent. Such pleas were not uncommon in this period of hardship. At the same time there seemed to be in the making some new notions (or, perhaps, a modified version of old expectations lying deeply buried in collective memory) about mutual obligations and responsibilities. Tenants of the Tepa zamindari at Rangpur made an extremely interesting statement: 'As they (tenants) had practically *maintained* their zamindar for many years the latter should consider it their *duty* to *pay back* some of the money in the years of hardship'. (italics mine).[56] The statement seems to indicate something of a transitional stage in the peasant world-view. It has moved away from an acceptance of the absolute right of the landlord, a right that he alone can modify according to his own discretion. The notion of mutual reciprocity has become more important as the underpinning of the natural order, equally binding on both sides. When the

52 Ibid, 11 February, 23 February, 24 February, 30 March 1931.

53 *Fortnightly Reports on Bengal*, 2nd half of April 1931. GOI, Home Poll 18–4/1931.

54 *The Amrita Bazar Patrika*, 23 June 1931 in *R N P* Bengal, week ending 27 June 1931.

55 *Donovan Papers* (CSASC), Monthly Travel Diary, entry for 17 April 1931.

56 *Report on the Land Revenue Administration*, p. 20.

landlord continues to extort rent in times of great distress, he violates his obligations and oversteps his rights. The notion of mutual obligations encompasses, however, a half-articulated questioning of this natural order itself. A basic and inequitous asymmetry in land relations, where the peasant's obligations are necessarily much heavier than the landlord's, is hinted at even when the peasant seems to talk of a fair natural order; he expresses this ambivalence when he says that he has 'maintained' his landlord so far. This comprehension, fleetingly attained, does not immediately lead to a serious questioning of the concept of mutuality. The tenant also seeks to invest rent with new attributes which make it appear more as a deposit placed with the zamindar which may be withdrawn at times of crisis. The statement as a whole is ambiguous and polyseimic: diverse, even contradictory, notions and levels of consciousness are collapsed and packed together.

The Congress remained faithful to its stand on agrarian protest. The usual social inhibitions were strengthened this year by the compulsions of the Pact. Prafulla Chandra Sen, the Gandhian leader from Arambagh, tried to organize an anti-settlement movement in November. He insisted that the slump had made it impossible for local peasants to bear the cost of settlement operations. There were fundamental problems with the very nature of the settlement itself. 'Settlement will in all probability cause the enhancement of rents and other cesses which at such a time will mean the exploitation of the poor and middle class peasants'. Jawaharlal, however, advised him to negotiate with the Government rather than launch a movement.[57]

The few Communists, who were still at large after the Meerut swoop, kept away from the rural scene. Harry G. Lynd, the Comintern agent, who came to India in February, laid down the line that the Communists should not work among the peasants directly but, rather, recruit them through work among mill-hands who had peasant origins and links.[58] The Communists, therefore, reaped no immediate benefit from the agrarian crisis and from an increasingly restive countryside.

While neither Congress leaders nor Communists were interested in a radical peasant movement, it is interesting that the men who

[57] Letter from Sen to Nehru, 12/11/31 and reply from Nehru, 16/11/31. *AICC Papers* P–6 of 1927/31.

[58] Dharani Goswami, *Ekti Krishak Bidroher Kahini, Parichay*, 1969.

were groping towards it were almost always described in Government reports as Congressmen preaching 'Bolshevik' ideas. A Ryots' Conference was held at Somra in Hooghly in May where a 'leading Communist' presided over an anti-landlord meeting.[59] Some local Congress leaders of Rajshahi tried to stir up Khas Mahal tenants in June. One of them even tried to mobilize Muslim tenants against a local landlord. Reports came in from several Eastern Bengal districts about a no-rent propaganda in December.[61] A large processison was taken out at Nadia with banners declaring: 'The land belongs to him who ploughs it'.[62] Much of this work was done by local leaders acting more or less on their own without any particular political affiliation, or by local Congressmen who decided to overstep the limits set by their headquarters. In the context of the deepening agrarian crisis their slogans and activities smacked of Bolshevism to an already nervous Government.

Such activities found a most fertile soil in Tippera. Located in Chittagong Division, Tippera is a well cultivated plain with highly alluvial soil, watered by numerous streams and rivers. Abundant rainfall made irrigation almost unnecessary.[63] The percentage of net cultivated area of land under double cropping was among the highest in Bengal.[64] Natural advantages put a high premium on land. Land disputes were common and fierce, leading quite often to riots and arson. A lot of land was under petty proprietors and permanent tenure-holders but the bulk was cultivated by tenants most of whom had occupancy rights.[65] Namasudras and Muslims were numerically preponderant among tenants and their numbers were growing. Both were hard-working, ambitious groups, keen on education and social upliftment.[66]

The spate of land or tenancy purchase which usually left little cash in peasant hands (but which denoted his prosperity and landholding rather than poverty) came to a rude halt when the slump wiped out

[59] GOI, Home Poll 35/50 of 1931.

[60] *Fortnightly Reports on Bengal*, 1st half of May 1931. GOI, Home Poll 18/5/1931.

[61] *Fortnightly Reports on Bengal*, 1st half of December 1931. GOI, Home Poll 18–12/1931.

[62] *Tegart Papers*.

[63] G. Webster, *District Gazetteer of Eastern Bengal; Tippera* (Allahabad, 1910).

[64] *Report of the Land Revenue Commission*, Vol. I, Appendix IX, Table I.

[65] *District Gazetteer of Eastern Bengal: Tippera*.

[66] E. Thompson, *Final Report on the Survey and Settlement Operations, Tippera* (Calcutta, 1920), p. 29.

profits from rice and jute cultivation. Credit became extremely difficult to obtain, even though, compared to Dacca or Mymensingh, interest rates were still quite low.[67] Thanks to the growing value of lands, rents had been rising over a long time and now their payment became a critical problem. Sahas and other non-cultivating trader-castes, on the other hand, continued to enjoy growing affluence. They had been buying up large numbers of intermediate tenures out of their commercial profits and many of them now evolved as considerable proprietors. Muslim and Namasudra cultivators, in contrast, very rarely had any trading interests.[68] The depression thus cancelled all the advantages which the Tippera peasant had. At the same time it aggravated existing structural imbalances. The crisis was one of threatened prosperity rather than one of growing poverty.

A Krishak Samiti (later renamed the Tippera Peasants' and Workers' Samiti) had been in existence at Comilla from 1919. Concerned, at first, with rather specific and limited tenant demands, it had become more or less defunct in the prosperous early 1920s. The entire picture changed from 1930; the heavy spate of borrowing at high interest rates in order to buy lands or tenancies came to an abrupt halt. Rice and jute prices crashed and in 1930 a flood washed away the entire crop at Brahmanbaria. The Samiti was quickly reactivated and considerably radicalized. Its leaders included Hindus and Muslims in equal numbers. Maulvi Mukleswar Rahman, Krishna Sundar Bhowmick, Maulvi Abdul Malek and Kamini Kumar Datta were the brains behind the movement and its chief financiers. Datta was an established pleader at Comilla town but he often went out to local villages to organize anti-Government meetings. A number of local Congress leaders like Hemprobha and Basanta Majumdar also became involved in a 'vilification campaign against the propertied classes.'[69] One of the first gestures of the reconstituted Samiti was to organize a huge procession of Comilla labourers and peasants from nearby villages to celebrate May Day. Men brandished the professional tools of their classes; ploughs, brooms, spades as well as banners proclaiming 'Down with the British Government'. A number of meetings were held to discuss a wide variety of issues: representation of cultivators on Councils,

[67] It was 24 per cent per annum, GOB, *Report of the Bengal Provincial Banking Committee, 1929–1930, Vol. I, 1930.*

[68] *District Gazetteer of Eastern Bengal: Tippera.*

[69] GOB, Home Confdl Poll, Confidential Branch -849/31 (1–9) of 1931.

release of Meerut prisoners, reduction of Union Board rates, and, most concrete of all, limiting the interest rate to a maximum of 6 per cent per annum. Muslim cultivators attended these meetings in large numbers.

An early issue from which the movement and the organization gathered strength was a dispute over the management of a market at Barura which was owned by the Law estate. Asimuddin Ahmad organized a boycott of the market and peasants eventually set up another market themselves. A no-rent campaign became very powerful at Nabinagar and Kasba thanas at Brahmanbaria. Samiti branches were opened at most villages and in some almost all ranks of villagers would enrol except the moneylenders. Samitis started a concerted social boycott of all moneylenders and demanded a surrender of loan contracts. A few mahajans were frightened enough to comply. Agricultural labourers were strictly forbidden to work under landlords wherever the no-rent movement was in progress. Intimidation checked the import of outside labour. Arbitration courts were set up to punish any violation of these arrangements. It is interesting to note how local Congressmen made effective use of Congress devices like social boycott and arbitration courts but used them in the service of a radical agrarian movement. Speakers urging 'socialist' or 'communist' doctrines were brought in from Calcutta. The Islamic dogma against usury was used to build up hostility against moneylenders, among indebted Muslim tenants. Meetings were usually held on Fridays after the Juma prayers near the mosque.[70]

Mahajans and landlords set up a Shanti Rakshini Bahini (Society for Preserving Peace) at Nabinagar. Its Secretary warned the Bengal Government about the spread of 'rank Bolshevism'. He wrote that the movement sought to combine all Muslim tenants against Hindu landlords, mahajans and traders. A major form of action was the boycott of a large number of zamindar-owned local bazars which now lost their supply lines. It is significant how very different forms of peasant struggles used the *hats* and bazars as their main arena. Payments of arrears of rent and debt had also been suspended. Landlords and mahajans were intimidated when they wanted to go to court to seek redress. 'Dispossession of land and cutting away of paddies' were also practised.[71]

[70] Letter from N.C. Bose to Tippera District Magistrate, 26 December, 1931—Confdl D.O. No. 100IC.

[71] Letter from Anil Behari Datta, Secretary, Shanti Rakshini Samiti, Nabinagar, Tippera, 4 December 1931 to Poll Secretary, GOB.

Towards the end of 1931 the movement crossed the district boundaries and began to spread into Noakhali and other adjoining districts. 'Some of the organizers of the peasant movement are Congressmen but they have no influence in Congress circles', wrote the District Magistrate of Noakhali. 'The fact is that local leaders of the Congress moved me to take drastic action against the organizers of the Peasants' meeting...'.[72] It is important to note that this letter was written at the beginning of 1932. Congress leaders therefore solicited Government help at a time when the second round of Civil Disobedience had already begun.

[72] Letter from Noakhali District Magistrate to Under-Secretary GOB, Poll Deptt. Poll Branch, Noakhali, 28 January 1932.

CHAPTER 4

1932–1934

The Soothing Shadow of the Big Rod[1]

'Civil Martial Law' was a complex of measures to combat the second round of Civil Disobedience. More than reflecting the attitudes of the new National Government in Britain, it was a response to experiences of the earlier movement within India.[1a] The framing of the policy in Bengal coincided with the Governorship of Anderson. The new Governor had served a ruthless apprenticeship in Ireland and he ably applied the lessons in Bengal, much to the relief of his demoralized colleagues.[2] Civil Martial Law was bolstered up by a free use of military forces. The 'pre-emptive strike', designed to smash the movement before it got off the ground, was complemented with more subtle forms of deterrents. The Government used increasingly sophisticated forms of propaganda to reassert its waning hegemony.

Between 1 January and 27 January 1932, 2670 men and women were convicted and 977 were committed as undertrials.[3] As many as 272 institutions were declared illegal within Bengal alone by the second week of January 1932.[4] The police systematically smashed

[1] Rajshekhar Basu, *Ulatpuran*, *Parasuram Granthabali*, Vol II (Calcutta 1969).

[1a] D.A. Low, *Civil Martial Law* in Low (ed.), *Congress and the Raj* (London, 1977).

[2] Reid, a senior official in the Bengal Government, recalled fondly the relief of having a strong man at the helm in those difficult days: the voluble admiration was close to what the public school fags had for their tough and manly seniors, *Robert Reid Papers*, MSS EUR E 248/2 (*a-c*), IOL.

[3] *Fortnightly Reports on Bengal*, 2nd half of January 1932, GOI, Home Poll 18/1/1932.

[4] *Bangabani*, 16 January 1932.

each salt-making attempt.[5] Public parks were closed to meetings[6] and all meetings and processions were dispersed by large bodies of armed police.[7] Even a 'charak sankranti' procession, part of a traditional religious celebration, led to shooting when Diwanganj villagers at Arambagh took one out in defiance of police orders.[8] Large-scale arrests and extraordinary police precautions aborted several district conferences.[9] Thé Congress session in Calcutta, planned for March 1933, was squashed by a police crackdown.[10] Within a month, there were three cases of firing: at the Nadia District Conference in June 1932,[11] at Masuria village at Contai in July when several people were shot dead, and within a few days of it, at Bandagora village in Midnapur in the course of the no-chowkidari tax movement.[12]

It was not enough to throttle the movement by removing active Congressmen and terrorists. More important was to squeeze dry the field of potential support and sympathy, to starve both forms of struggle of every kind of sustenance. The Bengal Government armed itself with twenty separate Acts and employed seven Government Departments to carry out the anti-terrorist campaign: Political, Judicial, Jail, Finance, Revenue, Education and Local Self-government.[13] Additional Government expenditure to combat terrorism alone rose from Rs 21,50,000 in 1931–2 to Rs 47,00,000 in 1932–3. In 1933–4 it further went up to Rs 53,75,000.[14]

Punitive police forces were deployed and collective fines were imposed on troublesome areas as both warning and punishment. Chittagong town and seven adjoining villages were bound down to pay the collective tax.[15] Tamluk and Sutahata in Midnapur,[16]

5 *The Amrita Bazar Patrika*, 22 April 1932.

6 GOB *Report on the Administration in Bengal, 1931–32* (Calcutta, 1933), p. 11.

7 For an account, see, for instance, *The Amrita Bazar Patrika*, 20 April 1932.

8 Ibid, 22 April 1932.

9 Ibid, 14 June 1932.

10 *Fortnightly Reports on Bengal*, 2nd half of March, 1933. GOI, Home Poll, 18 April 1933.

11 *The Amrita Bazar Patrika*, 9 August 1932.

12 Entries for 4 July and 12 July 1932, N.P. Mitra (ed.), *Indian Quarterly Register*, Vol. I, 1932 (Calcutta, 1932).

13 Anderson's report of 14 February, 1934. *Templewood Collection*, MSS EUR E 240/9 (IOL).

14 *Robert Reid Papers*.

15 *Fortnightly Reports on Bengal*, 2nd half of October, 1932. GOI, Home Poll, 18/13/32.

16 *Report on the Administration of Bengal*, p. 12.

Arambagh in Hooghly and Sonamukhi in Bankura also had the awesome punitive police posted on them (mostly Pathan Muslims in predominantly Hindu areas to increase communal divisions).[17] Six battalions of troops, including one British infantry battalion, were posted at Dacca, Comilla, Mymensingh, Rangpur, Bankura and Midnapur[18] to comfort overwrought nerves of officials.

The Acts, Ordinances and battalions notwithstanding, the British lion still seemed shorn of much of its former majesty. Crowds clashed with the police quite often, tax collection remained unsatisfactory and terrorism continued to spread, even among young women. An acknowledgement of their dwindling authority intensified the importance of customary rituals of obedience and deference. Midnapur villagers were forced to salute the British flag during route marches of troops, send 'dalis' or baskets of gifts and attend 'durbars' put up during these marches. Defiance led to flogging, loss of property, even rape.[19] Earlier the whole point about such genuflection had been their seemingly voluntary nature; a casual, absent-minded acknowledgement of these salutations, that seemed to pour forth spontaneously and willingly, setting forth most forcefully the well-established patterns of authority and obedience. A temporary breakdown of these patterns was both reflected in and necessitated the forced enacting of charades that had lost all meaning. A similar preoccupation with public spectacles to signify glory at a time when mass-level movements challenged their hegemony, probably led to the architectural expansion at New Delhi in the 1920s and early 1930s, and the Coronation fanfare of 1935. Such constant reiterations of loyalty were self-defeating. Not only were they painful reminders of the substance whose shadow they had become, they also stiffened and spread hostility among villagers from whom such acts were expected. 'I believe they increase hatred for the flag', wrote Bamford of the flag salutation parades, 'I do not mean that it . . . need involve bullying but I have little doubt that in practice it does'. Eventually Viceroy Willingdon tactfully suggested to Anderson that he should de-emphasize these measures.[20]

Coercion was not the only strategy to be employed. The Govern-

[17] *The Amrita Bazar Patrika*, 22 June 1932.

[18] *Fortnightly Reports on Bengal*, 2nd half of September, 1932. GOI, Home Poll 18/12/32.

[19] GOI,Home Poll 22/3/34 of 1934.

[20] GOI, Home Poll 55/34 of 1934.

ment seemed to have taken a leaf out of the Congress book to use propaganda in a loyalism restoration drive. Magic lantern and film shows were taken to villages for 'anti-Civil Disobedience' propaganda. Local officials and prominent non-officials organized lecture tours. Vigilance committees were set up by local bigwigs to guard against infiltration by the Congress and terrorists.[21] District level intelligence officers and Military Intelligence officers were advised to spend all their time in villages.[22] A Civil Obedience campaign was launched at Mymensingh.[23] The Government wanted to set up a Publicity Board where officials and prominent non-officials would come together for anti-terrorist propaganda work. The Board was to publish articles to counteract seditious literature and organize public lectures and meetings to justify Government action. Among prospective non-official members, the names of B.M. Sen (Principal, Presidency College) and Jadunath Sarkar (Vice Chancellor, Calcutta University and a leading historian) were proposed.[24] The Boy Scout institution was encouraged to catch schoolboys young, before they fell prey to terrorist recruitment.[25] Military officers suggested another expedient to absorb and channelize dangerous energies of schoolboys: organized games and house-system based competitive extra-curricular activities in schools.[26] The reproduction of certain public school traditions, albeit on a miniature scale, was expected to produce defenders of the Empire on the playgrounds of Bengali schools. All anti-nationalist elements and tendencies were thus put together to work with the Government machinery of repression and propaganda. It was a desperate mobilization of all possible resources. By the beginning of 1933 the Government at last felt itself coming out on top and in a stronger position than at any time since 1929.[27]

Civil Disobedience—Second Phase

The abrupt switching on and off, of the Civil Disobedience move-

[21] GOB, Home Confidential, Poll Poll 607 (1–15) of 1933.

[22] GOI, Home Poll 27/14/34 of 1934.

[23] Special AICC Bulletin, May 1932, *AICC Papers*, P 35/1932.

[24] GOB, Home Confdl., Poll Poll 384 (1–15) of 1932.

[25] Sir R.N. Mookerji, the loyalist industrialist, praised its 'salutary influence'. *The Statesman*, 13 January 1932. See also *Mr and Mrs Taylor Papers* (CSASC) for a letter from Mymensingh, 18 December 1934, describing the institution as an effective antidote to terrorism.

[26] *Robert Reid Papers*.

[27] *Report on the Administration of Bengal, 1932–33* (Calcutta, 1934), p. 1.

ment, dictated by the course of Gandhi's negotiations with the Government, fatally disrupted its development. When the Round Table negotiations finally ended in a fiasco and another round of struggle seemed inevitable in December 1931, revival became difficult in the face of the massive Government onslaught. The second round of Civil Disobedience never properly got into its stride.

The Congress Working Committee announced its decision to revive the movement from 1 January 1932. The organization, however, was smashed by the 'pre-emptive strike' before its preparations could mature at all. As early as April Anderson described the movement as 'practically dead'.[28] There was a month by month decline in conviction figures, in contrast to the trend in the first round of Civil Disobedience.[29] This, of course, would be more a result of the magnitude of the initial swoop which put almost all volunteers and participants between bars immediately after the movement began. Mass Civil Disobedience had to be suspended from May 1933. From August 1933 even individual Civil Disobedience was practically dead; Gandhi decided to give it up and devote himself to harijan welfare. The Burdwan Divisional Commissioner gave a rather macabre description of the stray incidents that occasionally occurred after this, 'these are the nervous twitching of the limbs after the parent body has actually died.'[30]

Salt satyagraha remained confined mainly to Tamluk and Contai at Midnapur.[31] Tamluk satyagrahis sent advance notices to the local police before each salt-making campaign through 'challenge letters'[32]—a non-violent adaptation, perhaps, of a traditional dacoit practice. Nationalist hartals were formidable only at Arambagh and Midnapur[33], while picketing at Calcutta and mofussil towns became increasingly difficult since arrests and assaults depleted the reserves of volunteers.[34] Traders in general withdrew whatever support they had offered earlier, 'Merchants and traders have rallied to the support of the Government'.[35] The situation was a little better at Bankura and Midnapur but even at Midnapur,

[28] Anderson's letter of 9 April 1932. *Templewood Collection*.

[29] *Report on the Administration of Bengal*, p. 13.

[30] GOI, Home Poll 18/10/1933.

[31] *AICC Papers,* P 35/1932.

[32] Report by Kamini Bala Adhikary, Director, Tamluk War Council *AICC Papers 4/1932.*

[33] *Report on the Administration of Bengal*, 1932–33, p. 10.

[34] PCC Report of 26 May 1932, *AICC Papers, 13/1932.*

[35] GOB, Home Confdl., Poll Poll FN 424/(1–19) of 1932.

bazar merchants drew up a charter in May 1933, supporting 'free trade'. 'This rapprochement', commented a Government report, 'between the trading and official communities is a welcome sign'.[36] The rapprochement continued much higher up as well. D.P. Khaitan, who was Birla's 'principal manager' and right-hand man, and who had so far been closely associated with nationalist activities, visited Anderson in May 1932: 'He left the distinct impression that whatever his attitude may have been in the past, he would be ready to co-operate with the Government in any constructive work'.[37] Traders' attitudes and decline of picketing did not, as yet, reverse the earlier import patterns. Boycott declined but it was not entirely dead. The sale of British piece-goods, sugar, paper, printing machinery and tobacco continued to decline and 'it is clear that the feeling of uncertainty created by the boycott, prejudices the placing of orders for new stocks.'[38]

Anti-Union Board and no-chowkidari tax struggles remained formidable at several places. The no-tax agitation was now broadened to include a refusal to pay the punitive tax. At Outshahi in Vikrampur, union courts were picketed almost entirely by women. At Tamluk 'female awakening' through the no-tax campaigns, picketing and processions was 'beyond expectation'.[39] The usual pattern earlier had been a flow of urban Congress women leaders into villages: now the movement depended much more on active participation, even leadership, by local women. Mahisya peasant or upper caste landholding families supplied most of the cadres. Kamini Bala Adhikary and Nitya Bale Gole were, for instance, 'dictators' of the Tamluk War Council.[40] Massive arrests of nationalist men, right at the beginning of the movement, necessitated such large-scale dependence on women. The public appearance of women from extremely conservative families and their daring political role did not lead to major upheaval within the domestic family structure. In fact the political participation of women, publicly and overtly, was in most cases approved by the family. This spelt a radical departure from the traditionally con-

[36] *Fortnightly Reports on Bengal*, 2nd half of June 1933. GOI, Home Poll 18/6/1933.

[37] Anderson's letter, 9 May 1932. *Templewood Collection.*

[38] *Fortnightly Reports on Bengal*, 2nd half of February 1932. GOI, Home Poll 18/4/1932.

[39] *The Challenge*, Calcutta, 29 August and 5 September 1932. *AICC Papers*, 4/1932.

[40] *The Amrita Bazar Patrika*, 14 June 1932. See also *AICC Papers*, Ibid.

servative social norms and values, and raises interesting questions on the relationship between politicization and emancipation, brought about by the national movement.

Remarkably enough, the revolution in womens' public role was accomplished without a corresponding change in the domestic milieu, personal relations or broader social rights for women. Neither was there any demand for such changes. Women saw their new role as the fulfilment of more traditional activities. Participation in the nationalist movement was perceived as more of a religious sacrifice.[41] Male comrades articulated and partly imposed this perception through a crop of nationalist literature which created an ideal type of the nationalist wife and mother whose public activities were actually meant to enrich domestic roles and duties.

No-tax led to large-scale confiscation and attachment of property. Half the subdivision withheld the payment of taxes at Arambagh between 1930 and 1933. The police in one case failed to take away attached properties since the local populace refused to provide them with means of transport. At another time properties actually had to be returned to owners as not a single person would bid for them at auctions.[42] The total value of properties attached for non-payment of taxes at Tamluk amounted to Rs 819.11 as. whereas the total amount of taxes due was Rs 107.2 as. The estimated loss of property at Arambagh was about Rs 10,000 for a total tax of Rs 300.[44] At Nadia, where the no-tax movement affected about ninety-eight villages, goods worth Rs 3068.10 as. were auctioned off for non-payment of taxes worth Rs 551.15 as. A large number of Union Boards and courts could not function at all.[45]

Arambagh villagers boycotted the Survey and Settlement operations. The arguments behind the boycott related mainly to the difficulties of bearing the expenses at a time of growing economic hardship. Small peasants also suspected that Settlement Officers, who accepted the hospitality of the village rich, would not conduct an impartial survey. About sixty villages were involved and opera-

[41] On this see Tanika Sarkar, 'Bengali Women and the Meaning of Politicization' *Indian Economic and Social History Review*, (1984).

[42] Hitesh Sanyal, *Arambage Jatiyatabadi Andolan, Anya Artha*, September-October 1974, p. 14.

[43] Civil Disobedience in Tamluk. *AICC Papers*, 4/1932.

[44] Arambagh War Council Report, Ibid.

[45] Nadia Jela Swadhinata Sangramer Itihas Rachana Samiti, *Swadhinata Sangrame Nadia*, pp. 176, 181.

tions had to be held up despite numerous raids, loot, arrests, torture and loss of property. At Nakunda village ten men were allegedly shut up for twenty-four hours in the April heat, without food or water in a 7 ft. × 5 ft. room. All the two hundred families of Talit village left home after sending prior notices to the Sub-Divisional Officer and feeding their standing crops to cattle.[46] During the agitations, Settlement operations had to be suspended in most villages. No transfer or eviction on the basis of new estimates and assessments could be made as long as the movement continued.[47]

Certain new forms of protest emerged particularly in cities and district towns during the flag-hoisting ceremony or through attempts to capture Government buildings. Every Monday, crowds, largely comprised of women, would rush to raise the national flag at the nearest official premises. Occasionally, quite large-scale efforts were made, again mostly by women, to take over the buildings and dislodge Government officers from them.[48] It was a fitting retort to random seizures of Congress offices. Both involved frequent clashes with the police and the employment of women was a device to minimize police assaults. There was also a simpler reason: lack of male adults in sufficient number due to earlier arrests.

The BPCC never formally sanctioned or initiated a no-rent movement. The police crackdown, however, had weakened central leadership and loosened its control over local branches and initiative. Many local-level leaders could no longer maintain their distance from peasant unrest now developing all around them. This was true even of disciplined Gandhian ashrams. These leaders found themselves waging an internal struggle: their internal discipline and fear of mob violence against the evidence of their own observations and their sympathies. Very often their sincere commitment to the cause of the rural poor would compel them to participate in local movements. At the end of 1932 rent suspensions had become 'rampant' at Arambagh 'and zamindars began to lodge complaints against defaulters'. At Kotalpur and Indas thanas in Bankura zamindars refused all applications for rent remission.[49] Landlords in Bankura had instituted more than 6000 suits against tenants who

[46] Arambagh War Council Report. *AICC Papers* 4/1932.

[47] Hitesh Sanyal, *Arambage Jatiyatabadi Andolan*.

[48] *Fortnightly Reports on Bengal*, 1st half of April 1932. GOI, Home Poll 18/6/1932. Also *Fortnightly Reports on Bengal*, 1st half of July 1932. GOI, Home Poll 18/10/1932.

[49] *AICC Papers* 4/1932.

were unable to pay rent because of the collapse of paddy prices.[50] All these places had powerful Gandhian centres, built largely upon their connections with poor peasants. The Arambagh Congress organ *Patra* grew stridently anti-zamindar in tone from 1932.[51] At Bankura 'a no-rent movement has been initiated in view of the economic distress prevailing in some of the villages'.[52] At Kotalpur and Patrasayar thanas at Bankura the Congress upheld peasant threats to withhold rent if no remission was granted.[53] A no-rent resolution was passed at the Atrai thana Congress Conference at Rajshahi on 22 August 1932.[54] Congress Committees at Jalpaiguri, Sylhet and Tippera, also encouraged these moves.[55] Tenants at Pathimpasha village of Bhanu Bill at south Sylhet had been locked in a long-drawnout conflict with their zamindar over rent. The Congress was trying to mediate when the police arrived there with elephants to eject Manipuri and Muslim tenants. The elephants trampled down their houses along with the Congress office.[56] Many of these tenants had been active in Civil Disobedience under the leadership of Baikuntha Sharma.[57] Such conjuncture between the Congress agitation and agrarian protest, was, however, infrequent and intermittent. Moreover, they were confined mainly to sound Gandhian bases where the training in discipline and non-violence would confine protest to appeals, petitions and efforts at arbitration. If a no-rent agitation was indeed unavoidable then at least it would remain non-violent.

As repression removed top-ranking leaders and turned every single form of satyagraha into a full-scale conflict, the composition of participants went through some significant changes. The proportion of urban, educated, middle class young men decreased even further, while participation by women from similar and also from rural peasant background increased. When the police fired on a crowd of satyagrahis at Munshiganj in Dacca, Muslim weavers joined in the fray and attacked the police.[58] Kalipada Das

[50] *Congress Bulletin* of 28 March 1932.

[51] Hitesh Sanyal, *Arambage Jatiyatabadi Andolan*.

[52] *The Challenge*, 29 August 1932.

[53] *The Challenge*, 20 June 1932.

[54] *The Challenge*, 29 August 1932.

[55] *Special AICC Bulletin,* March 1932. *AICC Papers* P 35/1932.

[56] *Amrita Bazar Patrika*, 20 April 1932.

[57] *AICC Papers* 4/1932.

[58] *Fortnightly Reports on Bengal*, 2nd half of January 1932. GOI, Home Poll 18/1/1932.

Karmakar, the third Dictator of the Arambagh war council, led a 'huge procession of workers and peasants' against the police station. The purpose, interestingly enough, was to celebrate May Day. On 2 May about a hundred Santals and 'other workers' went on a march at Dinajpur to hoist the national flag. Somra Bhagat, a tribal leader at Alipur Dooars in Jalpaiguri, had his house burnt down by the police when he insisted on disobeying an Emergency Notice in April 1932.[59] A handful of Congressmen at Noakhali had organized a procession at Hasanabad village in Tippera. When the police fired on the crowd a large number of villagers (Hindus and Muslims) joined the demonstrators and shouted *Bande Mataram* as well as *Allah O Akbar*.[60] A number of Santals from Akra, Balurghat subdivision at Dinajpur, violently resisted the arrest of some of their men on criminal charges, braving police fire. Officials claimed that they were all confirmed nationalists and attributed their resistance to the spirit of Civil Disobedience.[61]

Police firing killed several men during the National week celebrations at Masuria village in Tamluk in July 1932. The local Shabar community (untouchables and snake-charmers by profession) made up a song which they went around singing in other villages. The song cursed and abused the police and recalled the fate of Peddie, Douglas and Garlick. 'When brothers and sons of the land are dying why doesn't a single brick hurt you?' they asked. At Masuria, 'all the "babu-bhayas" are the adopted sons of the police', was their allegation.[62] It is interesting to note the way in which social superiors and anti-nationalist elements are conflated together, so that the same group is accused of a double crime. Popular perception identified nationalism with a rising essentially of the poor. This was a way of appropriating the movement as their own. It also provided fresh scope for questioning and indicting social enemies, and, by implication, the social order. A process of displacement shifted the basic charge of oppression to the charge of betrayal, since this would be a crime easier to identify with a broader and more general nationalist consensus.

Muslim participation in the movement was not negligible. Quite a

[59] *AICC Papers* 4/1932.

[60] *Bangabani*, 16 February 1932.

[61] *Fortnightly Reports on Bengal*, 1st half of July 1932. GOI, Home Poll 18/10/1932.

[62] Prabodh Chandra Basu, *Medinipur Jelar Bhagawanpur Thanar Itibritta*, p. 159.

high proportion of radical nationalist newspapers had Muslim proprietorship and almost exclusively Muslim circulation. *Al Kalam* (Urdu daily from Calcutta), *Hind-e-Jadid* (Urdu daily, Calcutta), *Abhijan* (Bengali monthly), *Azad* (Bengali weekly, Noakhali), *Hamdard* (Urdu daily, Calcutta), *Masik Mohammadi* (Bengali monthly, Calcutta), *Mohammadi* (Bengali weekly, Calcutta), *Moslem* (Bengali weekly, Calcutta), *Mussalman* (English daily, Calcutta) and *Watan* (Urdu daily, Calcutta)—all were described as 'Extremist' and had circulation figures above 1,000.[63]

Sufi Abdul Qadia, a pro-Government religious leader of the Ahmadiyya sect, was worried by the fact that 'there is a great deal of unorganized discontent among the Muslim peasantry' which might turn to the advantage of the Congress. Discontent was being stoked, he thought, by Muslim villagers who had begun to associate with detenus. Their ranks were swelled by a large influx of Deoband seminary students, who had recently returned to their home villages. Hussain Ahmad, an ex-student of Deoband, went to Calcutta to preach boycott and use of khadi. There was a strong possibility that 'the Mullahs in the mofussil, who are the products of Deoband are being influenced by him . . . in making anti-British propaganda in the village.'[64]

Civil Disobedience was particularly successful among Bogra Muslims. A district with the largest Muslim population in the province, Bogra was one of the most fertile tracts in the country, with a healthy climate and a small incidence of droughts and famines. It had a substantial body of small landholders and about 90 per cent of its tenants had occupancy rights. The number of landless peasants was growing but the total was still very small. The bulk of the labourers had to be imported from Rajshahi, Murshidabad and Nadia.[65] The unusual distribution of land and tenancy rights somewhat cushioned the effects of depression. This might have been a part of the reason behind the large-scale involvement of Muslim villagers in Civil Disobedience, an unprecedented development for a Muslim majority district.

On the whole, however, disjunction rather than co-operation was the rule. Dissociation became a serious problem for Hindu politicians of all hues when the Communal Award on electoral seat

[63] GOI, Home Poll 53/1/35 of 1935.

[64] GOI, Home Poll 39/11/1933.

[65] J.N. Gupta (ed.), *District Gazetteers of Eastern Bengal and Assam*: Bogra (Allahabad, 1910), pp. 31, 82, 87.

allocation was announced in 1932. The Poona Pact, a result of Gandhi's negotiations with Ambedkar, made their position worse. Of the eighty seats allotted to general Hindu constituencies, thirty were now reserved for untouchables or depressed castes. Caste Hindus were left with only fifty general constituencies as against 119 Muslim seats in a house of 250—a situation which put them permanently in a position of minority.[66]

The Bengal Congress decided to abide by Gandhi's decision and resigned itself to the situation rather than follow Malaviya out of the Congress. Congressmen, nevertheless, were deeply worried about electoral prospects, given the long-standing communication gap with untouchables and Muslims. The Bengal Hindu Sabha had conducted a campaign to protest against the Award and the Pact, arguing that the cultural and material importance of the Hindus should, in all fairness, outweigh the simple numerical superiority of Muslims. Eminent Hindus, including a number of nationalists, petitioned the Secretary of State to argue their case against the Communal Award. 'The Hindu minority of Bengal claim their due weightage of representation as a recognized Minority right'. The core of the argument referred to the 'enormously prominent part they (the Hindus) have played under British rule in the intellectual, cultural, political, professional and commercial life of the Province'. The petition also mentioned their superior contribution to provincial revenues which was far in excess of their proportional numerical strength. The Secretary of State was reminded that Hindus 'are overwhelmingly superior culturally while their economic preponderance is equally manifest'. Signatories, calling themselves 'representative Hindu leaders', were an interesting assortment: Rabindranath Tagore, Sir P.C. Ray, Rai Jatindra Nath Chowdhury (President, Bengal Provincial Hindu Sabha), Badridas Goenka (Director, Reserve Bank of India), Jugal Kishore Birla, Sarat Chandra Chatterji and many others.

Great anxieties were assiduously churned up by the Hindu press about Muslim assaults on the sexual purity of Hindu women. A Women Protection Committee of the Bengal Provincial Hindu Sabha was set up[67] to foster paranoid fears. 'Nari niryatan' or oppression of Hindu women became a recurrent motif; in North India the counterpart of women in Hindu propaganda would be the cow endangered by Muslim design. The Bengal Congress, which

[66] GOB, *Report on the Administration of Bengal 1931–32*, p. 27.

[67] *Akhil Bharatiya Hindu Mahasabha Papers*—G8 (NMML).

had close and amicable relations with the Hindu Sabha, did not initiate a counter-campaign to mitigate the effects of such propaganda.

The distance from the untouchables also boded ill for Congress electoral chances. Many Muslims and Namasudras of Faridpur had welcomed anti-Civil Disobedience measures. All over East Bengal 'backward castes' as a whole, remained indifferent to the movement.[68] The Congress tried to find ways out of the impasse. As after Chauri Chaura, there was by 1933–4 a bifurcation of energies into electoral work on the one hand, and rural welfare and harijan uplift work on the other. This time, however, Harijan welfare was a strategy designed largely to improve Congress electoral prospects. The aim of electoral politics, too, had changed. There was now a serious attempt to participate in government and seek political power, however limited, within the given system. Secretary of State, Hoare, wrote to Anderson in April 1933, 'I am glad to hear what you say as to the possibility of the Congress leaders working for the reforms honestly and not for wrecking'.[69] A British official remarked gleefully, 'It is amusing to note the eagerness with which the Congress Party is awaiting the White Paper. I really believe that at long last their followers are coming to their senses.'[70]

Sen Gupta was dead and Bose had been forced to leave the country by 1934. The absence of the two main agitators left direction in the hands of the Big Five: men who had had remarkably little to do with the Congress movement while it was on but who, for this very reason, were found to be best-equipped to lead the organization back to the safer and sober excitement of electoral politics. B.C. Roy began to negotiate with Ansari and Bhulabhai Desai from April 1934 to revive the Swarajist Party.[71] It was time now 'to fumble in a greasy till and add the ha'pence to the pence.'

Gandhians went back to their ashrams with vastly enriched personal prestige but with hardly any new ideas in mind. Charka and minor relief work could hardly cope with the spreading waves of rural protest. National education had dwindled to such an extent that in 1934 there was a proposal to discontinue the official annual reports on its state. In 1933 there were only nine national schools in

68 GOB, Home Confidential, Poll Poll FN (1–19) of 1932.

69 Hoare's letter of 7 April 1933, *Templewood Collection*.

70 Baker's note, 8 March 1933. *E.B.H. Baker Papers* (CSASC).

71 N.P. Mitra (ed.) *Indian Annual Register*, April 1934, (Calcutta, 1935).

Bengal; all were considered to be politically harmless.[72]

The Macdonald Award and the Poona Pact lent a special urgency to harijan upliftment. From June 1933 Bengal Gandhians did begin serious work among Harijans. Their work, however, would never assume the proportions of a serious social movement. A Congress anti-untouchability drive had been very active at Dubrajpur in Bankura. Its aspirations were tragically belied when a common feast, organized by Congressmen, was disrupted since untouchable Bagdis and Haris refused to eat food cooked by Bauris.[73] Bauris were classified as ritually more unclean than Bagdis and Haris, who jealously guarded the slender distinction in ritual ranking as the only signifier of dignity and self-respect. Barisal Namasudras refused 'to risk levelling down with the genuine untouchables such as sweepers and "doms"'.[74] The factors that define the subaltern's self-awareness need not only be elite groups exerting domination from above; it may equally be classes and groups that lie even lower down in the hierarchy and the distance from whom delineates the living space which a subaltern group reserves for itself. There are wheels within wheels in the highly intricate and delicately balanced caste structure which stubbornly would not melt away at the magic touch of Gandhian goodwill. Congress efforts to create an integrated social base for itself and to reach down to the lowest categories within Hindu society, had always to contend with protest movements from below that refused to confine themselves to the straitjacket of Gandhian non-violence.

Revolutionary Terrorism: The Ebb Tide

The entire machinery of repression and propaganda of the Bengal Government was deployed, as we have seen earlier, to flush out a handful of young men and women. Throughout the years 1928–32, there was no room for official complacency about revolutionary terrorism. However, the Fortnightly Report on Bengal observed in the first half of September, 1932, that terrorism was on the wane. As if to mock such reports, the Pahartoli fighting took place at Chittagong the next fortnight and Watson, the editor of the *Statesman*,

[72] GOI Home Poll 101/34 of 1934.

[73] *Fortnightly Reports on Bengal*, 1st half of June 1933. GOI Home Poll 18/7/1933.

[74] *Fortnightly Reports on Bengal*, 1st half of December 1933. GOI Home Poll 18/14/1933.

was shot at in Calcutta.[75] The pattern repeated itself in August 1933. The Fortnightly Report noted a distinct improvement in the situation in the first half of August. In the second half of the month, Burge, the Midnapur District Magistrate, was assassinated.[76]

Till the end of 1933 about forty-two 'akhras' of an 'objectionable' nature continued to survive; twelve in the Presidency Division, twenty-four in Rajshahi, four in Dacca and two in Chittagong.[77] Urban centres around Calcutta harassed the police well into 1933. Bepin Ganguly, 'at present the most dangerous of all absconders' operated from Diamond Harbour, Baranagore and Barnipur. Khagen Chatterji's group at Baranagore-Majilpur and Satcowripati Roy's group at Jaynagore were considered 'dangerous'. The Howrah District Magistrate reported in May 1933 that terrorism was actually spreading in his area; seven different groups operated from there.[78] Such minute, fragmented groups could hardly aspire towards really large-scale operations. The danger of individual target selection remained, however, and no single police operation, however intensive, could eliminate the problem.

Even after the death of Surya Sen in 1933, terrorism continued to spread. It moved into the Feni subdivision that connected Tippera with Chittagong. The Rajshahi Anushilan and the Dacca Shri Sangha remained fully active. The Tippera Hill Tracts were considered a sanctuary and at Rajshahi Harijan work was allegedly a cover to harbour terrorists.[79]

Such tenacity thoroughly terrorized officials and the entire European community in Bengal. O.M. Martin, the Rajshahi District Magistrate, did not dare to move a step without a posse of armed guards around him. He lived in great fear of the woman terrorist in particular, who seemed to him to be deadlier than the male of her species.[80] Donovan, the Barisal District Magistrate, left his post and quit the country in a hurry. A pretext was trumped up by the administrative personnel to save him from embarrassment but 'it is

[75] *Fortnightly Reports on Bengal*, 1st and 2nd halves of September, 1932. GOI, Home Poll 18/12/1932.

[76] *Fortnightly Reports on Bengal,* 1st and 2nd halves of August, 1933. GOI, Home Poll 18/9/1933.

[77] Note by Bellety and George, 7/11/33. GOB, Home Confidential, Poll Poll 831/33 of 1933.

[78] GOB Home Confidential, Police Police 420 (1–25) of 1933.

[79] *Fortnightly Reports on Bengal*, 1st half of March 1934. See also 18/7/1934, 2nd half of July 1934. GOI, Home Poll 18/3/1934.

[80] Martin's letter of 6 May 1932. *O.M. Martin Papers* (CSASC).

perfectly clear', wrote Anderson, 'that he had lost his nerve and was becoming hysterical'.[81] Mrs Taylor, wife of the Inspector General, Bengal Police, wrote from Mymensingh in November 1933, 'We have come back to a state of seige . . . . We are again prisoners in the constant care of armed guards'.[82] Panic was so great at Chittagong that a force of several thousand policemen had to be stiffened by regular troops and a Royal Navy flagship came up to the harbour to raise sagging morale.[83] Secretary of Hoare wrote to Anderson with sympathy: 'People of England are prepared to go to great lengths . . . lest further outrages may lead to a really dangerous Black and Tan atmosphere.'[84]

While the European community in Bengal remained panic-stricken, Anderson, who had to ride a similar storm in Ireland, knew from experience that the worst was over. He was not daunted even by Burge's murder which he described as a 'purely temporary setback'. The impasse on information seemed to have been removed at last. Multi-pronged repression and propaganda methods began to pay dividends. Middle class Hindus in troublesome areas like Midnapur were collectively branded and treated as suspects and as potential or actual terrorists.[85] Except at Chittagong, this eventually broke the back of urban Hindu middle class support and sympathy that had so far provided both the breeding ground and the shelter for terrorists. Apart from repression and an erosion of political interest due to the waning of Civil Disobedience, depression might also have constituted one of the factors behind a growing de-politicization of middle class Bengalis. Declining prices could have lulled the fixed-income professional groups into a sense of complacency and political apathy.

A powerful and unambiguous expression of the process of rejection was Rabindranath's *Char Adhyay* which came out in October 1934. An over-suspicious Government report initially described it as 'rabidly anti-Government and pro-terrorist'.[86] The impression must have been corrected soon enough since no steps were taken

[81] Anderson's letter, 9/4/1932. *Templewood Collection.*

[82] Mrs Taylor's letter, 7/11/1933. *Mr & Mrs Taylor Papers.*

[83] *Bomb and Pistol in a Bengal Presidency. Robert Reid Papers.*

[84] Hoare's letter, 14/10/1932. *Templewood Collection.*

[85] Even Anderson described measures taken against the Midnapur Hindu community as 'pretty drastic'. For an account of the many humiliations and restrictions inflicted on them see Anil Bhanja in A. Mitra (ed.), *Communist Holam* (Calcutta, 1976).

[86] GOI.Home Poll 55/1/35 of 1935.

against the book. The key to Tagore's thinking on terrorism may be found in the introduction of the novel: instead of the commonly used Bengali term for terrorism (*Santrashbad*, a literal translation) he concocts a new and far more emotive term: '*bibhishika pantha*' which means 'path of nightmare'.[87] Indranath, the terrorist 'dada' recalls Sabyasachi of *Pather Dabi* in his stature as supreme leader. His power, however, depends on very different qualities: deviousness, nihilism and a predilection for cruelty and violence. Indra's creed is a deeply pessimistic one. Love and agony for an enslaved country are conspicuous by their absence. Revolutionary sentiments are described as a 'sublime death wish' and the true glory of the martyrs is located in dying nobly, without hopes for a better future, since the country itself is moribund. There is no positive, affirmative cause to uphold. Even Indra's actions against the British are inspired by an 'impersonal sentiment' for they are 'the greatest among all western races . . . I applaud their human qualities.[88]

Atin, the rich, handsome, sensitive admirer of Ela, the beautiful revolutionary heroine, had been forced to join the revolutionary group because this was the only way of reaching out to her. He describes young revolutionaries as people without autonomy or will; they evoke the image of thousands of puppets dancing blindly and mindlessly to the tune of a heartless puppeteer. The other archetypal terrorist is the bestial Batu who easily turns informer. The two major positive characters in the novel are Ela and Atin, whose reasons and emotions have rejected the terrorist path but who are still trapped in it because it leaves them with no freedom or option. For Atin, this involvement at first means an agonizing denial of all the richness of his sensibility. Later, it represents a descent to the lowest depths of falsehood, meanness, distrust and an obsessive love for power. The path which began with an impersonal, awful discipline, ends up with the total destruction of all human values.

The novel in some ways, is a continuation of attitudes and concerns portrayed in *Ghare Baire* which Tagore wrote in 1914 to comment on Extremist nationalism and the beginnings of terrorism.[89] The most important aspect of the earlier novel was the moral degeneration of a woman through her interest in militant politics and her involvement with an Extremist politician. When

[87] Rabindranath Tagore, *Char Adhyay* (Calcutta, 1934), Introduction.

[88] Ibid., pp. 36, 42–43.

[89] A sensitive discussion of this novel is to be found in P.K. Datta's unpublished paper.

two teenaged girls assassinated the District Magistrate of Comilla in 1931, political involvement of women reached new heights. This explains, to a great extent, Tagore's rejection of terrorism. It may also partly explain fears about the consequences of radicalism among erstwhile radical, urban, educated, middle class nationalists. Young women, who took their place besides men as comrades-in-arms, epitomized a surprising combined uneven development in the field of social relations. In a generally conservative milieu, which still confined women (with or without some education) to the nursery or the kitchen, terrorist women seemed to have skipped several stages of development. Pritilata Waddedar planned and led the Pahartali attack at Chittagong, Kalpana Dutt jumped bail and, dressed in male clothes, was in hiding in the Chittagong forests with a group of male comrades and Suhashini Ganguly lived as the wife of a man, who was a mere acquaintance, to provide shelter to Chittagong absconders. Terrorist women themselves froze the revolution at this point and did not extend it to any transformation of broader human relations. They did not even justify their revolutionary actions on grounds of equality in political choice and protest. They sought to explain their unconventional behaviour in terms of a religious sacrifice at a time of exceptional national crisis.[90] Terrorism seemed to release, with unbearable clarity, all the latent violence associated with the principle of *Shakti* which is invoked and deeply feared at the same time in Bengali tradition. It created an ambivalence which was not easily resolved, however much terrorists themselves used traditional religious digits to explain their behaviour.

For Tagore, however, there was no ambiguity, there was only revulsion. In matters relating to the dignity of women he was often in advance of his times, upholding the inviolability of a woman's integrity, the delicacy and purity of her sensitivity. But the concept of woman's integrity had very definite bounds; it must be fully compatible with colour, beauty, love and her essential femininity. Nationalist discipline, angry, militant political concerns do not match the attributes of that femininity. When Ela confesses her mistake in taking to terrorism, Atin declares triumphantly: 'At last I see the girl who alone is real. You reign at the heart of home with a fan in your hand and preside over the serving of milk, rice and fish. When you arrive with dishevelled hair and angry eyes to an arena where politics has the whip hand, you are not your normal self but

[90] Pritilata Waddedar, *Chattogram Biplaber Bahnisikha* (Calcutta, 1974).

are unbalanced, unnatural . . .'. A woman's role is carefully sex-bound; it is 'a world of sweetness (which) . . . may appear narrow on the surface but in reality it has boundless depths in it . . . it is not a cage . . . . Up to now women have served while men have provided the means of livelihood. Anything to the contrary is shameful.'[91]

Chittagong, for a long time, proved a glorious exception to this general trend of turning away. Not only was Hindu, urban, middle class support retained in the teeth of the most severe strain, but help came, unsolicited, from areas and groups which had little to do with terrorists elsewhere. Absconders were pushed for shelter to villages around Dhalghat and Patya. These were methodically combed and villagers brutally punished on suspicion but they steadfastly refused to give up the absconders. 'The villages within half a dozen miles of Dhalghat are the centre of revolutionary organization. It was through the active support of the inhabitants of these villages that Surya Sen and his party were able to make their plans'.[92] Villages were promised remission from punitive fines in exchange for information but the device failed completely.[93] When Tarakeswar Dastidar escaped into Bidgram in March 1933 with a police party at his heels, villagers were hauled up before police officers and warned of dire consequences. They still remained silent. 'The reason that the majority of the inhabitants of all these villages were disloyal, was that for the last two years they had actively supported and admired Surya Sen. It was in the villages of this area the previous three years that Jugantar assassins were trained. From these villages they set out to commit their murders and returned to shelters which . . . were safe, only because they had the wholehearted sympathy of the villagers.' Only after the capture of Surya Sen was this passive resistance broken.[94]

Chittagong terrorists were totally dependent upon the goodwill and courage of men and women from very different walks of life—people with whom they had never worked before, but who still rose magnificently to the occasion. At Khelaghat, an old boatman Tarini

[91] *Char Adhyay*, pp. 98, 68, 70. For a discussion of this novel see Tanika Sarkar: 'Bengali Middle Class Nationalism and Literature: A Study of Saratchandra's Pather Dabi and Rabindranath's Char Adhyay', in D.N. Panigrahi (ed.), *Economy, Society and Politics in Modern India* (New Delhi, 1985).

[92] GOI, Home Poll 27/14/34 of 1934.

[93] *Fortnightly Reports on Bengal*, 1st half of March 1933. GOI, Home Poll 18/3/1933.

[94] GOI, Home Poll, 27/14/34 of 1934.

Majhi, gave invaluable help to survivors from Jalalabad.[95] A Muslim peasant offered shelter to absconders at Anwara village.[96] Surya Sen was once hurriedly taken by a Muslim boatman to the house of a Muslim peasant where he hid for some time.[97] Bijoy Sen took shelter in his home village after Jalalabad. When a police party questioned the predominantly Muslim poor peasants of the village they all lied and insisted that Bijoy had been in the village from before the Jalalabad episode. A Muslim servant of the family though tortured would not change his story.[98] A poor Muslim family hid Ambica Chakravarty, ignoring a reward of Rs 5000 for information about him.[99] Sections of Chittagong's Buddhist community were also suspected of sympathy and support.[100]

On terrorists themselves the experience could not but leave a profound impact. Necessity had thrust upon them a sudden and pressing need for help from unexpected quarters. That gradually created a new understanding of mass contact and a broader concept of the meaning and purpose of revolution. The enforced reliance on and prolonged existence among the rural poor deepened this. Those of them who were spared execution pondered upon this experience in their prison cells or in their exile in the Andamans. It is no accident, after all, that almost all Chittagong convicts turned to the Communist Party when they were released.[101] Repression alone did not finish off terrorism as a creed and political option. The experience of Chittagong absconders and other hunted young men and women during the most critical phase of repression brought home to them that their movement was leading to a blind alley.

Surya Sen was arrested in February 1933 and executed along with Tarakeswar Dastidar in January 1934. His martyrdom indicated the end of the era of classic revolutionary terrorism. With his band of followers he had attained the highest peaks which pure terrorist efforts could ascend. In the attempt, the limits of their enterprise had also been revealed with burning clarity. Terrorists themselves

[95] Probodhranjan Sen, *Biplobayojane Tarini Majhi Ebong Aro Aneke* in Sachindranath Guha (ed.). *Chattogram Biplaber Bahnisikha* (Calcutta, 1974), p. 101.

[96] Sudhin Das, *Smriti Tarpan,* p. 109.

[97] Manindralal Majumdar, *Smritir Aloke Agniyug*, pp. 139–8.

[98] Badal Sen, *Smritikatha*, pp. 260–1.

[99] Ashru Datta, *Ambica Chakravarty*, p. 335.

[100] *Fortnightly Reports on Bengal*, 1st half of March 1934. GOI, Home Poll 18/3/1934.

[101] Niranjan Sen, *Bengal's Forgotten Warriors* (Bombay, 1945).

had been forced to transcend the limits of strictly individual, secret terror.

The decline of the terrorist creed did not simply mean the end of a romantic dream. The Bengal Government was at last rid of an enemy which had shaken its administration and the confidence of its officers to the core, which had been most successful in destabilizing the political situation in the stormy years between 1930 and 1934. The Agniyug did not survive just as a bitter-sweet memory, as an inspiring example which had lost its relevance. Aspects of the heritage got linked up with later political traditions of the country. They were resurrected again and again in movements of very different hues. If a section of revolutionary terrorists got absorbed within the Communist Party, sections of Bengal's Communists too, went back to those traditions and incorporated them.

Peasant Protest

Paddy prices came down to twelve annas per maund towards the end of 1932.[102] Jute sold at Rs 2.8 as. per maund when the cost of cultivation was somewhere around Rs 6.[103] Basic inequities within rural power relations were thrown up in sharper relief against the backdrop of the economic crisis. Government officials noted that a 'non payment complex is spreading among agriculturists in Bengal', which was 'at first due to *sheer inability to pay* but has now become the result of *an unwillingness to recognize any duty* to pay'[104] (italics mine). As we have seen earlier, peasants recognized that their actions challenged fundamental power categories and norms. They worked out the meaning and argument behind such acts. The authorities found their conceptualizing more alarming than their actions. 'The Government regards with considerable anxiety the growing tendency among agriculturists and wage-earners . . . to regard the payment of rent and other legitimate dues as a liability.'[105]

Attacks on existing structures of authority took many forms. Dacoities in the countryside swelled in scale and strength of organization.[106] Significantly, their maximum incidence occurred in

[102] *Fortnightly Reports on Bengal*, 2nd half of December 1932. GOI Home Poll 18/15/1932.

[103] *Economic Problems of Bengal*, Memorandum submitted to GOB by Bengal National Chamber of Commerce, 10/1/1933, p. 23.

[104] GOB, Home Confidential, Poll 873/33 (1) of 1933.

[105] GOB, Home Confidential, Poll 112 (1–6) of 1933.

[106] See reports in *Bangabani*, April numbers, 1932.

places like Tippera and Mymensingh[107] where distress was especially acute and where peasants, too, were extremely restive. Some of the militancy and social questioning would have rubbed off on dacoits of these areas who were more dispossessed peasants than petty, professional criminals. Those dacoities had some unusual features. At East Madaripur (Faridpur) around Gourhati thana, these and 'other offences against property' had continued for several months in 1932 in 'almost an epidemic form'. When criminals were rounded up, it was revealed that they constituted a centralized gang that recruited villagers from other parts of Faridpur as well as from Barisal under Moharali Sardar.[108] The form of organization—wide-ranging recruitment under a single leader—and the form of action—'offences against property', in months of particularly acute peasant crisis, bring them nearer to a sort of 'social banditry'. A dacoity took place at Balshid (Nabiganj thana at Tippera) in May 1933 when the house of a taluqdar-cum-mahajan was attacked by a crowd of about a hundred men who were his own tenants and debtors. In the clash a son of the house was killed and a lot of debt bonds were looted.[109] Villagers organized themselves in an armed band at Damodarhat thana (Balurghat, Dinajpur) in Agradigun village and attacked a police camp that had been set up to collect long-pending debts in the locality.[110] The dividing line between stable organization and sporadic violence was very thin and uncertain; one kind of activity would easily flow into the other stream, given the relative infancy of organizational work and the intensity of economic distress. It is possible that while tenants' associations depended more on tenants of some substance and more secure occupancy rights, the dacoities mobilized poor tenants or agricultural labourers. The distinction, however, was not absolute.

Kishoreganj had a tradition of anti-mahajan violence—classified elsewhere as dacoities and rural crime by officials—which was already organized on anti-Hindu lines. Strong police action in July 1930 had suppressed the debtors' movement for the time being. It was revived from March 1932 in an expanded form. No-rent demands were added to the withholding of debt and interest

[107] *Fortnightly Reports on Bengal*, 1st half of March 1934. GOI, Home Poll 8/3/1934.

[108] *The Amrita Bazar Patrika*, 18 August 1932.

[109] *Fortnightly Reports on Bengal*, 1st half of May 1933. GOI, Home Poll 18/6/1933.

[110] *Bangabani*, 5 April 1932.

payment.[111] Some mahajan houses—mostly Hindu—were burnt and the house of a Hindu dafadar-cum-moneylender, Nand Kumar Goswami of Banagram, was set on fire. The police expected the beginnings of serious communal trouble from this.[112] Violent and open crowd action characterized Kishoreganj events as well as episodes recorded as dacoities. It was the anti-Hindu content that made officials include it within the domain of recognized politics while similar action against property elsewhere would be branded as crime.

Bands of Santal peasants armed themselves and roamed around the Dinajpur countryside. A police party visited Chakram village at Balurghat, Dinajpur (an area marked by tribal participation in Civil Disobedience) to see if local Santals were preparing illicit liquor. Santals resisted their entry, a formidable clash occurred and several men were injured on both sides.[113] A few months later the Dinajpur District Magistrate complained that Santals tended to assemble in huge, threatening bands, flourishing their bows and arrows, at the slightest provocation. When the police went to Gangarampur village to disperse one such gathering, Santals shot at them with bows and arrows. The Sub-Divisional Officer of Balurghat recommended an immediate regulation banning the use of bows and arrows to control this menace.[114]

Malda Santals had a history of sharecropper agitation, combined with a movement for Hinduization.[115] Jitu Santal engaged in his last combat on 3 December 1932. As had been planned much earlier, a large band of Santals marched up to the historic city of Pandua, occupied the ruins of the Adina mosque and 'conducted there a debased form of Hindu worship' to transform the mosque into a temple. Jitu, who now called himself Gandhi, declared the end of the British raj and proclaimed his own Government from within the mosque.[116] A pitched battle followed between his men and a large group of armed police who opened fire after the Santals refused to come out. Three Santals, including Jitu himself, were

[111] *Fortnightly Reports on Bengal*, 1st half of March 1932. GOI, Home Poll 18/5/1932.

[112] GOB, *Report on the Administration of Bengal 1931–32.*

[113] *Bangabani*, 27 February 1932.

[114] GOB, Home Confidential Police Police 669 (32) (1–6) of 1932.

[115] See above. For a connected study of the entire movement, see Tanika Sarkar, 'Jitu Santal's Movement in Malda, 1924–32; A Study in Tribal Politics,' in Ranajit Guha (ed.) *Subaltern Studies*, Volume IV (Delhi, 1985).

[116] Mitra (ed.), *Indian Quarterly Register*, Vol. I (1932), 14/12/1932.

shot dead, while a constable was killed by a poisoned arrow.[117]

Malda Santals were oppressed by an unusually heavy burden of rent, illegal cesses and abwabs. Legal processes were distorted and manipulated by landlords to cheat them of their holdings. The process was accelerated during the depression. A report from the Settlement Officer of Malda after the Adina incident confirmed that in recent years about 20,000 Santals had lost their occupancy rights and most of them had become *adhiars*.[118] Dispossession was not just an economic catastrophe; it had strong cultural connotations as well. 'A Santal's land not only provides economic security, but is a powerful link with his ancestors; and this applied to newly occupied areas no less than the old, for he will not take possession till the spirits approve. The land is a part of his spiritual as well as his economic heritage'.[119] The right to a tract of land which provided for his livelihood and which the spirits had blessed and made secure, was, therefore, inviolable. This is what the Santals tried to establish through crop looting in September 1928.

Jitu's Hinduization drive derived some of its basic notions from the proselytizing wave of the Hindu Sabha that swept over Malda at this time and which reached him through the mediation of Kashishwar Chakravarty. 'In Shikarpur', declared a Sanyasi, 'we will not keep either Santals or Muhammadans any longer'. Traditional Santal practices like the use of pigs and hens, had to be discarded as reprehensible.[120]

The location of the Adina mosque within the Barind may have contributed to its choice as an obvious target for an aggressive Hinduization campaign. Not only was it the second largest Muslim religious building in India, it was also a major centre of pilgrimage. As such it was of particular importance for Hindu Sabhas as a site which would be worth 'recovering'.

The autonomy of Jitu's movement revealed itself, however, in the incorporation of very different attitudes, some of which had nothing to do with the Hindu Sabha message. If Jitu nurtured hostility against Muslims, he also had deep contempt for lower

[117] *Statesman*, 16 December 1932.

[118] *Final Report on the Survey and Settlement Operations in the District of Malda*, 1928–35, pp. 40, 46, 72, 75.

[119] W.J. Culshaw and W.G. Archer, 'The Santal Rebellion', in *Man in India*, VOL. XXV (December 1945), p. 215.

[120] GOB, Poll Conf. FN 629 (1–3) of 1926. Evidences of Karo and Hakim Hembrum.

castes and untouchables.[121] There is an intermeshing of apparently contradictory social and political strands; while the attitude towards Christians and Muslims certainly reflected Hindu Sabha messages, contempt for 'Domes' and 'Chamars' denoted assent to the values and attitudes of the traditional Hindu society which surrounded them at Barind and which the Hindu Sabhas were trying to eliminate in their quest for an integrated, unified Hindu community.

The internalization of dominant Hindu attitudes does not indicate a simple model of Sanskritization. Even when Hindu religion and the caste structure are accepted, there is, on another plane, a notion of continuous struggle where Hindu overlords and local oppressors are implicitly pitted against Santal peasants. Jitu promises that zamindaris would be absent in the coming Utopia; he alone will exact a fixed tribute. Hindus constituted the prominent landholding class at Barind and a rejection of zamindari undoubtedly implied a protest against their dominance. 'All the land will be ours' was a slogan that was repeated again and again.[122]

It is interesting that even though non-tribal political forces in Malda were represented by Swarajists and Hindu Sabha activists who had little use for Gandhi, Jitu himself accepted him as an overarching authority. He appropriated Gandhi's image for himself and used his symbols. He would give 'darshan' to his disciples, sitting at the charka. At the Adina mosque he called himself Gandhi and proclaimed Gandhi's 'raj'.[123] A selective use of nationalist messages and symbols expressed the independence of tribal politics with regard to Swarajist and Hindu communal forces, and of the limits beyond which manipulation from above failed to work.

The reappropriation of 'desh' (homeland) was a theme that occurred again and again in the Dol's preaching: 'Jitu says that the present Raj will not remain, that Desh will come. The English Raj has gone. Our Raj, our Desh is coming', and so on.[124] The conceptualization of 'desh' had within it several strands of meaning. The anti-foreign message had been vigorously broadcast in villages by different segments of the Bengal Congress since Non-Co-operation. To the Santal, however, the message had been familiar for a very long time. He had his own memories of anti-British

[121] Ibid.
[122] Ibid.
[123] *Statesman*, 16 December 1932.
[124] GOB, Poll Conf. FN 629 (1–3) of 1926. Evidence of Malta and Meghrai.

struggles, of the great Santal rebellion of 1855. At the same time, within the broader framework of liberation from British rule, the focus, for Jitu, was on the freedom the Santals had to attain by themselves. His messages were meant exclusively for the Santal community, the fight at Adina mobilized Santals alone. The notion of a specifically Santal 'desh' was implicit in Jitu's discourse. The new order that he tried to project corresponded to an ancient Santal vision of a perfect state of freedom in its most significant aspects.[125]

The new order was to be achieved, and the new raj proclaimed, with the occupation of the Adina mosque. The act of occupation was finally undertaken in 1932 because, due to its coincidence with Civil Disobedience, rumours about the collapse of the Government poured into the district. It seemed a propitious moment to initiate the final battle. The political moment attained a supremacy of its own, overwhelming specific class objectives. It is, indeed, a point of some significance that unlike 1928 the agrarian question was not directly at issue in December 1932. Since the entire ritual battle rested on a belief in a magical transformation of the world, anything else would have been extraneous at that supreme movement.

The 1932–4 period was marked also by the emergence in large numbers of associations and organizations to give an enduring shape to peasant grievances and demands. Most tenant organizations shared a common resistance to rent and interest payment.[126] The growth of rather similar associations or Proja Samitis at the same time among the same sections, seemed to give them the appearance of a single, unified movement with a centralized leadership. There was, however, never a common leadership or a consciously united movement. Tenants were mobilized under diverse influences, their organizations revealed a lot of internal variations and their struggles also remained separate.

The Krishak O Sramik Samiti (the name probably indicates the influence of the WPP) revived the peasant agitation at Tippera from February 1932. The Samiti had close links with the local Congress and the personnel of the two organizations overlapped frequently. Maulvi Mukleswar Rahman, Krishna Sundar Bhowmik, Qazi Abdul Latif, all were Samiti leaders as well as prominent members of

[125] See Tanika Sarkar, 'Politics of Tribal Protest'.

[126] Associations were particularly numerous in Noakhali, Tippera, Mymensingh, Faridpur, Jessore, Bogra, Rajshahi, Rangpur, and in parts of Midnapur. *Report on the Administration of Bengal, 1932–33.*

the local Congress.[127] The Samiti was banned in early February[128] but the agitation continued up to 1934. It was directed against local moneylenders and demanded a revision of the Tenancy Act.[129] At Bogra and Noakhali, local Congress leaders like Rajibiddin Tarafdar advocated rent and interest reductions.[130]

Congress involvement in agrarian struggles elsewhere was the exception rather than the rule. A few Communists (or men suspected of Communist connections) on the other hand, began in this direction almost for the first time. A Hooghly ryots' meeting was organized by suspected terrorists who wore red shirts and distributed pamphlets issued by the 'Plough Army'.[131] A number of Peasant Association meetings at the Sadar subdivision in Burdwan were presided over by 'that notorious Communist Bhupendra Nath Datta'. A Kanthi Mahakuma Sramik O Krishak Samiti was set up at Contai in 1933, which distributed extremely radical pamphlets among tenants. Demands for land nationalization and minimum wages were added to the more usual demands for no-rent and no interest. It probably intended to expand the scope of recruitment and to mobilize agricultural labourers as well as tenants.[132]

More influential and powerful agitators were 'some half-literate village notables, generally quite honest—but apt to mix up religion, politics and economics'. Men who had long enjoyed a position of traditional social and religious hegemony among peasants of their own localities now emerged as organic leaders of agrarian agitations. 'There is no dearth of Maulvis and Maulanas, Mahatmas and Saints nowadays', commented Ghuznavi bitterly.[133] The Tangail agitation at Mymensingh reveals how local religious authority inspired political struggles. It is not just a question of political manipulation from above by religious leaders. Neither is it a clear case of a political struggle dressed up in a religious garb, that hoodwinks an ignorant and devout rural populace into political

[127] *Bangabani*, 3 February 1932.

[128] Ibid., 16 February 1932.

[129] *Fortnightly Reports on Bengal*, 1st half of may 1933. GOI, Home Poll 8/6/1933.

[130] *Fortnightly Reports on Bengal*, 1st half of February 1934. GOI, Home Poll 18/1/1934.

[131] *Fortnightly Reports on Bengal*, 1st half of June 1933. GOI, Home Poll 18/6/1933.

[132] Ibid., 1st half of July 1933. GOI, Home Poll 18/7/1933.

[133] Ghuznavi's Note of 22 February 1933. GOB, Home Confidential Poll Poll 161 (29–67) of 1934.

action. Peasants would not compartmentalize the sacred and the profane, the political and the magical, in their own conception. A single unified authority would usually lay down the law and decide strategies about all problems, mundane as well as metaphysical. Just as the family 'guru' would control matrimonial alliances as well as the Puja ritual, similarly, the village priest or 'maulvi' might well be the natural and final authority on problems of economic crisis and of political protest.

Maulana Abdul Hamid of Bhasanir-char—the 'Maulana Bhasani' who was to play a significant role as a populist leader for over forty years in East Bengal—told a huge crowd, assembled for Id prayers at Tangail, that if they followed him in large enough 'numbers and attacked the properties of the Hindu Raja of Santosh, they would acquire the merit of a Haj pilgrimage'. The attack was prevented by the prospect of severe action under an Ordinance. Meetings continued where printed circulars were distributed, advising the setting up of village organizations to protect tenant rights. Hamid was externed. After his release, he started a movement in the Government forests at Tangail aimed at a wholesale cutting down of trees. 'While he refrained from telling them openly to withhold payment of just dues, he was advising them quietly to do so and to cut down trees . . . for their own use'. He was externed again. Hamid's authority astonished the upper-class politician Ghuznavi who observed that Maulanas like him did not have even a basic acquaintance with Arabic religious texts.[134] Officials suspected that 'his (Hamid's) ambition is to play the role of a local Gandhi'.[135]

There had been no lack of self-styled Gandhis in troubled times like these who, along with the 'Maulanas and Maulvis' and the many 'Babas' of Northern India, fulfilled a particular social function in the countryside. We have seen how Jitu Santal had proclaimed himself a Gandhi. A conflation of Gandhi's charisma with their own, of the broad national movement with their own local struggles, would have added greater certainty and weight to the aims of these grass-roots leaders. The Gandhian movement thus often provided a convenient backdrop against which a host of subaltern groups would engage in their own struggles with a vague sense of identification with the broader upsurge whose purposes had been transmitted to them through disjointed bits of rumour.

[134] Ghuznavi's Note of 22 February 1933. GOB, Home Confidential Poll Poll 112 (1–6) of 1933.

[135] GOB, Home Confidential Poll Poll 885/1933.

Hamid had, from the beginning, alienated the Government by attacking a Government forest as well as a Hindu zamindar. Some other rural agitators would try to avoid war on both fronts. They would seek to appease the government by condemning the Congress or the terrorists. Even Hamid had opened a meeting by a speech replete with anti-terrorist denouncements which at first fooled Bell, the Sub-Divisional Officer. Ghuznavi, however, warned Bell that 'under the cloak of helping with anti-terrorist propaganda, he (Hamid) has been sedulously preparing the ground for a mass agrarian revolt.'[136] Bell was convinced by these arguments and Hamid was externed by the authorities. The ostensible purpose of the All Bengal Raiyat and Debtors' Conference organized by Maulvi Abdul Rashid at Rajshahi was to solicit Government relief for cultivators and a proposal was made to adjust the rent rate to the value of the staple crops. Rashid made all the expected loyalist noises and gestures but the District Magistrate remained wary. 'Personally, I do not like the looks of the Maulvi . . . he has a shifty eye and the looks of a professional agitator'.[137] Reversing its earlier policy, the Government by 1933, was ready to treat all agrarian agitators as potentially dangerous forces, even if they constituted the most formidable political rival of the Congress in the countryside.

Land Revenue Administration reports had noted the growth of no-rent tendencies in different zamindaris without undue concern up to 1931. They happily observed that tenant relations were more or less cordial on Government lands. As the slump persisted and tenant resistance hardened everywhere, the Government became more sensitive about its role as the final defender of colonial property relations and as a formidable landlord in its own right. It was admitted that 'the Court of Wards estates and the Khas mahals were in the same position as the private zamindaris'.[138] The growing identity of interests dictated a severe policy towards tenant agitations of all colours. An official recommended the policy of extreme vigilance to all District Officers in a note of February 1933, 'But for such action it would have been impossible to stem the spread of communism in my own district of Tippera . . . . The extremist section is now anxious to organize the masses and to excite them against Government as also against the present capitalist form of society'.

[136] Ibid.

[137] GOB, Home Confidential Poll Poll 112 (1–6) of 1933.

[138] *Report on the Land Revenue Administration, 1931–32.*

Another Government officer flatly refused to grant any validity to no-rent demands since tenants could still pay rent 'without starving or abandoning cultivation'. District Officers were told to step up propaganda on behalf of rent payment since no-rent movements were politically dangerous and since the Government itself was vitally affected as a Khas mahal landlord.[139] It is interesting that no-rent moves, from whichever quarters, were supposed to lead, fatally and inevitably, towards Communism.

Workers and Communists

Strikes were rather minor affrays during these years and their numbers steadily declined. There were thirty-three labour disputes in 1933 as against forty-one in 1932.[140] Disciplined and purposeful direction gave way to sporadic clashes; nearly every dispute turned into a violent encounter. Waverly Mill workers in the 24 Parganas attacked the manager and clashed with the police who fired on them in January 1933.[141] Calcutta Corporation conservancy staff, coolies and carters went on a strike in April 1933 to demand a pay rise. When the police fired and arrested about a hundred and fifty coolies, the crowd was joined by three thousand carters and a thousand labourers of various descriptions, who paralysed road traffic and showered bricks on the police.[142] Prabhabati Das Gupta organized strikes in some jute mills in November 1932. These failed and about three hundred mill-hands were dismissed. Some of these men made a bomb attack on 22 November on houses of people 'who had incurred their displeasure.'[143]

Anger dissipated itself rather too easily in this manner and sustained strikes became difficult to organize. Repression and the threat of retrenchment took their toll on labour militancy while workers who held jobs were somewhat pacified by falling prices. Given this context, Government worries and large-scale preventive measures may seem excessive. From early 1933 detailed reporting on labour matters was recommended; knowledge about this field

139 GOB, Home Confidential Poll Poll 112 (1–6) of 1933.

140 GOB, *Report on the Administration of Bengal 1932–33.*

141 *Fortnightly Reports on Bengal*, 1st half of January 1933. GOI, Home Poll 18/1/1933.

142 Mitra (ed.), *Indian Quarterly Register, 1933, Vol. I*, 29 April 1933.

143 *Fortnightly Reports on Bengal*, 2nd half of November, 1932. GOI, Home Poll 8/14/1932.

gained a sudden priority in official concerns. The Communist Party was banned in July 1934, just five years after the Meerut arrests.[144] Action was advised against a large number of unions and political organizations, affiliated to the Red Trade Union Congress.[145]

The Government reacted more to certain latent potentialities and possibilities rather than to an actual threat. Leftists were coming together with plans for sustained organizational work. The earlier pattern—leaders taking charge of struggles just before, or even during a strike, was changing. There was now an interest in long-term union building. Leftists began to revive old links—among jute, railway and corporation workers, for instance—and new bases were sought among transport workers, stevedore labourers and others. The process formed a part of a fresh and very important reorganization within the Communist Party which was on the point of regaining its old ascendancy among workers.

An 'Open Letter' of the Chinese, British and German Communist Parties had advised Indian Communists in 1932 to consolidate an illegal, united Communist Party of India. *The Imprecor* document of 1934 advised Communists to participate in all mass movements and win terrorists over to their side. Criticism of Congress leaders was to coexist with prospects of joint struggles.[146]

Equipped with this broader framework, Abdul Halim formed the Workers' Party in Bengal (as a part of the Workers' Party of India) in February 1932. It had established itself by 1933 as the recognized Communist group, enjoying Soviet confidence and support, and representing the Third International in India. The WP came to control several key unions: the E.B. Railway Workers' Union, City and Motor Transport Workers' Union, Bengal Jute Workers' Union, Match Factory Workers' Union and so on. The Party formed local cells in factories and study circles among workers of jute and textile mills, docks, railways, engineering workshops and glass factories.[147] Long term politicization—though not broad cultural education either among leaders or among cadres—and not intermittent regulation of strikes, became the perspective.

Elaborate conspiracy charges against Communists had exploded the Congress allegation that Communists were anti-national. The W P persisted with criticism of Gandhi, and especially of the

[144] Ibid., 2nd half of July 1934.GOI, Home Poll 18 7/1934.

[145] GOI. Home Poll 7/20/34 of 1934.

[146] Williamson's Confidential Report, *India and Communism. Hallet Collection.*

[147] GOI, Home Poll 7/20/34 and KW of 1934.

Bengal Congress leadership. The main basis of the critique had now shifted to the abandonment of the mass upsurge and Gandhi's tendency towards compromise. A League Against Gandhism was formed around 1934, which organized several meetings to criticize the Congress on these grounds. The authorities became anxious about such an ultra-nationalist critique of Gandhi. An ironical situation developed when the police arrested Abdul Halim, Saroj Mukherji and Ranen Sen for disrupting a meeting of the Reception Committee of the Congress.[148] Arrests of Congress members during 1942, when Communists briefly supported the British War effort, have been kept fully alive in national memory. The coin had another side which has been relegated to deliberate amnesia.

Soumyendra Nath Tagore summed up the anti-Gandhi polemic very lucidly in a pamphlet which was immediately banned by the Government. He located Indian capitalist interests behind the compromise and disruption of the mass upsurge. He made an interesting assessment of Civil Disobedience from which Communists had dissociated themselves earlier on, 'The masses have advanced much more in their struggle against the Imperial Government than what had been ordered by the Congress'.[149] It postulated in an embroynic form certain notions about mass nationalist politics that have gained considerable significance in recent historical writings: the evidence of two distinct and parallel levels of elite and subaltern anti-imperialist struggle. These may get braided together and may even overlap but the elite leadership continuously tries to contain and control the more radical stream of mass militancy.

Despite the recent scars of repression, despite the iron frame of a very Stalinist frame of political understanding and a rather economist conception of mass struggle (even that, nevertheless, was a desperately difficult enterprise under the circumstances) Communists in Bengal were about to enter the forefront of mass movements. A recognition of such possibilities inspired the Government's ban on the infant Party, at a moment when all restrictions on the Congress were being lifted.

[148] Ibid.

[149] S.N. Tagore, *Samrajyabad Birodhi-i-Congress Virodhi* (Calcutta 1935).

Conclusion

These six years then, were years rich in promise. Yet they constituted, at the same time, a peculiarly fragmented experience. The several strands of political activity remained disjointed even when they all challenged, in different ways, the colonial state and its property relations.

The earlier phase of mass nationalist struggle, in contrast, seems to indicate a broader range and a greater cohesion. The Congress leadership was more united, terrorists had suspended their separate course of action to join the mass upsurge and Hindus and Muslims were engaged in a common crusade under the banner of Khilafat Non-Co-operation. This unity was expressed in a powerful wave of anger against the State at the grassroots level, whatever its divisive potential was for national politics. Rangpur Muslim peasants set up a 'Swaraj Thana' under a 'Gandhi Daroga' [1]—a classic inversion of the significata of authority. O.M. Martin, the District Magistrate at Noakhali, found the anger of Khilafatist leaders and Muslim villagers much more unnerving than Congress activities. He even asked Congress volunteers to step up their messages about peace and non-violence in the hope that this would keep matters under control. [2]

Congress leaders like Sen Gupta organized powerful labour movements such as the Assam Bengal Railway strike. Jute mill workers often courted arrest in Calcutta during the last phase of the movement. During the week ending on 5 January 1922, only 39 out of 349 arrests in Calcutta were from among students. One hundred and twenty three were mill hands. 'The remaining persons arrested were boat *majhis* and low class Muhammadans from the suburbs'. [3]

[1] Rajat K. Ray, *Social Conflict and Political Unrest in Bengal, 1875–1927* (Delhi, 1984).

[2] *Martin Papers.*

[3] GOB, Poll 14 (1–20) of 1922.

Congress leaders were ready to work among peasants with a self-confidence and sureness of touch that seemed to be sadly inhibited in the 1930s. Militant peasant struggles over issues like forced indigo cultivation strengthened and extended the range of possibilities.[4]

The heady vision of Swaraj within a year had inspired sweeping millenarian hopes. Such a conceptualization of the struggle was made possible by a filtering of Gandhian messages and commands through indigenous peasant codes of beliefs and practices. Ramrajya possibly corresponded to a millenium and Gandhi was the messianic leader, leading his flock towards it. Charka and boycott could be the prescribed ritual that needed to be observed for a magical transformation of the world. The process of appropriation imparted an exceptional unity and intensity to popular participation. The Bengal Government worried much more about movements among peasants and tribals of Chittagong, Tippera, Rangpur and Midnapur than it did about the formidable anti-Union Board agitation under Sasmal. 'The spirit of violence and contempt of all authority . . . was not of the leaders but of the masses'.[5] Nearly seven hundred prisoners broke out of the Rajshahi Central Jail on 24 March 1921. 'The story had gone round that a new Raj was to be inaugurated and all prisoners released, so they anticipated this millenium by liberating themselves.'[6]

There was little labour or tribal participation in Civil Disobedience. Hindu-Muslim joint action did not remotely approach earlier proportions and the real strength of the organized Congress movement lay primarily among middle-ranking Hindu peasants in a few pockets of south-west Bengal. The Provincial Congress leadership resolutely avoided peasant struggles. Bitter factional squabbles continued to plague the leadership and terrorists pursued their own separate path. While the Congress swept the 1937 polls over most of the country, in Bengal (as in Punjab) it won the majority of Hindu seats but was still relegated to an overall minority position because of its total failure in Muslim constituencies. In both provinces, the clear coincidence of class and communal divisions was partly responsible for the failure which could only have been overcome through a close Congress association with radical peasant struggles.

[4] On this see Sumit Sarkar, 'The Conditions and Nature of Subaltern Militancy'.

[5] GOB, Poll Confidential, 395 (1–3) of 1924: *History of Non-Co-operation movement in Bengal.*

[6] *Robert Reid Papers.*

The possibility of future partition was implicit in the relatively poor Congress electoral performance in both provinces in 1937.

Yet Civil Disobedience, too, had frequently implied the construction of a new moral universe, a reordering of the everyday world of domination and deference. Subordinated groups like peasants, workers or women cannot really acquire resources for active protest or defiance without a sharp break within their cognitive categories about relations of power and a conceptualization of a radically new order, which may seek to sanctify and legitimize itself by harking back to a supposedly older and more authentic norm. We have seen how a mere derisive smile of an embattled peasant or worker at a moment of struggle—a smile that is improvised under exceptional circumstances and is not a regular part of a ritual inversion of order—can indicate the end of the world to the threatened authorities. Yet the scope of such defiance was restricted and broken, again and again, by other compulsions and alliances that pulled different classes, religious and political communities apart.

The Bengal Congress, then, failed to live up to its expected role as an effective umbrella. A wide spectrum of political options emerged, perhaps, as a direct corollary. The most interesting consequence, significantly shaping the political movement in Bengal to this day, was the development of a distinct and viable Left alternative.

Bibliography

PRIVATE PAPERS

India Office Library and Records London

Birkenhead Collection: Correspondence with Jackson.
Halifax (Irwin) Collection: Telegrams and letters from and to Secretary of State; Correspondence with persons in India.
Templewood (Hoare) Collection: Correspondence with Jackson; Correspondence with Anderson.
Hallet Collection.
Robert Reid Collection.

Centre of South Asian Studies, Cambridge

Benthall
O. M. Martin
J. T. Donovan
Tegart
W. C. Sharpe
Taylor
Baker

Nehru Memorial Museum and Library, New Delhi

Purushottamdas Thakurdas
B. P. Singh Roy
Raja of Santosh
Aswini Coomar Banerji
Bidhan Chandra Roy

INTERVIEWS

Shantimoy Ray (Calcutta, 1976)
Pramatha Bhowmick (Calcutta, 1976)
Saibal Gupta (Calcutta, 1978)
Bhupal Panda (Calcutta, 1978)
Robi Mitra (Calcutta, 1978)
Ranen Sen (Calcutta, 1978)
Muzaffar Ahmad (interviewed by P. C. Joshi—courtesy Gautam Chattopadhyay)

Abdul Razzak Khan (interviewed by P. C. Joshi—courtesy Gautam Chattopadhyay)
Dhiren Mazumdar (courtesy Gautam Chattopadhyay)
Sushil Chatterji (courtesy Gautam Chattopadhyay)
Parimal Roy (Rome, 1977).

Nehru Memorial Museum and Library transcripts

Bhupati Mazumdar
Satcouripati Roy
Kamala Dasgupta
Prabhabati Dasgupta
Shibnath Banerji
Nellie Sengupta
Pannalal Dasgupta
Anil Baran Roy
Satish Dasgupta

OFFICIAL RECORDS

Government of India

Public and Judicial Proceedings, 1928–1934 (POL)
Home Political Proceedings, 1928–1935 (NAI)
Meerut Conspiracy Case Proceedings (NMML Microfilm)

Government of Bengal

Home Confidential, Political Department, Political Branch, 1928–1934 (WB SA)
Home Confidential, Police Branch, 1928–1934 (WB SA)

OFFICIAL PUBLICATIONS

Royal Commission on Labour in India (1930), Vols. 1, V

Government of India

Census of India, 1931, Vol. V (Bengal)
D. Petrie, *Communism in India, 1924–1927* (reprinted, Calcutta, 1972)
H. Williamson, *India and Communism 1928–1935* (Seen in Hallet Collection)
H. W. Hale, *Political Trouble in India, 1917–1937* (reprinted Calcutta, 1937)

Government of Bengal

Report of Bengal Provincial Banking Enquiry Committee (1930) *Report of Land Revenue Commission* (Floud), (1940)

Terrorism, Civil Disobedience and the Calcutta Corporation (1934)
Proceedings of the Bengal Legislative Council, 1927–1929
Annual Reports of the Administration of Bengal 1925–26 to 1934–35
Bengal District Gazetteers: Dacca, Mymensingh, Tippera, Faridpur, Bakarganj, Noakhali, Chittagong, Rangpur, Rajshahi, Bogra, Jessore, Khulna, 24 Parganas, Midnapur, Howrah, Hooghly, Bankura.
Bengal District Gazetteers 'B' Volumes (Statistical Abstracts, 1921–22 to 1930–31) for above districts.
Final Reports on Survey and Settlement: Birbhum, Burdwan, Dinajpur, Faridpur, Tippera.

RECORDS AND PUBLICATIONS OF POLITICAL AND BUSINESS ORGANIZATIONS

All India Congress Committee Papers (NMML)
Akhil Bharatiya Hindu Mahasabha Papers (NMML)
Annual Reports of the Indian National Congress (1928–29, 1931).
Annual Reports of the Indian Chamber of Commerce (Calcutta, 1928–33).
Bengal National Chamber of Commerce, *Economic Problems of Bengal* (Memorandum to Government of Bengal, January 1933)

NEWSPAPERS AND PERIODICALS

The Amrita Bazar Patrika (Calcutta)
The Statesman (Calcutta)
Forward (Calcutta)
Advance (Calcutta)
Bangabani (Calcutta)
The Ananda Bazar Patrika (Calcutta)
Modern Review (Calcutta)
Prabasi (Calcutta)
Parichay (Calcutta)
N. N. Mitra (ed.) *Indian Quarterly Register* (Calcutta, (1927–1937)

CONTEMPORARY PAMPHLETS AND LITERATURE

(The pamphlets, many of them anonymous, are arranged in chronological order as far as possible. The place of publication is Calcutta, unless otherwise specified.)

Maulvi Sheikh Idris Ahmed, *Krishaker Marmabani* (Malda, 1921) (IOL)
Munshi Kumar Ali, *Jatiya Gan* (Comilla, 1926) (IOL)
Abed Ali Mian, *Desh Shanti* (Ranapur, 1926) (IOL)
Muhammad Faizul Kabia, *Jatiya Kabita* (Chittagong, 1926) (IOL)
Syed Asadullah Shirazi, *Biplabi Tarun* (1928) (IOL)

Swami Jnanananda, *Patnabhali Satyagraha* (Barisal, 1928) (IOL)
Anon, *Youths of Bengal* (Mechuabazar, Calcutta, December 1929) (IOL)
Munshi Mohammad Yasin Howladaa, *Jamidarer Daya, Prajar Sashan* (Barisal, 1929) (IOL)
Mohammed Mayauddin Hamidi, *Krishker Unnati* (Khulna, 1929) (IOL)
Anon, *Jaubaner Dak* (1929) (IOL)
Narayanchandra Bandopadhay, *Shree Bhaonta* (1930) (IOL)
Abdul Chhamed Mian, *Desh Boka Part I* (Mymensingh, 1930) (IOL)
Anon, *Peasant Uprising in Kishoreganj* (1930)
Baikuntha Das, *Matri-Adesh* (Silchar, 1930) (NAI)
Satish Dasgupta, *Bharate Samyavad* (1930) (IOL)
Leaflet by *Akhalia Congress Committee, Assam* (1930) (BM)
Lakshikanta Kirtania, Kumud Bhattacharji, *Ganer Bahi Loter Gan* (Mymensingh, 1930) (IOL)
Bhupendra Kishore Rakshit Roy, *Chalar Pathe* (1930) (IOL)
Bijoylal Chattopadhyay, *Damaru* (1930)
Charubikash Datta, *Rajdrohir Jabanbandi* (1930) (IOL)
Anon, *Purna Swadhinata Chai Keno?* (Sylhet, 1930) (IOL)
Mukunda Das, *Karma Kshatra* (Kasipur, 1930) (IOL)
Santwana Guha, *Agnimantre Nari* (1930) (IOL)
Land and Order in Midnapur (Non-Official Enquiry Committee Report, 1930) (BM)
Bandopadhyay, *Mukti Pathe* (Mahishbathan, 1931) (IOL)
Anon, *Shanti Kothay?* (1931) (IOL)
Nagendranath Das, *Phansi* (1931) (BM)
Narendra Chaudhuri, *Muktir Sandhan* (Sylhet, 1931) (BM)
Shri Kal Bhairab, *Bhairabi Chakra* (c., 1931) (IOL)
Bijoylal Chattopadhyay, *Kalar Bhari* (1931) (IOL)
Dwijendramohan Dasgupta, *Swadhinata Sangrame Dakshin Srihatta* (Dakshin Srihatta Congress Committee, 1931) (IOL)
Anon, *Desher Dak* (1931). (IOL)
Santwana Guha, *Bhangar Pujari* (1931) (IOL)
Ramniranjan Guha Roy, *Pujar Upahar – Banglar Katha* (*c.* 1931) (IOL)
24 Pargana Jela Rashtriya Sammelan, Indubhushan Ghoshalan Abhibhasan (June 1931) (IOL)
Pratap Chandra Maiti, *Swaraj Sangeet* (*c.* 1931) (IOL)
Somnath Lahiri, *Samyavad* (1931) (IOL)
Anon, *Sabash, Bimal, Sabash*! (July, 1931) (IOL)
Sachindranath Sanyal, *Deshbashir Prati Nibedan* (Santipur, *c* 1931) (IOL)
Jnanenjan Neogi, *Biplabi Bangla* (1931) (IOL)
Amarendra Sen, *Kshete Paina Keno?* (Dhubri, 1931) (IOL)
Nababganj Yuba Sammilani – Pramathanath Bandopadhayer Abhibhasar (1931) (IOL)
Prabhatmohan Bandopadhyay, *Mukti-pathe* (1931) (IOL)

Banjir Ahmed, *Bandir Bansi* (1931) (IOL)
Sheikh Muzaffar Ahmad, *Banglar Patan* (Chittagong, 1931) (IOL)
Yashodalal Acharya, *Mayer Dak* (Barisal, *c.* 1931) (IOL)
Nagendranath Das, *Shoka-Sindhu* (*c* 1932) (IOL)
Nagendranath Das, *Deshbhakta* (*c* 1932) (IOL)
Nagendranath Das, *Dineshar Shesh* (*c* 1932) (IOL)
Mukunda Das, *Path* (Barisal, *c* 1932) (IOL)
Anon, *Let the Dogs Bark—Caravan Passes On* (1932) (IOL)
Kazi Nazrul Islam, *Chandrabindu* (1932) (IOL)
Hemendralal Roy, *Rikta Bharat* (1932) (IOL)
Sureshchandra Dhar, *Deshapriya Jatindramohan* (Calcutta, 1933)
Mehbul Ahmed, *Hindu Musalmaner Hangamar Kabita* (Chittagong, 1933) (IOL)
Anon, *Swadhin Bharat* (1933) (BM)
Deshapriya Jatindramohan Sengupta—His Life and Work (1933) (IOL)
Arun Chandra Datta, *Yuger Bangla* (1933) (IOL)
Nagendranath Das, *Rakta–Pataka* (*c* 1933) (IOL)
Anon, *Jago! Jago! Shaktipujaa Din Agoto Oi* (1933) (IOL)
Deshapriya Jatindramohan (1934) (IOL)
Provincial Anti-Terrorist Conference, Town Hall, Calcutta, 16 September 1934 (1934)
Soumendranath Tagore, *Samrajyabad Birodhi-i Congress Birodhi* (1935) (NAI)
Rakta Chai! Rakta Chai! Shudhu Rakta Chai !!! (n.d.) (IOL)
Swadhin Bharat (n.d.) (IOL)
Saratchandra Chattopadhyay, *Pather Dabi* (Calcutta, 1926)
______, Sarat-Sahitya-Sangraha, Vols. VIII, XIII.
Jibanananda Das, *Rupashi Bangla* (Calcutta, 1932)
Rabindranath Tagore, *Char Adhyay* (Calcutta, 1934)
______, Letters to P. C. Mahalanobis and Dilip Roy (*Desh*, 1965, 1976)
______, *Rachanabali*
______, *Patrabali*
______, *Gitanjali*

UNPUBLISHED THESES AND RESEARCH PAPERS

Chattopadhyay, Gautam, *Role of the Bengal Legislature in India's Struggle for Freedom* (ICHR Project)
De, Jatindranath, *The History of the Krishak Praja Party in Bengal*, 1929–47 (Delhi University thesis, 1978)
Lambert, Richard D., *Hindu-Muslim Riots* (University of Pennsylvania thesis, 1951)
Rule, Pauline, *Crime, Society and the State in Colonial Calcutta c 1860–1940* (University of Melbourne thesis, 1982)

MEMOIRS, BIOGRAPHIES, ARTICLES AND GENERAL WORKS

Ahmed, Abdul Mansur, *Amar Dekha Rajnitir Panchash Bachhar* (2nd ed., Dacca, 1970)

Ahmad, Muzaffar, *Amar Jivan o Bharatar Communist Party Part II* (Calcutta, 1974)

Alavi, Hamza, 'Peasants and Revolution' in Miliband and Saville, ed., *Socialist Register*, 1965

Bagchi, Amiya, *Private Investment in India, 1900–1939* (Cambridge, 1972)

———, 'Reflections on Patterns of Regional Growth in India during the period of British Rule (Occasional Paper No. 5, 1976, Centre for Studies in Social Sciences, Calcutta)

Bandopadhyay, Bibhutibhusan, *Aranyaka* (Calcutta, n.d.)

Bandopadhyay, Manik, 'Jiyanta' (1950), in *Manik Granthabali*, Vol. VII (Calcutta, 1972)

Bandopadhyay, Nripendrachandra, *At The Cross-Roads* (Calcutta, 1950)

Bandopadhyay, Saroj, *Bikikinir Ghat* (Calcutta, n.d.)

Basu, Prabodhchandra, *Medinipur Jalar Bhagawanpur Thanar Itibritta* (Calcutta, 1976)

Behl, Vinay, 'Tata Iron and Steel Compani ke Sramik Andolan, 1920–28' in *Anya Artha*, 1978

Bengal Anti-Communal Award Movement (Calcutta, 1939)

Bhattacharji, Pradyumna, *Samajer Matra Ebang Tarashaṇkar Upanyas: Chaitali Ghurni* (Ekshan, Calcutta, 1975)

Blyn, George, *Agricultural Trends in India 1891–1947* (Pennsylvania, 1966)

Bose, Atul, *Medinipurar Boma o Biplab* (Calcutta, 1962)

Bose, Santipriya, *Banglar Chasi* (Calcutta, 1944)

Bose, Sisir, ed., *Subhaschandra Bose—Correspondence 1924–32* (Calcutta, 1967)

Bose, Subhaschandra, *The Indian Struggle* (Calcutta, 1935, 1964)

Brahmachari, Bankim, *Swadhinata Sangrame Sutahate* (Midnapur, 1977)

Broomfield, J. H., *Elite Conflict in a Plural Society: Twentieth Century Bengal* (Berkeley, 1968)

———, 'The Forgotten Majority: The Bengal Muslims, September 1918', in D. A. Low, ed., *Soundings in Modern South Asian History* (London, 1965)

Brown, Judith, *Gandhi and Civil Disobedience: The Mahatma in Indian Politics, 1928–34* (Cambridge, 1977)

Chakravarty, Dipesh, 'Sasipada Banerji: A Study in the Nature of the First Contact of the Bengali Bhadralok with the Working Classes of Bengal' (Centre for Studies in Social Sciences, Calcutta, Occasional Paper No. 4, 1975)

———, 'Conditions for Knowledge of Working Class Conditions' in Ranajit Guha (ed.) *Subaltern Studies II*

______, 'Communal Riots and Labour: Bengal's Jute Mill Hands in the 1890s' in *Past and Present*, (1981)

______, 'Trade Unions in a Hierarchical Culture: The Jute Workers of Calcutta, 1920–50' in Ranajit Guha (ed.) *Subaltern Studies III*

______, 'On Deifying and Defying Authority: Managers and Workers in the Jute Mills of Bengal' in *Past and Present*, (1985)

Chakrabarti, Narendranarayan, *Netaji Sanga o Prasanga* (Calcutta, 1963).

Chandra, Bipan, *Nationalism and Colonialism in Modern India* (New Delhi, 1979)

Chatterji, Partha, *Bengal 1920–1947: The Land Question* (Calcutta, 1984)

Chattopadhyay, Bhola, *Aspects of Bengal Politics in the 1930s* (Calcutta, 1969)

Chattopadhyay, Gautam, *Communism and Bengal's Freedom Movement, Vol. I, 1917–29* (New Delhi, 1976)

Chattopadhyay, Tushar, *Swadhinata Sangramar Bish Bacchar* (Calcutta, 1975)

Chaudhuri, Benoybhushan, 'Agricultural Production in 19th Century Bengal' in *Bengal Past and Present*, (Calcutta, 1969)

______, 'Agrarian Movements in Bengal and Bihar, 1919–39',. in B. R. Nanda, (ed.) *Socialism in India* (New Delhi, 1972)

______, 'Process of Depeasantisation in Bengal and Bihar, 1885–1947 in *Indian Historical Review*, July 1975)

Chaudhuri, Sukhbir, *Peasants and Workers' Movement in India, 1905–29* (New Delhi, 1971)

Communist Holam (Midnapur, 1976)

Culshaw and Archer, 'The Santal Rebellion' in *Man in India*, (December 1945)

Das, Narendranath, *History of Midnapur*, Part II (Calcutta, 1962)

Dasgupta, Ajit, 'Jute Textile Industry', in V. B. Singh (ed.) *Economic History of India* (Bombay, 1965)

Dasgupta, Hiralal, *Swadhinata Sangrame Barisal* (Calcutta, 1972)

Dasgupta, Ranjit, 'Structure of Labour Market in Colonial India in *Economical and Political Weekly*, (Special Number, 1981)

De, Sureshchandra, *Swadhinata Sangrame Nawabgunj* (Calcutta, 1972)

Dubey, V., *Railways*, in V. B. Singh, (ed.) *op. cit.*

Dutta, Bhupendra Kumar, *Biplaber Pada Chirha* (Calcutta, 1953)

Dutta, Kalpana, *Chittagong Armoury Raiders* (Bombay, 1945)

Fuchs, Stephen, *Rebellious Prophets* (Bombay, 1965)

Gallagher, J. 'Congress in Decline, 1930–39', in Gallagher, Johnson, Seal, (eds.) *Locality, Province and Nation* (Cambridge, 1973)

Gandhi, M. K., *Collected Works*, Vol. XXXVI (Government of India, 1970)

Ganguli, Prafulchandra, *Biplabir Jivan-Darshan* (Calcutta, 1976)

Ghatak, Adharchandra, *Nandigram Itibritta* (Calcutta, 1964)
Gopal, S., *Jawaharlal Nehru: A Biography, Vol. I* (Bombay 1976)
Gordon, Leonard, *Bengal: The Nationalist Movement 1876–1940* (Delhi, 1974)
Goswami, Dharani, 'Ekti Krishak Bidroher Kahani' in *Parichay*, (Calcutta, 1969)
———, 'Bharatar Communist Andolanar Tirishar Darshak' in *Parichay* (Calcutta, 1973)
Goswami, Gopinandan, *Medinipurer Shaheed Parichay* (Gopalpur, Midnapur, 1977)
Goswami, Tulsi, *Footprints of Liberty* (Calcutta, 1971)
Guha, Nalinikishore, *Banglay Biplab-bad* (Calcutta, 1923, 1954)
Guha, Ranajit, *A Rule of Property for Bengal* (Paris, 1963)
———, *Elementary Aspects of Peasant Insurgency in Colonial India* (Delhi, 1983)
———, (ed.) *Subaltern Studies*, Vol. I–IV (Delhi, 1982–86)
Guha, Sachidranath, *Chattogram Biplaber Bahnisikha* (Calcutta, n.d.)
Gupta, Parthasarathi, *Imperialism and British Labour Movement* (Macmillan, 1975)
Gupta, Pramatha, *Je Sangramer Shesh Nai* (Calcutta, 1971)
Habibulla, B. D. *Sher-e-Bangla* (Barisal, 1962)
Hardiman, David, *Peasant Nationalists of Gujarat: Kheda District 1917–34* (Delhi, 1981)
Huq, M. Azizul, *The Man Behind The Plough* (Calcutta, 1939)
Islam, Mustapha Nurul, *Bengali Muslim Public Opinion As Reflected in the Bengali Press, 1901–30* (Dacca, 1973)
Jeffrey, Robin, (ed.,) *People, Princes and Paramount Power* (New Delhi, 1978)
Kanungo, Hemchandra, *Banglay Biplab Prachesta* (Calcutta, 1928)
Karnik, V. B., *Indian Trade Unions—A Survey* (Bombay, 1960)
Laushey, D. M., *Bengal Terrorism and the Marxist Left* (Calcutta, 1978)
Low, D. A. (ed.) *Congress and the Raj* (New Delhi, 1977)
Macpherson, Kenneth, *The Muslim Microcosm: Calcutta, 1918–35* (Wiesbaden, 1974)
Mazumdar, Satyendranarayan, *Amar Biplab Jignasa* (Calcutta, 1973)
Momin, Abdul, *Kolkataye Garoan Dharmaghat* (Mulayan, Calcutta, 1970)
———, *Chatkal Sramikar Pratham Sadharan Dharmaghat* (Kalantar, Calcutta, 10–12 August, 1970)
Moore, R. J., *Crisis of Indian Unity* (Oxford, 1970)
Outshahi Oramer Itibritta (Calcutta, n.d.)
Pal, Pramathanath, *Deshapran Sasmal* (2nd ed., Calcutta 1961)
Pandey, Gyanendra, *The Ascendancy of the Congress in Uttar Pradesh, 1926–34* (Delhi, 1978)
Rasul, Abdulla, *Krishak Sabhar Itihas* (Calcutta, 1969)

Ray, Prafulla Chandra, *Life and Experiences of a Bengal Chemist* (Calcutta, 1932)

Ray, Rajat, *Social Conflict and Political Unrest in Bengal, 1875–1927* (Delhi, 1984)

Ray, Ratnalekha, *Change in Bengal Agrarian Society, c 1760–1850* (Delhi, 1979)

Ray, Subodh, (ed.,) *Communism in India—Unpublished Documents 1925–34* (Calcutta, 1972)

Ray, Suprakash, *Bharater Biplabik Sangramer Itihas* (Calcutta, n.d.)

Revri, C, *The Indian Trade Union Movement* (Delhi, 1976)

Saha, K. B., *Economics of Rural Bengal* (Calcutta, 1930)

Sanyal, Hitesh, 'Arambage Jatiyatabadi Andolan' in *Anya Artha*, (Calcutta, 1974–75)

_____, 'Dakshin-Paschim Banglay Jatiyatabadi Andolan' in *Chaturanga*, (Calcutta, 1976–77)

Sarkar, Sumit, *Swadeshi Movement in Bengal, 1903–08* (New Delhi, 1973)

_____, 'The Logic of Gandhian Nationalism: Civil Disobedience and the Gandhi-Irwin Pact, 1930–31' in *Indian Historical Review*, (July 1976)

_____, 'The Conditions and Nature of Subaltern Militancy: Bengal from Swadeshi to Non-Cooperation *c* 1905–22', in Ranajit Guha, (ed.,) *Subaltern Studies III*.

Sarkar, Tanika, 'The First Phase of Civil Disobedience in Bengal, 1930–31' in *Indian Historical Review*, (July, 1977)

_____, 'Kolkatay Pratham Barricade *Baromas*, (Calcutta, April 1980)

_____, 'Politics and Women in Bengal: The Conditions and Meaning of Participation' in *Indian Economic and Social History Review*, (21 i, 1984)

_____, 'Bengali Middle Class Nationalism and Literature: A Study of Saratchandra's Pathar Dabi and Rabindranath's Char Adhyay', in D. N. Panigrahi, (ed.) *Economy, Society and Politics in Modern India* (Delhi, 1986)

_____, 'Jitu Santal's Movement in Malda, 1924–32: A Study in Tribal Protest', in Guha, (ed.,)*Subaltern Studies* II

Sasmal, Bimalananda, *Swadhinatar Phanki* (Calcutta, 1967)

Sen, Asok, *Iswarchandra Vidyasagar and His Elusive Milestones* (Calcutta, 1977)

Sen, Niranjan, *Bengal's Forgotten Warriors* (Bombay, 1945)

Sen, Ranen, *Banglay Communist Andolaner Pratham Yug* (Mulayan, Calcutta, 1975)

Sen, Shila, *Muslim Politics in Bengal, 1937–47* (New Delhi, 1976)

Sen, Sukomal, *Working Class of India: History of Emergence and Movement* (Calcutta, 1977)

Simmons, C. P., 'Indigenous Enterprise in the Indian Coal-Mining Industry, c 1835–1939' in *Indian Economic and Social History Review*, (April-June 1978)

Singh, Ananta, *Agnigarbha Chattogram* (Calcutta, 1968)
Singh, Bhagat, *Why I am an Atheist* (ed.) Bipan Chandra, (Delhi, 1979)
Swadhinata-Sangrama Nadia (Krishnanagar, 1973)
Swadhinata-Sangrama Sutahata (Midnapur, 1977)
Tegart, C., *Terrorism in India* (London, 1932)
Tomlinson, B.R., *The Indian National Congress and the Raj, 1920–42* (Cambridge, 1976)
Waliullah, Mohammad, *Yugavichitra* (Dacca, 1967)

Index